American Literature and Culture in an Age of Cold War

American Literature and Culture in an Age of Cold War

A CRITICAL REASSESSMENT

EDITED BY

STEVEN BELLETTO

AND

DANIEL GRAUSAM

UNIVERSITY OF IOWA PRESS

Iowa City

University of Iowa Press, Iowa City 52242

www.uiowapress.org
Printed in the United States of America

Design by Richard Hendel

The University of Iowa Press is a member of Green Press Initiative and is committed to preserving natural resources.

Printed on acid-free paper

Library of Congress Cataloging-in-Publication Data
American literature and culture in an age of cold war: a critical reassessment / edited by Steven Belletto and Daniel Grausam.
p. cm.
Includes bibliographical references and index.
ISBN-13: 978-1-60938-113-4 (pbk)
ISBN-10: 1-60938-113-0 (pbk)
1. American literature—20th century—History and criticism. 2. Cold War in literature. I. Belletto, Steven. II. Grausam, Daniel, 1975–
PS228.C58A44 2012
810.9′3582825—dc23 2012006953

CONTENTS

ACKNOWLEDGMENTS

We would like to thank our contributors for their generosity and labor, and for their patience as we were completing this volume. Charlotte Wright and the entire staff at the University of Iowa Press have been wonderful. Special thanks go to Joe Parsons, both for his initial interest and for his ongoing support and wise counsel.

INTRODUCTION

CULTURE AND COLD CONFLICT

STEVEN BELLETTO AND

DANIEL GRAUSAM

What Is Cold War Culture?

When in June of 2010 news broke concerning a long-term undercover Russian spy operation in the United States, the media had their summer blockbuster. Nearly every news story or radio broadcast featured some variation of "not since the Cold War," mused about whether the conflict had ever really ended, and commented on the oddity of this espionage ring. The television critic for the *New York Times*, for one, noted the aesthetic shape of the "quaint," "Cold War–style" spy operation, and joked that there would soon be a "Real Russian Spies of New Jersey" reality show.[1] The story soon emerged: nearly a dozen Russian agents had been under deep cover in the United States, tasked with integrating themselves into American society. Some did so by becoming average members of the American middle class, and in some cases so complete was their transformation that their identity started to seem the end, rather than the means, of their mission.

It was all textbook Cold War thriller, if indeed a bit quaint-seeming: hadn't we seen this all before? The Rosenbergs. Klaus Fuchs. Aldrich Ames. Weren't spies supposed to be from a bygone era? And yet there was the espionage ring in all its pulp glory—the *Newsweek* headline announced that it was "Part John le Carré, Part Austin Powers." It was as if the Russian spies were taking their cues from film, rather than the other way around: as the employer of one of the accused noted, the story seemed "straight from a movie."[2] The whole affair could indeed have been straight from the film *Salt*, released just a few weeks later, which featured Angelina Jolie as a Russian mole inside the CIA. (Despite half-serious speculation in the blogosphere, it turned out that the real Russian spy ring was not in fact an elaborate marketing campaign by Sony Studios.)[3]

Directed by Phillip Noyce, who brought Tom Clancy's *Clear and Present Danger* and *Patriot Games* to the silver screen in the 1990s, *Salt* seemed almost too fitting in the summer of 2010. Part seat-of-the-pants thriller, part feminized reworking of Bond ingenuity, part kitsch (there is a secret

Russian castle where child agents train in isolation), the film paralleled the real spy ring: on the one hand it was deadly serious, on the other it was too campy to be believable. The frightening possibility of losing control of the American nuclear arsenal coexisted with scenes of children lining up to kiss the ring of their grizzled Soviet spymaster.

The point of a tour through *Salt* is not, of course, to suggest that we should take our historiographic cues from Hollywood, or that we should necessarily seek to extend the Cold War's descriptive reach past 1989 or 1991 (although there may be good reasons to do so).[4] Rather, what *Salt* exemplifies is a confusion about just what the Cold War and its culture were and are. Indeed, the real story of the spy ring seemed less an example of contemporary espionage than an assemblage of the classic features of high Cold War cinema. There was the striking female lead Anna Chapman, described in the media as if she were a Bond Girl (the *New York Post* headline read, inevitably, "From Russia With Love") along with reports of invisible ink and secret communication networks. Capping it all off was the reason one person simply couldn't believe that her neighbors were foreign agents: they had perfect hydrangeas in their front yard.[5] For the neighbor, the mundane fact of the well-kept hydrangeas invalidates the fantastically romantic possibility that spies live on the block; for the cultural critic, this screams of the cinematic Cold War, in which the humble hydrangea played a key role as a Communist cover. In a famous early scene of *The Manchurian Candidate* (1962), arguably the classic film of American Cold War culture, U.S. troops being brainwashed in Manchuria are tricked into believing that they are in New Jersey listening to a Ladies' Club presentation on the growing of hydrangeas. Once again, the quotidian crashes against the improbable, and there seems a profound confusion of realms—just where does history end, and imaginative aesthetic production begin? Anna Chapman, for instance, could populate the pages of a Don DeLillo novel: since her return to Russia she has hosted a television program called *Secrets of the World* and has sported lingerie and a gun on the cover of the Russian version of *Maxim*. It isn't that, Bond-like, sex is in the service of espionage, but rather that secret agency qualifies you, if you are especially attractive, to sell your sexuality. In this case, the provocative agent was now "qualified" to wear the luxury lingerie brand Agent Provocateur on the cover of the premier soft-core men's magazine.

The Russian spy ring and *Salt* appeared after we had begun work on this collection, but they confirmed our sense that the time was right for a critical reassessment of Cold War culture. We believe that the confusion surrounding the spy ring was due in part to the fact that the full cultural impact of the Cold War remains unprocessed, and that some of the operative paradigms for understanding the culture of the Cold War were contributing to, rather than alleviating, such confusion. It was time to foreground the wide variety of ways in which we might understand the Cold War's shaping power. Collecting the work of some of the very best cultural critics writing about the period, what follows reveals the multiple ways in which American cultural production from the late 1940s to the present might be understood in relation to the Cold War. While they have benefitted from much of the pioneering work done on American Cold War culture, the following chapters offer a critical engagement with reigning paradigms and a series of suggestive revisionist claims.

Cold War Literary and Cultural Studies

Ann Douglas claimed in 1998 that literary critics do not make the Cold War "central" to their work on post-1945 American literature, even though two key concepts they employ—postmodernism and postcolonialism—are "inexplicable outside the context it [the Cold War] supplies."[6] Douglas had a point: in 1998 the Cold War was still seen as an explanatory paradigm for a relatively small subset of postwar cultural production. And it was also true that some work on Cold War culture did not necessarily extend its focus to literature. This was the case in two excellent collections that revised our understanding of postwar culture. In Lary May's *Recasting America: Culture and Politics in the Age of Cold War* (1989), one chapter (of fourteen) dealt at length with a work of literature (Ralph Ellison's *Invisible Man* [1952]).[7] Although the scope of *Recasting America* has made it essential reading for those interested in Cold War culture, there is a tacit sense that literature might be of the Cold War only if it engages in overtly political concerns. *The Other Fifties: Interrogating Midcentury American Icons* (1997) does feature sustained analyses of novels but, tellingly, does not even include the term *Cold War* in its index, although some of the contributions explicitly engage Cold War politics.[8] The book's editor Joel Foreman hoped to avoid characterizing the 1950s as defined merely by "massively invasive systems of repression operating most powerfully at the level of ideology" and so downplayed the conceptual importance of the Cold War, ironically collapsing its meaning into "systems of repression."[9] Clearly, not all cultural production from 1947 through 1991 can be explained via the Cold War, but it is equally the case that the Cold War was influential in ways not solely reducible to arguments about psychological and aesthetic power struggles.[10] What Douglas was calling for was a systematic way of linking literary analysis with what the Cold War could mean or do (and she in fact gives examples of "cultural historians attempting literary methods of reading . . . but falling short").[11] Nearly fifteen years later, it is hard to believe that such a clarion call was ever needed. We now have a formidable list of monographs, essays, collections, and conference presentations that examine the literature of the last sixty-five years in relation to the Cold War.[12] Just since 2000, there have been more than twenty-five monographs devoted to Cold War literature—and this number does not include book collections, countless individual essays, or the many monographs predominantly about Cold War film or cultural history.[13]

In fact, work was well under way before Douglas's essay appeared. The three books which marked a cultural turn in Cold War studies were, perhaps fittingly, clustered around the fall of the Berlin Wall and the collapse of the Soviet Union. These are Elaine Tyler May's social history *Homeward Bound: American Families in the Cold War Era* (1988), and two works of literary and cultural criticism, Thomas Schaub's *American Fiction in the Cold War* (1991) and Alan Nadel's *Containment Culture: American Narratives, Postmodernism, and the Atomic Age* (1995). Although May is not primarily concerned with literature, *Homeward Bound* is a favorite starting point for literary critics writing on the period because it reveals how private life was shaped by geopolitical dynamics. George Kennan's influential formulation of containment led to an American foreign policy concerned with preventing the spread of Soviet-sponsored Communism abroad and with maintaining a U.S. sphere of influence. May uncovers a domestic equivalent. As she puts it, "In the domestic version of containment, the 'sphere of influence' was the home. Within its walls, potentially dangerous social forces of the new age might be tamed, where they could contribute to the secure and fulfilling life to which postwar men and women aspired. . . . More than merely a metaphor for the cold war on the homefront, containment aptly describes the way in which public policy, personal behavior, and even political values were focused on the home."[14] *Homeward Bound* is one of the reasons why *containment* now evokes a powerful cultural dimension of the Cold War as well as foreign policy. If the term means checking the spread of Communism around the globe, resulting in the Korean and Vietnam Wars and various interventions in the Middle East, Latin America, and elsewhere, it likewise names the construction of domestic consensus.

Schaub's *American Fiction in the Cold War* describes the rise of a new liberalism that developed in the wake of revelations about Stalinist Communism. If Communism had once been imagined as a powerful alternative to fascism, midcentury history convinced some Western intellectuals that Communism and fascism were parallel forms of totalitarianism. This shift helps illuminate, according to Schaub, "the true labor of fiction throughout this period . . . the struggle to develop a new relation between art and politics."[15] After demonstrating that postwar literary critics and their aesthetic values were informed by Cold War politics, Schaub shows how fiction that seems distinct from Cold War culture—for instance, work by Flannery O'Connor and John Barth—ought to be understood in light of the "liberal narrative." Barth's *The End of the Road* (1958), in which "the political is entirely obscured by philosophical discourse," can be shown to be "reproducing a contemporary view of liberalism's complicity with the horrors of Nazism and Stalinism."[16] Schaub's sense that there could be a different kind of politics at work in American fiction explains why later scholars have suggested, as Adam Piette puts it, that *American Fiction in the Cold War* "launched Cold War literary criticism."[17]

But the book that exemplifies the first phase of Cold War literary criticism is Nadel's *Containment Culture*—it is telling that seven of the eight chapters that follow are indebted to its claims and legacy. Like Schaub, Nadel looks at some texts that do not seem overtly political: J. D. Salinger's *The Catcher in the Rye* (1951) or the film *The Ten Commandments* (1956), among others. While nobody would say that such works are explicitly *about* containment, Nadel reveals how they engage with the norms of containment articulated by Kennan and implemented by the Truman and Eisenhower administrations. In a series of detailed analyses, Nadel shows how what he calls "large cultural narratives" could affect personal stories and then charts the breakdown of the logic of cultural containment from the 1960s on. As with Schaub's work, one reason that Nadel's blending of cultural criticism with rigorous close reading has been so influential is that it made visible new relationships between aesthetics and politics. Schaub and Nadel highlight a political and aesthetic culture of chastened liberalism that sought to contain dissent, and their powerful readings led to a virtual consensus among literary scholars that Cold War culture meant what Nadel named "containment culture." For many critics, Cold War culture *is* containment culture, and vice versa, which leads to a narrative of the Cold War as a principal context only for the culture of the long 1950s. And while critics learned from Nadel, too often they lacked the subtlety of his readings: for Nadel, the early postmodernism of the 1960s helped us to see that containment culture was never as all-powerful or successfully repressive as some would have it.

The second phase of Cold War literary criticism, which emerged in the early 2000s, acknowledged the pioneering work done by Schaub, Nadel, and others but theorized the Cold War's relationship to culture without relying primarily on the containment model. Understanding American literature and culture in a global frame, this second phase mirrored an increasing interest in the global Cold War on the part of historians.[18] Christina Klein's *Cold War Orientalism: Asia in the Middlebrow Imagination, 1945–1961* (2003) analyzes the relationship between domestic culture and the third world, and shifts attention from the containment model to what she calls the "global imaginary of integration," which illuminates another way in which the rest of the world was viewed during the Cold War. As she explains:

> Where the global imaginary of containment drew on the residual internationalism of the right, with its vision of bulwarks between nations and a mortal conflict between communism and capitalism, the global imaginary of integration drew on the residual internationalism of the left, which imagined the world in terms of open doors that superseded barriers and created pathways between nations. It constructed a world in which differences could be bridged and transcended. In the political rhetoric of integration, relationships of "cooperation" replaced those of conflict, "mutuality" replaced enmity, and "collective security," "common bonds," and "community" became the preferred terms for representing the relationship between the United States and the noncommunist world.[19]

Focusing on integration allows Klein to read various texts as being informed by the Cold War without equating them with the impulses of containment. A range of middlebrow work featuring international adoption narratives, for instance, foregrounds "the idea of alliance among independent parties—the model of postwar integration—rather than the idea of an empire unified by blood and force."[20] This in turn suggests another connection between personal life and the Cold War: "In part because the family balanced emotional unity with internally structured hierarchies of difference based on age, it served as a model for a 'free world' community that included Western and non-Western, developed and underdeveloped, established and newly created nations."[21]

The idea that cultural texts might reveal a relationship between "established and newly created nations" is evident in another significant book of the second phase, Leerom Medovoi's *Rebels: Youth and the Cold War Origins of Identity* (2005). In Medovoi's account of the postwar rise of the concept of identity, the rebellious young are important because they navigate the schizophrenia of a consensus culture committed to individual freedom: the "young American rebel [serves] as guarantor of the nation's antiauthoritarian democratic character."[22] Noting the political rebellions occurring around the world as Africa, Asia, and Latin America began to decolonize, Medovoi shows how the rebel was also connected to global democratic freedom. Turning from a "dichotomous" view of the Cold War, Medovoi reminds us that "by the mid-1950s, the 'three worlds concept' had become the globe's dominant topological imaginary," and that by 1960, forty countries (with a collective population of over 800 million) had revolted against colonialism to create "newly sovereign 'national characters.'"[23] These new national characters served as key ideological battlegrounds of the Cold War, as evidenced by phenomena such as the People-to-People Program, which aimed to win the "hearts and minds" of these varied populations.

Rebecca M. Schreiber's *Cold War Exiles in Mexico* (2008) extends this project of globalizing American Cold War culture by analyzing the work of writers, filmmakers, and visual artists who were blacklisted or otherwise exiled from the United States during the Cold War and found new creative lives in Mexico. A by-product of the U.S.-Soviet rivalry but crucially not defined by it, this is a different archive of Cold War texts (the work of Willard Motley, for example) and leads to a new way of viewing Cold War cultural production. As Schreiber writes, "the work of Cold War exiles constitutes a form of critical transnationalism that challenged official versions of U.S. national culture from the mid-1940s to the mid-1960s."[24] Jodi Kim's *Ends of Empire* (2010) likewise argues that "Asian American critique unsettles and disrupts the dominant Manichaean lens through which the Cold War is made sense of and in turn generates meaning. . . . [By] conceptualizing Asian American critique as an *unsettling hermeneutic* [*Ends of Empire*] generates a new interpretive practice or analytic for reading Asian American cultural production."[25] Attuned as it is to the real effects of a conflict sometimes rendered abstractly, Asian American cultural production can change the way the Cold War is conceptualized: from an Asian American perspective, for example, the Cold War can look like a civil war "*within* the selfsame western modernity."[26]

Other recent books have assumed the global frame of the Cold War while focusing primarily on American or Anglo-American literature. Arthur Redding's *Turncoats, Traitors, and Fellow Travelers* (2008) shows how domestic U.S. culture exists in a transnational context, so that, for example, W. E. B. Du Bois's "postwar activist, literary, and theoretical work remains compelling and might best be understood as a provocative and engaged critical response to the global Cold War, which itself can hardly be analyzed without a keen eye to its racial dimensions."[27] Furthermore, Paul Bowles's well-known depictions of existential crisis and loss in places such as North Africa "mark the limitations of imperial power."[28] Adam Piette's *The Literary Cold War* (2009) focuses on British and American writers but ranges around the globe, following Graham Greene and Mary McCarthy to Southeast Asia or Allen Ginsberg to the Arctic. Piette figures the Cold War relationship between aesthetics and politics in surprising ways, as when he writes of the "Arctic Cold War," emblematized in the construction of the Distant Early Warning (DEW) line across a four thousand-mile stretch in Alaska and Canada. As Piette puts it, "the Arctic came to symbolize the Cold War, secret, inaccessible, bitterly cold, hiding within its wastes enormous bases such as Thule in Greenland, incredible surveillance systems and mind-numbingly powerful weaponry."[29] It was likewise the place for Ginsberg to meditate on the Cold War; in 1956, he sailed through the polar regions as a trainee yeoman on the USNS *Pendleton*, part of the Military Sea Transportation Service, the body responsible for constructing the DEW line. Noting that Ginsberg travels to this netherworld between the United States and the Soviet Union just after his Russian-born mother has died, Piette echoes the connections drawn between the familial and the political in May and Klein; analyzing Ginsberg's journals, he concludes there is a "struggle between familial and superpolitical readings. . . . Ginsberg accepts the mystifying invisibility of the Cold War as a pastoralizing dream of peace."[30] Some of the more recent work in Cold War literary studies, then, takes the global imaginaries of containment, integration, and three worlds as powerful, but not necessarily exclusively explanatory, paradigms.

Cold War Criticism Now

As we have demonstrated, the containment thesis has enormous power for critics engaging the long 1950s. While there are some highly visible examples of state sponsorship and control of cultural production—most notably the House Un-American Activities Committee (HUAC) in Hollywood, television censorship, or the revelations of CIA funding for the literary magazine *Encounter*—"containment" has often functioned as a metaphor in literary studies, a way of registering anxiety about dissent, visibility, and surveillance. In the present volume, William J. Maxwell's opening essay is simultaneously an example and a critique of the containment paradigm. Building on the work of historian Ellen Schrecker, Maxwell looks beyond the highly visible public spectacle of McCarthyism to understand the era as one shaped by "Hooverism," that is, FBI domestic surveillance. Perhaps the most surprising aspect of the day-to-day operations of state surveillance is its interest in the world of books. Shamed by its failure to catch sufficiently in advance Max Lowenthal's damning *The Federal Bureau of Investigation* (1950), the FBI subsequently infiltrated the American publishing industry. Punning on the George W. Bush–era idea of Total Information Awareness, Maxwell dubs this FBI effort Total Literary Awareness, a program that has left behind an extensive archive of FBI interest in African American cultural production. Maxwell reveals the machinery of cultural containment, but his key examples also show how ineffective this FBI surveillance turned out to be; works of the imagination, it turns out, don't reveal their Communist sympathies in any straightforward way.

Catherine Gunther Kodat's examination of the career of Edwin Denby reveals that our paradigms for understanding Cold War culture are at least in part the consequence of the figures we have privileged. Although Denby was a vital part of the New York arts scene, he is remembered primarily for one subset of his writings—his dance criticism—rather than his four volumes of poetry. By considering both the poetry and Denby's writings on dance, Kodat gives us new ways of understanding Cold War culture. A conventional approach might well link Denby's commitment to neoclassical values in ballet and his formalist poetics to his homosexuality: such established and circumscribed forms of aesthetic expression might allow Denby to hide queerness. Yet as Kodat notes, Denby's poetry is surprisingly open about male-male desire, so the homology between formal aesthetic control and political oppression breaks down when the poetry is taken seriously. Restrictive aesthetic forms—the sonnet, in Denby's case—might function as glass houses rather than as wooden enclosures.

One of the recurring critiques directed at Communism was that it represented a hitherto unknown centralization of power. But in Daniel Belgrad's account, the centralization of power is a defining feature of modernity, rather than a mere Communist aberration in its history, and he demonstrates the continuities between fears of Communism abroad and anxieties about centralized power in the United States. From World War II onward, some American intellectuals claimed that democracy must be a means as well as an end, and in their view deliberate and centralized social planning threatened it. For Belgrad, this anxiety helps us to understand the emergence of American postmodernism in new ways, and he tracks a cultural narrative critical of centralized authority, with reference to the idea of feedback loops. Cybernetics and ecology both understood the complexity of the systems they sought to model and argued that rational technocratic control threatened to destroy the very democracy it sought to defend. Belgrad shows how a commitment to seeing the universe as a self-regulating system of interconnection informs major works of music, literature, and social theory, and in so doing offers us a new way of comprehending the rise of postmodernism within a Cold War context.

Andrew Hoberek's chapter situates Frank Herbert's 1965 novel *Dune* in an ever-evolving Cold War U.S. foreign policy. Kennedy's administration moved away from a foreign policy based on containment to one in which the path to global success lay in winning the hearts and minds of developing nations, and in suggesting to the developing world that American help was the path to modernity itself. What is particularly telling is that *Dune* reveals how this change was sold to the American public, as it shows us how modernization theory offered a way for America to think of itself as a global but—crucially—nonimperial power, while simultaneously reanimating a sense of domestic potentiality that had seemed increasingly fragile in the era of the gray flannel suit. In Hoberek's allegorical reading of *Dune*, the third world is marked less by the absence of modernity than by its potential for arrival, and thus becomes the ground on which the American middle class can recuperate its agency.

Linking the United States with the globe is also one of the tasks of Karen Steigman's chapter. Joan Didion has often been represented as a conservative political thinker, and her work has been placed in a longer history of colonial and imperial romance. But Steigman's chapter offers us a somewhat different Didion. The unlikely pairing of Didion with Gayatri Chakravorty Spivak suggests a shared project: what is the historical nature—and proper form—of intimacy between first- and third-world feminists? Steigman argues that Didion's *A Book of Common Prayer* (1977) charts the "impossible intimacy" of the privileged American woman Charlotte Douglas, who comes to the fictional Central American country of Boca Grande but fails to register or understand its politics, even as she herself affects them. Didion demonstrates how Charlotte and her arms-brokering lawyer of a husband are implicated in the seemingly relentless series of revolutions in Boca Grande and in the American Cold War state writ large; both geopolitics and personal relations are figured as the imbrication of the first and third worlds.

Christine Hong's examination of narratives chronicling the 1950 seizure and subsequent loss of Pyongyang by UN forces reminds us that the Cold War was quite hot and that the Korean War complicates the explanatory power of the containment paradigm. Furthermore, narrative fiction plays a crucial role in understanding a conflict that is both ongoing and forgotten. As Hong points out, the notion of exile, along with its associated postcolonial theory, is inadequate for understanding the work of Korean American authors: in these cases, the relationship to an authentic home is complicated by the lack of a definitive resolution to conflict. Hong claims that we can read the work of Korean American authors through the lens of counterintelligence, suggesting a reciprocal relationship between literary and state-sponsored narratives of a past that is not yet over. Richard Kim's *The Martyred* (1964) is a rich site for such consideration. Not simply fiction about the Korean War, it is finally a novel about the Korean War as a narrative battlefield, concerned as it is with the work of South Korean intelligence operatives tasked with narrating the atrocities of North Korea against its Christian population.

Leerom Medovoi's chapter turns conventional accounts of the era as a bipolar ideological conflict on their head by instead foregrounding the Cold War as part of the long biopolitical remapping of the world. The claim that Communism and Nazism were parallel forms of totalitarianism, in that both sought to organize every aspect of their populations' lives, made possible an understanding of Communism not simply as an ideological argument about economics but as the enemy of humankind itself. In this formulation, Communism was committed to the creation of a class of racialized subhumans. What distinguishes Medovoi's argument is the way in which a war against totalitarianism, a war that often took the form of an argument about totalitarianism's links to racism, was itself committed to the logic of racial hierarchy. Totalitarianism was bad because it imagined some life as subhuman, yet antitotalitarianism frequently racialized its ideological opponent, thereby ironically committing itself to the very dynamic it was ostensibly criticizing.

Alan Nadel revisits his foundational work on American Cold War culture by considering how the Cold War was revivified in the Reagan era;

if Hoberek pointed out how the "Eastern" could function in the 1960s to reenergize domestic ambitions, Nadel asks us what it means that in the Reagan era such work could only happen in "a galaxy far, far away." For Nadel, the original *Star Wars* trilogy is a crucial text for understanding the logics of the Reagan era, and in particular for examining how Reaganism found ways of reinvigorating a story of Western power and conquest that had seemingly disappeared during what Jonathan Schell has called "the time of illusion," a decade (the 1970s) defined by epic failures abroad (Vietnam, the oil crisis) and at home (Watergate).[31] Nadel returns to his influential formulation of "Containment Culture" to see in the Vietnam era a continued exposure of the contradictions of Cold War culture, contradictions that were suppressed during the 1950s and exposed in the 1960s. The illumination of these contradictions helps, in Nadel's account, to explain the "virtual demise" in the 1960s of the Western, the most prolific of American popular genres, and the aesthetic corollary to the political mythology of the high Cold War. In his analysis, the original *Star Wars* trilogy tried to resolve how we might reinvigorate both the Western and the story of the West when the informing political situation had changed so dramatically.

NOTES

1. Alessandra Stanley, "Cold War–Style Spying Is Back (How Quaint)," *New York Times* (13 June 2010): C1.

2. Jerry Markon and Philip Rucker, "The Suspects in a Russian Spy Ring Lived All-American Lives," *Washington Post* (30 June 2010). Web.

3. *Salt*, DVD, directed by Phillip Noyce (Sony Pictures, 2010).

4. See for example Nikhil Pal Singh, "Cold War Redux: On the 'New Totalitarianism,'" *Radical History Review* 85 (Winter 2003): 171–81.

5. Scott Shane and Charlie Savage, "In Ordinary Lives, U.S. Sees the Work of Russian Agents," *New York Times* (28 June 2010). Web.

6. Ann Douglas, "Periodizing the American Century: Modernism, Postmodernism, and Postcolonialism in the Cold War Context," *Modernism/Modernity* 5, no. 3 (September 1998): 71–98, 75.

7. Lary May, ed., *Recasting America: Culture and Politics in the Age of Cold War* (Chicago: University of Chicago Press, 1988).

8. Joel Foreman, ed., *The Other Fifties: Interrogating Midcentury American Icons* (Urbana: University of Illinois Press, 1997).

9. Ibid., 3.

10. One powerful recent example is Mark McGurl, *The Program Era: Postwar Fiction and the Rise of Creative Writing* (Cambridge, MA: Harvard University Press,

2009), which argues that the defining context for postwar American fiction was the system of higher education.

11. Douglas, "Periodizing the American Century," 85.

12. This change is reflected in a more recent interdisciplinary collection, Douglas Field, ed., *American Cold War Culture* (Edinburgh: Edinburgh University Press, 2005), which has detailed readings of various novels and films. Other recent collections that offer readings of literature contextualized by the Cold War include Andrew Hammond, ed., *Cold War Literature: Writing the Global Conflict* (New York: Routledge, 2006); Josh Lukin, ed., *Invisible Suburbs: Recovering Protest Fiction in the 1950s United States* (Jackson: University Press of Mississippi, 2008); and Andrew Hammond, ed., *Global Cold War Literature: Western, Eastern and Postcolonial Perspectives* (New York: Routledge, 2012).

13. See Suzanne Clark, *Cold Warriors: Manliness on Trial in the Rhetoric of the West* (Carbondale: Southern Illinois University Press, 2000); Timothy Melley, *Empire of Conspiracy: The Culture of Paranoia in Postwar America* (Ithaca, NY: Cornell University Press, 2000); Edward Brunner, *Cold War Poetry* (Urbana: University of Illinois Press, 2001); D. Quentin Miller, *John Updike and the Cold War: Drawing the Iron Curtain* (Columbia: University of Missouri Press, 2001); Marcel Cornis-Pope, *Narrative Innovation and Cultural Rewriting in the Cold War Era and After* (New York: Palgrave, 2001); Camille Roman, *Elizabeth Bishop's World War II–Cold War View* (New York: Palgrave, 2001); Jacqueline Foertsch, *Enemies Within: The Cold War and the AIDS Crisis in Literature, Film, and Culture* (Urbana: University of Illinois Press, 2001); Deborah Nelson, *Pursuing Privacy in Cold War America* (New York: Columbia University Press, 2002); Robin Peel, *Writing Back: Sylvia Plath and the Cold War* (Madison, NJ: Fairleigh Dickinson University Press, 2002); Christina Klein, *Cold War Orientalism: Asia in the Middlebrow Imagination, 1945–1961* (Berkeley: University of California Press, 2003); Bruce McConachie, *American Theater in the Culture of the Cold War: Producing and Contesting Containment* (Iowa City: University of Iowa Press, 2003); Michael Davidson, *Guys Like Us: Citing Masculinity in Cold War Poetics* (Chicago: University of Chicago Press, 2003); David Seed, *Brainwashing: The Fictions of Mind Control* (Kent, OH: Kent State University Press, 2004); Leerom Medovoi, *Rebels: Youth and the Cold War Origins of Identity* (Durham, NC: Duke University Press, 2005); Julia Mickenberg, *Learning from the Left: Children's Literature, the Cold War, and Radical Politics in the United States* (New York: Oxford University Press, 2006); Matthew Frye Jacobson and Gaspar González, *What Have They Built You to Do?* The Manchurian Candidate *and Cold War America* (Minneapolis: University of Minnesota Press, 2006); Rebecca M. Schreiber, *Cold War Exiles in Mexico: U.S. Dissidents and the Culture of Critical Resistance* (Minneapolis: University of Minnesota Press, 2008); Arthur Redding, *Turncoats, Traitors, and Fellow Travelers: Culture and Politics of the Early Cold War* (Jackson: University Press of Mississippi, 2008); Daniel Cordle, *States of Suspense: The Nuclear Age, Postmodernism, and United States Fiction and Prose* (Manchester, UK: Manchester Univer-

sity Press, 2008); Eric Keenaghan, *Queering Cold War Poetry: Ethics of Vulnerability in Cuba and the United States* (Columbus: Ohio State University Press, 2009); Adam Piette, *The Literary Cold War: 1945 to Vietnam* (Edinburgh: Edinburgh University Press, 2009); Ann Sherif, *Japan's Cold War: Media, Literature, and the Law* (New York: Columbia University Press, 2009); David Caute, *Politics and the Novel During the Cold War* (Piscataway, NJ: Transactions Publishers, 2010); Jodi Kim, *Ends of Empire: Asian American Critique and the Cold War* (Minneapolis: University of Minnesota Press, 2010); Daniel Grausam, *On Endings: American Postmodern Fiction and the Cold War* (Charlottesville: University of Virginia Press, 2011); Derek C. Maus, *Unvarnishing Reality: Subversive Russian and American Cold War Satire* (Columbia: University of South Carolina Press, 2011); and Steven Belletto, *No Accident, Comrade: Chance and Design in Cold War American Narratives* (New York: Oxford University Press, 2012).

14. Elaine Tyler May, *Homeward Bound: American Families in the Cold War Era* (New York: Basic Books, 1988), 14.

15. Thomas Schaub, *American Fiction in the Cold War* (Madison: University of Wisconsin Press, 1991), 191.

16. Ibid., 163, 178.

17. Piette, *The Literary Cold War*, 6.

18. See for example Odd Arne Westad, *The Global Cold War: Third World Interventions and the Making of Our Times* (Cambridge: Cambridge University Press, 2005); and Gilbert Joseph and Daniela Spenser, eds., *In from the Cold: Latin America's New Encounter with the Cold War* (Durham, NC: Duke University Press, 2007).

19. Klein, *Cold War Orientalism*, 41.

20. Ibid., 146.

21. Medovoi, *Rebels*, 146.

22. Ibid., 3. As Medovoi writes, "Although containment undoubtedly represents a central political logic of Cold War culture, I believe that the three worlds imaginary generated a rival logic of emancipation whose consideration offers a more dialectically complex understanding of the era" (*Rebels*, 337, n. 29).

23. Ibid., 11.

24. Schreiber, *Cold War Exiles in Mexico*, 202.

25. Kim, *Ends of Empire*, 5.

26. Ibid., 24.

27. Redding, *Turncoats, Traitors, and Fellow Travelers*, 60.

28. Ibid., 112.

29. Piette, *The Literary Cold War*, 79.

30. Ibid., 80.

31. Jonathan Schell, *The Time of Illusion* (New York: Vintage, 1976).

Rethinking Domestic Cultures

1

TOTAL LITERARY AWARENESS

WHY COLD WAR HOOVERISM PRE-READ AFRO-MODERNIST WRITING

WILLIAM J. MAXWELL

In the upshot of World War II, it first appeared that the subject of this chapter, the Federal Bureau of Investigation's invasive surveillance of African American authors, would go the way of the 1919–20 Palmer Raids, a relic of the anticommunist emergency flushed from Bureau memory. "The world that the [FBI] faced in September 1945 was very different from the world of 1939 when the war began," the Bureau's self-produced on-line history sensibly remarks.[1] African Americans, tasting "equality during wartime labor shortages, had developed aspirations and the means of achieving these goals [that they] had lacked before the war."[2] Harry Truman of half-Southern Missouri, elevated to the White House after Franklin Delano Roosevelt's sudden death, was privately less sympathetic to black aspirations than the fallen president. Yet the realpolitik of a regionally fractured Democratic Party and a Soviet-challenged national image pushed his administration to employ honeymoon capital to widen the cracks in white supremacy opened by wartime organizing. In 1946, Truman appointed the board of the first federal Civil Rights Commission. Inside a year, its integrated membership had produced the landmark report *To Secure These Rights*, recommending presidential measures to eliminate religious and racial segregation. In 1948, Truman gave Southern Democrats hell by endorsing the Commission's advice to desegregate the U.S. military. As viewed by the late Malcolm X biographer Manning Marable, these overtures lured African Americans into a shortsighted, long-lasting accord with Cold War liberalism.[3] As viewed by the FBI, they were an immediate challenge to display egalitarian bona fides.

Marching ahead of the army, the Bureau honored its black troops in the October 1947 issue of *Ebony*, Afro-America's highest-circulation source of positive images. The unsigned, splashily illustrated cover story "Negro FBI Agents in Action" cautioned that Bureau employees doing "highly confidential work cannot be publicly identified."[4] This was a handy dodge for an institution that employed all of fifteen black investigators between

1919 and 1956.[5] J. Edgar Hoover's publicity-seeking Crime Records Division nonetheless permitted flattering portraits of two racial exceptions: James E. Amos, one of the Bureau's "crack agents," and Sam Noisette, the director's "personal aide," a self-described soul brother to Hoover who worked the door to his boss's inner sanctum.[6] Amos is painted as a hard-bitten encyclopedia of G-man wisdom, a "gray and balding" survivor of gangland battles who "has gum-shoed for the FBI for the past 26 years."[7] His assistance in writing "an unhappy finis to Marcus Garvey's dramatic 'Back to Africa' movement" suggests the inconvenient truth of his hiring before the Hoover administration.[8] Hoover's younger protégé Noisette, by contrast, is cast as the trusted doorman of the national security/publicity state, "the greeter to thousands of Americans who come to Washington to see how the world's most scientific anti-crime agency works."[9] Between the heading "Front Man for the FBI" and the handsome photo of Noisette attending to criminological relics in the director's reception room, Hoover's postwar Bureau clarifies its comfort with black window dressing, the personal aide rivaling the crack agent as the representative black FB eye.

Not long after the *Ebony* piece, however, the Bureau's favorite African American employees were widely known to work on retainer, far from headquarters. From January to October 1949, FBI spies shined in the notorious Smith Act trial of twelve Communist Party leaders arrested for advocating the violent overthrow of the United States. All twelve were found guilty as charged under the 1940 statute, and the verdict was upheld by the Supreme Court's *Dennis* decision of 1951, an opinion virtually outlawing American Communism. Ellen Schrecker, the prominent liberal chronicler of McCarthyism, suggests that the trial was a painful blend of barricades shouting match and literary-critical seminar. Anticommunist prosecutors and Communist theoreticians loudly clashed over the layers of double-talking "Aesopian language" in the Marxist-Leninist canon. As in the original Red Raids of 1919–20, crescendos of rhetorical violence in leftist writing were presumed guilty of the performative, and legal briefs were thick with selections from the Bureau's vast library of radical publications.[10] Yet what clinched the jury's guilty verdict was the personal touch of well-rehearsed FBI informers—or loyal "informants," in the sanitizing terminology promoted by their Bureau handlers. African American William Cummings, a Toledo, Ohio, auto worker who entered the Communist Party for the FBI in 1943, was one of seven witnesses chosen to take the stand from a casting call of sixty. According to his testimony, vicious Marxist literature rhymed with informal party schooling, which "taught militants that one day the streets would run with blood."[11]

Cummings was not the only African American infiltrator working for Hoover. A disproportionate percentage of the FBI's approximately one thousand informers in the postwar Communist Party were black, about half of these salaried professional anticommunists for reasons of conviction or necessity.[12] Recruiting African American sources was preferred as the Bureau schemed to transform the party's staunch antiracism into an existential threat. The "lingering obsession with white chauvinism protected black members from suspicion," FBI historian Kenneth O'Reilly explains, since "white communists who accused Negro comrades of working for the FBI often found themselves accused of racism and drummed out of the party."[13] Federal Loyalty Board and McCarthy committee hearings thus often hosted the likes of William O. Nowell, once one of the party's longest-serving African American recruits, a graduate of Soviet cadre schools who appeared on behalf of the U.S. government at over forty trials and hearings between 1948 and 1954. Manning Johnson, formerly an experienced party manager, received $4,500 a year from the Justice Department for his eagerness to lie "a thousand times" to defend national security.[14] Lola Belle Holmes pulled in speaker's fees from the ultraconservative John Birch Society after testifying at the Smith Act trial of black Communist Claude Lightfoot.[15] Julia Clarice Brown, a Clevelander who named 120 names of ex-comrades before the House Un-American Activities Committee (HUAC), offered a race-first defense of her double-faced cohort in *I Testify: My Years as an F.B.I. Undercover Agent* (1966). "There can be no doubt," she proclaimed, "that the real and ultimate goal of Soviet strategists is the absolute domination of world humanity by a Caucasian Communist elite."[16] In Brown's calculation, Soviet premier Nikita Khrushchev had more in common with Alabama's segregationist governor George Wallace than either could afford to admit.

Making cases and headlines, Brown and similar Bureau informers helped to create an aura of undercover daring seductive enough to diminish the attractions of James Amos and other aging FBI idols of the gangster era. Shape-shifting spies starred in the breakthrough Bureau entertainments of the early 1950s, finally unseating the self-consistent gangbusters of the FBI fictions of the 1930s. *I Was a Communist for the FBI*, declared the informer-hero of the eponymous 1951 film, charitably cast as a documentary for the purposes of its Academy Award nomination. FBI mole Herbert Philbrick (the introducer of Julia Brown's book) revealed how *I Led Three Lives: Citizen, "Communist," Counterspy* in a lucrative 1952 memoir adapted for television until 1956. By the middle of the decade, Cold War secret agents had completed the burial of perhaps the Bureau's greatest fiction, the New Deal "public hero" (a burial anticipated, in fact, in *Ebony*'s equal praise for Amos and Noisette, the latter more Man Friday than hard-boiled G-man). The public enemy plot had given way to an "espionage plot" feeding off the corpse of Soviet spying, a security threat in fact largely removed from American territory by 1951, the year Senator Joseph McCarthy first denounced an immense Communist conspiracy and in turn invented "one of the most consequential conspiracy theories in U.S. history."[17] Projected in sepia tone, the FBI's new model protagonist looked oddly like the narrator of Ralph Ellison's *Invisible Man* (1952), a great American novel shorn of its extensive Bureau references before the last draft. Ellison's talkative leading man matched the FBI's as a clever screen for clashing ideological impressions, resurrected from the party underground to speak on the frequencies of anticommunist consensus. Hoover pugnaciously shielded his rising class of spy-heroes, black and white, from "pseudoliberal" criticism. "You find reference to [informants] in the Bible," he insisted to the readers of *U.S. News and World Report*.[18] Along the way, he defended the African American informers who played a willful part in persecuting W. E. B. Du Bois, Paul Robeson, and several of the other black artists discussed later in this chapter. Here as elsewhere, the story of the FBI's close engagement with Afro-modernism is not in every respect a black-and-white morality tale.

Uncovering the deepest logic behind the victory of the FBI spy-hero means reinspecting the Bureau's zealously literary part in the racial politics of the long McCarthy era, which is the focus of the pages that follow. Aspects of this role flowed from the micropolitics of Hoover's break with Truman, a president unforgivably wary of "building up a gestapo" in the United States and guilty of establishing the CIA in 1947, a detested Bureau rival from the start.[19] Hoover repaid Truman's differences from FDR with a spotlit appearance before HUAC, dramatizing his fresh partnership with antiadministration Red-baiters dismayed by the measured pace of liberal anticommunism.[20] Testifying that HUAC and the FBI shared a paramount goal, "protection of the internal security of the nation," Hoover renounced his primary alliance with executive power by blessing the congressional McCarthyite tactic of "prescriptive publicity" against Soviet penetration.[21] For the remainder of the Truman administration, the FBI disdained both special service to the president and the remnants of the Democratic New

Deal that once fostered it. In their place, the Bureau slipped its secret file on Truman to his Republican opponents and arranged to protect state security in concert with a grateful Republican Congress.[22] Following the outbreak of the Korean War, this Congress bucked Truman's veto in order to pass the Internal Security or McCarran Act reauthorizing the Bureau's custodial detention program. Its descendants on Capitol Hill approved or sweetened every yearly FBI budget request until Hoover's death.[23] Beneath the director's ostentatious nonpartisanship, the soul of the FBI's antiradical politics reenlisted in the GOP.

Almost at once, however, the Bureau's technical assistance to McCarthyism exceeded the requirements of Hoover's feud with the Democrats. In Ellen Schrecker's account, the FBI scrambled to occupy "the bureaucratic heart of the McCarthy era." "Had observers known in the 1950s what they have learned since the 1970s, when the Freedom of Information Act opened the Bureau's files," she speculates, "'McCarthyism' would probably have been called 'Hooverism.'"[24] Schrecker's case for Cold War Hooverism depends on a high regard for the functioning of the FBI's charismatic bureaucracy, its design, management, and marketing of a "machinery of political repression" able to install reactionary anticommunism as a touchstone of good government.[25] Providing undercover informers to prosecutors was just one part of the apparatus. Under a secret "Responsibilities Program" established in 1951, the Bureau dispatched file-based, not-for-attribution "blind memoranda" to governors and other "appropriate authorities," warning of possible Communists on the payroll.[26] Well-honed Bureau techniques for indexing dissent directly fed the classic sin of the blacklist, fingering over four hundred public employees for firing, most of them school and university teachers. The names that the FBI could not legally name for state officials it delivered to the Boy Scouts, the Red Cross, and other wholesome quasi publics.[27] At least until 1953, when Hoover began to fear the senator's sloppiness, the FBI supplied Joseph McCarthy's Permanent Investigations Subcommittee with everything it could: public praise; back-channel political advice; prejudicial information on enemies culled from the Bureau archives; and former FBI agent Don Surine as chief investigator.[28] In the McCarthy who fell from grace, Hoover met an anticommunist more media-drunk than himself, and he did not enjoy the reflected glare. Even HUAC, the director wrote, seemed to care more for "headlines . . . than ultimate security."[29] Ironically, thanks to Hoover's relative discretion, his term as McCarthyism's comptroller-in-chief only enhanced his charismatic appeal. Buoyed by popular anticommunism, public esteem for the director reached its apex, envisioning an untouchable among law-and-order untouchables. In the appraisal of one contributor to *Kids' Letters to the F.B.I.* (1966), a little classic of youthful obedience, Jesus was indeed a "hero," but "Mr. Hoover has done more toward helping to keep down juvenile delinquency, as well as other crimes."[30]

Hoover was worshipped less earnestly by the minority of American liberals revolted by McCarthyism in any guise, their discontent galvanizing unprecedented open criticism of the Bureau—and unprecedented Bureau pushback. The publication of Max Lowenthal's *The Federal Bureau of Investigation* (1950), the first vigorously unauthorized history of the institution, is a cautionary case in point. Over five hundred pages, a decade in the making, and released in the same year as the Bureau's first "Ten Most Wanted" list, Lowenthal's book mounts a lawyerly case against the FBI's aura as "the infallible watchdog of American security and liberty."[31] The Hoover Bureau's appetite for "rumors, suspicions and gossip," Lowenthal concludes, "is the realization of the fear expressed" by the FBI's earliest skeptics, the congressmen who confronted President Theodore Roosevelt with the worry that the Bureau "might some day adopt practices habitual to political police systems in Europe but abhorrent to a democracy."[32] Lowenthal, an ex–Supreme Court clerk, onetime congressional aide, and close friend of President Truman, derived little comfort from the quiet approval of his indictment at the White House: word alone of his book's appearance attracted a prodigious Bureau counterattack. Wilting under fire, sales of *The Federal Bureau of Investigation* failed to break 7,500, disappointing distinguished independent publisher William Sloane.[33] Considered in relation to the history of FBI literary surveillance, however, the book thrived as the inspiration for the intensified Bureau counterliteratures of the 1950s, which were approaching a peak of their own.

Hoover, furious that his reader-agents failed to pick up the scent of Lowenthal's history prior to an advance notice in *Publishers Weekly*, had plunged into a firing mood even before the book's release. "Mr. Hoover, if I had known this book was going to be published," swore Louis Nichols, head of the crime records division, "I'd have thrown my body between the presses and stopped it."[34] Nichols mended fences with Hoover by supervising an instant refutation. Within the "Seat of Government," the FBI's modestly nicknamed Washington headquarters, this pre-rebuttal of Lowenthal's charges planted the seeds for the most successful Bureau self-narrations of the 1950s: Hoover's own *Masters of Deceit* (1958), with two million paperbacks sold, and Don Whitehead's rose-tinted *The FBI Story* (1956), written inside a Bureau office furnished with hand-picked case summaries. Beyond FBI headquarters, Walter Winchell and other columnists friendly to the Bureau immediately adopted the pre-rebuttal's talking points, their objections reinforced in planted editorials ("Smearing the FBI," charged the *New York Herald Tribune*). Head agents at the Bureau's local field offices were directed to discourage bookstores from stocking Lowenthal's title. One up-and-comer proposed that G-men remove copies from public libraries but was shot down with the news that stolen books might be replaced, doubling sales. The book's author was kept under constant FBI surveillance; during one of his out-of-town business trips, Lowenthal's wife awoke to a 3:00 AM call from a team of agents. Bureau allies denounced him on the floor of Congress as a treasonous New Deal relic and dragged him before an executive session of HUAC.[35] A *Nation* piece with an immortal title—"The FBI Reviews a Book"—noted the mystery of the session's transcript, which was publicly released, without clarification, "just one day before Mr. Lowenthal's book went on sale."[36]

All of this extraordinary literary-critical activity indeed took place in advance of *The Federal Bureau of Investigation*'s printing. "Perhaps coincidentally, perhaps not," journalist Curt Gentry remarks, "the page proofs of the book vanished from the motorcycle sidecar of a messenger en route from the printer to the publisher."[37] Absolutely noncoincidental in the Lowenthal affair is the expansion of FBI literary surveillance into an agenda I call "Total Literary Awareness." Half a century before the Pentagon's controversial Total Information Awareness (TIA) program, an abandoned effort to aggregate and "data-mine" all electronic predictions of terrorist activity, the Bureau's undeclared "TLA" program sought precocious knowledge of all published threats to the state—especially those threats to the state of the Bureau's reputation. Cold War Hooverism's hyperactive counterliterary meddling thus did not end with the bowdlerization of State Department libraries abroad, enforced by Bureau crony Roy Cohn during a 1953 tour of European capitals. Back in the United States, the impulse was to know enough of domestic publishing to screen suspicious books before they reached the shelves. As we will see, TLA equipped FBI literary surveillance with newfound reach and muscle but dramatically failed to regulate the whole of U.S. literature. Recently released Bureau files disclose that the postwar swell of Afro-modernist writing was far better mapped and appreciated by Hooverism than previously acknowledged, yet it was also less containable by such state interference than might be expected.

Some of the tentacles of Total Literary Awareness have been unraveled by literary historian Claire Culleton. Delving into the Bureau's 234-page file on commercial publisher Henry Holt, she uncovers evidence of Hoover's "custodial relationship" with the pillars of the Cold War book market.[38] Holt employees sent the Bureau all manner of literary foreknowledge, from book proposals to page proofs to advance copies, so much material that an editorial staffer wrote Hoover with the news that "I am beginning to feel like a member of the FBI myself."[39] Predictably, Hoover and his ghostwriters were asked to provide blurbs for *The Hidden Russia* and other anticommunist titles. Just as often, however, the Bureau was granted uncommon rights of pre-refusal. Holt editor Milt Hill, for example, asked for "advice as to whether we should do or not" a McCarthy autobiography, receiving a green light since it "would be a friendly book from a Bureau standpoint."[40] Books less kind to the Bureau were rejected with its help at Holt and other firms. The manuscript of Fred Cook's muckraking *The FBI Nobody Knows*, eventually published in 1964, was refused at Random House (home of *The FBI Story*) after Bennett Cerf shredded professional ethics by forwarding a copy to Hoover.[41] Editorial informants such as Cerf, recruited in the wake of the Lowenthal embarrassment, made it practically impossible to criticize the FBI through a major New York publisher without costly delay. With the FBI fed the minutes of editorial board meetings at *Time* and *Life*, *Fortune* and *Look*, the *Reader's Digest* and the *Daily Worker*, points along the full spectrum of U.S. print culture were opened to Bureau pre-awareness.[42] To adapt Louis Nichols, there was now most always a body poised to throw itself between the presses.

Critical nonfiction was the initial target of the Bureau's Cold War campaign to impose itself between unflattering portraiture and the American public. Yet the Afro-modernist FBI files of the period demonstrate that Total Literary Awareness also kept watch over imaginative literature. Judging from Lorraine Hansberry's file, the FBI refused to believe that playwrights deserved to choose who reviewed their trial runs.[43] Just escaped from the University of Wisconsin to freelance writing in New York City, Hansberry's otherwise overlooked contributions to small labor papers inspired a 1952 security check, the trigger of a 1,052-page file that closed only with copies of her premature obituary (U.S., Federal, Hansberry, document of July 21, 1952). Exposing its sensitivity to young literary talent, the FBI leapt into coordinated national action when hearing of her intent to attend a Montevideo peace conference in 1953. The "Washington field office is requested to examine the files of the Passport Division of the United States Department of State," Hansberry's Bureau file attests, "in an effort to obtain all available background material on the subject, any derogatory information contained therein, and a photograph and complete description" (document of March 30, 1953). The Milwaukee office unproductively rummaged through her Wisconsin transcripts for other crumbs of scandal, while Chicago discovered her family's prominence in the city's racially fractured real estate market (document of March 14, 1953). New York revealed her independent employment as an "instructor of a class in Literature of the Negro" at the progressive Jefferson School, and traced her residence to Bleecker Street in Greenwich Village, this literature's downtown office since the Harlem Renaissance (document of December 18, 1953). For all their prescient interest, none of the Bureau's field offices predicted Hansberry's posthumous emergence as a voice of lesbian feminism, uncharacteristically missing the implication of her draft play for Sappho, *Andromeda the Thief.* Neither could they envision her dismissal by later black nationalists for sins of "leftwing accommodation to middle-class ideology."[44] What Black Power revisionist Peniel Joseph describes as her "unusual biography—an upper-middle-class black woman who abandoned a comfortable existence for identification with the racially and politically oppressed"—in fact struck the Bureau as a typical profile of present literary danger.[45]

By the mid-1950s, male gazers at the New York branch of the Bureau were familiar enough with Hansberry's everyday life and looks to record her adoption of an "'Italian' cut" hairstyle (document of October 11, 1956). The Bureau's premature discovery of *A Raisin in the Sun*, the play that made her famously young and gifted, was par for this course. In 1958, a year before *Raisin*'s Broadway debut, Hoover ordered New York's special agent in charge to "promptly conduct [a] necessary investigation in an effort to establish whether the play . . . is in any way controlled or influenced by the Communist Party and whether it in any way follows the Communist line" (document of September 5, 1958). Thus, no academic lectures were required for the Bureau to expect the militancy beneath Hansberry's crossover appeal: her Security Index card was preparation enough (document of September 5, 1958). The file ingredients that follow Hoover's edict approximate the contents of a drama fanatic's scrapbook. Clipped reviews and playbills track *Raisin*'s tryouts through the provinces, documenting the conquest of New York one outpost at a time. Reports from the *New Haven Register* and *Journal-Courier* on the play's Connecticut run are carefully cut and pasted, but the highest aim is seeing a trial production in the flesh (document of January 23, 1959). Since the Bureau's New Haven office failed to witness the show for itself, "Philadelphia is requested to designate an Agent [*sic*] to attend in order that a true picture of the play's content can be obtained and properly analyzed" (document of January 29, 1959). When the FBI's long experience in deciphering Afro-modernism met the rushed demands of Total Literary Awareness, only a Bureau-trained reader was thought up to the task.

The particular reader selected, a Philadelphia-based special agent whose name has been lost to Freedom of Information Act (FOIA) censorship, fulfilled his assignment at the Walnut Theater with a notably sensitive four-page review. Sustaining interpretive positions while describing narrative arcs, volunteering minutely witty descriptions of characters and costumes, this talented ghostreader bids for a place in the upper echelon of FBI English heads. The receptive insight of his review—it would receive a noninflated A in many college classes—flowed from inspiration beyond the call of police duty. With its swelling existential vocabulary, the reviewer's sketch of a super-articulate Hansberry character searching for "a means of self-expression and self-identification" indeed doubles as a confession of unfulfilled literary need (document of February 5, 1959). A G-man Flaubert, the reviewer might as well have admitted that Mademoiselle Younger, *c'est moi*. The rigorous demands of TLA precognition, this is to suggest, did not always prevent FBI readers from succumbing to the spell of black expression.

The reviewer begins with reference to a plot summary previously published in the *Philadelphia Daily News*, the equivalent in a Bureau file of dismissive in-text citation. What comes after, the agent's independent analysis of Hansberry's well-made play, will not respect the obvious. Hoover's orders to measure *Raisin*'s debts to Communism are thus dispensed with respectfully yet swiftly. "The play contains no comments of any nature about Communism as such," the reader certifies, "but deals essentially with negro [*sic*] aspirations, the problems inherent in their efforts to advance themselves, and varied attempts at arriving at solutions" (document of February 4, 1959). The review takes flight when party lines give way to the intersection of racial and dramatic tensions: "The contrasting proposals for solutions are set up through the character delineations of the widowed mother, her son, and her daughter. The specific bone of contention which is the central theme of the plot is the sum of $10,000 received by the widow as a result of the death of her husband" (document of February 5, 1959). Themes, plots, and bones may be conflated, but the Bureau reviewer insightfully sketches the interiors of Beneatha, the Younger family's quick-witted medical-student daughter, searching for an attractive partner in racial uplift "under the amused and tolerant scrutiny of the other women"; George Murchison, her ardently assimilationist suitor captured by his "over narrow, over emphatic ivy league [*sic*] clothes"; and Joseph Asagai, his principled Nigerian rival, quickened by anticolonial ambition to "overthrow the rule of European nations, find political freedom, . . . and make [his] own future" (document of February 5, 1959). "Africa," continues the reviewer, "is a matter which is only dimly comprehended by the other members of the family": this lack of understanding matches the mostly white audience at the Walnut, only a handful of whom "appeared to dwell on the propaganda messages" (document of February 5, 1959). As it happened, New York audiences were little more attuned to *Raisin*'s layers of Pan-Africanism, muted by Hansberry's South Side Chicago setting, the familiar scene of domestic naturalism's native sons. A mysterious Philadelphia FBI agent may thus have gotten at the play's budding black internationalism first, encouraged by TLA policy to forward the news to Washington prior to Hansberry's Broadway debut. Communism as such was a welcome absence in *Raisin*, this police-reviewer assumed, yet the play's love match between Nigeria and black Chicago required early exposure to federal authorities, then prioritizing U.S.-Africa policy under the Eisenhower administration's new Bureau of African Affairs.[46]

Dozens of less thoughtful FBI agents spent workdays in the grip of TLA investigations, packing the personal files of Afro-modernists only suspected of literary intent. Again and again, Bureau critics provided emerging black writers of the Cold War with some of their earliest notices, often fault-finding and hidden from productive use, yet eager for any sign of professional development. For example, the 1951 file of Alice Childress, Hansberry's sister playwright in the orbit of Paul Robeson's journal *Freedom*, reflects an FBI agent's study in the Billy Rose Theatre Collection of the New York Public Library. Knowing that Childress had been trained in drama "since her Junior High School days," this Bureau researcher applied the scholarly lessons of FBI archivism, poring over catalogs for hints of original plays of her own.[47] Lance Jeffers's file of 1949,[48] 187 pages devoted to the poet whom Trudier Harris called a "black nationalist without a movement,"[49] prepares for publications to come by combing every credit hour of his creative writing major. As of 1950, a memo reveals, Jeffers was "working toward a Bachelor of Science degree in writing" at Columbia, "and his schedule consists of 20 points composed of English, composition, and French" (U.S., Federal, Jeffers, document of January 26, 1950). "To date," reported an anxious agent, hovering like a tuition-paying parent, "he has earned 69 points of the necessary 124 points which are needed for graduation" (document of January 26, 1950). In the instance of Calvin Hernton's 1955 file, meanwhile, the Bureau confessed its interest in books with no chance of reaching a publisher.[50] Tracking the cofounder of *Umbra* magazine even while he was an MA candidate at Fisk, Bureau pre-readers took seriously the typically self-admiring efforts of a student novelist (bohemian male subgenre) to write what he knew best. Unassumingly titled *The Recognition of Man*, Hernton's manuscript-in-progress is described as "the story of two individuals who are attending a college or university. One of these individuals is principally interested in exploitation of any persons over whom he can gain control, while the other is a poor but hard working character who is attempting to get an education, and who takes occasion throughout the book to explain to the other character the difference between right and wrong as concerns the various phases of life which the average person will encounter" (U.S., Federal, Hernton, document of March 14, 1955). Interviewed by a Bureau team despite this off-putting thumbnail, Hernton pled artistic myopia, promising he was "not interested in Communism and [advising] that his principal interest is in his writing and because of this he does not know what goes on around him" (document of March 14, 1955). Pre-reading even more ghostly materials occupied the agents assigned the case of Julian Mayfield in 1954, the year the actor-novelist relocated to Puerto Rico.[51] After observing that "the subject stayed in his house most of the time and appeared to occupy much of his time by typing," the hunt was on to discover the polished results (U.S., Federal, Mayfield, document of November 30, 1955). Though it failed to learn precisely "what material the subject was typing" in Naranjito, the FBI lingered close enough to hear literary sounds from Mayfield's rooms until 1974, with his novels *The Hit* (1957), *The Long Night* (1958), and *The Grand Parade* (1961) paving the way for his service as a speechwriter for Kwame Nkrumah, Ghana's founding postindependence president (document of November 30, 1955). The CIA for its part took an interest in Mayfield that has been sensitive enough to be censored until the present, "pursuant to an Executive Order."[52]

Better-established Afro-modernists with first publications under their belts also faced TLA speed-reading, the greater intensity of the chase signaling their graver threat. Author-critic J. Saunders Redding,[53] wanted by the Bureau from 1953 to 1968, managed to produce *To Make a Poet Black* (1939), a landmark social history of African American literature, without Bureau preknowledge. The success of his postpassing novel *Stranger and Alone* (1950), however, left him with many acquaintances willing to talk with the FBI, nameless cronies prone to recommending "that any writing or lecturing done by the applicant be reviewed before being presented" (U.S., Federal, Redding, document of February 27, 1953). The need for such vigilance stemmed not from Redding's hedged attraction to Communism but from the ambiguous politics of his passionate intensity, the product of an artistic temperament supposedly marinated in racial grievance. Redding is depicted as "a person who is very emotional and high-strung," and these "traits come out in his writings, which deal with the disadvantages and handicaps of being a Negro" and are thus subject to interpretation "in a very different light than the author may have intended to impart" (document of February 27, 1953). Willard Motley's file,[54] a toxic amalgam of Bureau curiosities about black cosmopolitanism and black queerness, nears its 1967 conclusion with news of the novelist's withering life in Mexico, stranded abroad by the homosexuality "provisions . . . of the Immigration and Nationality Act" (U.S., Federal, Motley, document of March 18, 1954). "Gone into full retirement," dependent on the income "from the paper-back edition of 'Let No Man Write My Epitaph' [*sic*]," he was said "to keep a group of young boys about him and only spasmodically work on a new book" (document of March 7, 1961). Motley's writing in its "raceless" prime attracted vigorous forms of TLA scrutiny from 1951 on. A confidential report accurately revealed that Motley's second book, a novel "about soldiers home from the wars and tentatively titled 'They Fished All Night' is being gestated on an Oregon ranch" (document of March 18, 1954). Surveillance of Motley's usual literary neighborhood in Chicago followed an informant's hands-on account of the making of *Knock on Any Door* (1947), the bestselling portrait of an Italian altar boy turned gangster: "the story contains certain passages describing in minute detail a homosexual act. . . . It would be rather difficult to depict in such graphic style an act which had not been experienced by the narrator" (document of March 18, 1954). The queer milieu of Motley's work hours presented not only sexual opportunities for the author, concluded another source, but also "personality portraits for projection in his writings, much [*sic*] of which deal with sociological problems and adjustment" (document of March 18, 1954). Slumming through the Motley file, Total Literary Awareness plunged the Bureau into the cultural dynamism of Chicago's interzone, a space where social fictions sprang from interracial sexual exchanges marginal enough to dodge total policing.

Not every Afro-modernist file initiated in the long McCarthy era—the busiest period in the history of Bureau counterliterature—opens with fingerprints of the FBI's post-Lowenthal resolve. Given the sheer number of these files, twenty-two in all, holes in the TLA blanket should be expected. Ralph Ellison's collection, opened in 1950, busied itself with the security challenges of his White House visits and American Academy in Rome fellowships. (Early versions of *Invisible Man* did not return the Bureau's relative kindness.)[55] E. Franklin Frazier's and Charles S. Johnson's employment by UNESCO sparked mandatory loyalty investigations in 1953 and 1952, respectively; so did William Pickens's work for the "Interracial Section" of the U.S. Saving Bonds program in 1947.[56] Andy Razaf (file opened 1949), Shirley Graham Du Bois (1950), Lonne Elder III (1954), Frank London Brown (1955), and writer-cartoonist Ollie Harrington (1951), his dossier active into the twenty-first century, were pursued as garden-variety unionists or Communists before their artistic ambitions assumed equal billing.[57] Uncommon black Beat Bob Kaufman (1950), a radical "of the waterfront" rumored to have been "expelled from the CP for degeneracy," received much the same treatment (U.S., Federal, Kaufman, document of June 21, 1956).[58] William Gardner Smith (1951), Ollie Harrington's fellow Francophile, was recognized as the author of *The Last of the Conquerors* (1948), yet he was initially sought for Socialist Workers Party membership (U.S., Federal, Smith, document of May 5, 1951).[59] *The Crisis of the Negro Intellectual* (1967) eventually infiltrated the Bureau library, but Harold Cruse (1950) was first recruited as an undercover Communist Party informant. He proved willing to name names of onetime comembers, but nothing more (U.S., Federal, Cruse, document of November 26, 1956).[60] Hoyt Fuller's (1954), Amiri Baraka's (1957), and James Baldwin's (1958) files took shape and weight only in the 1960s, and are most accurately measured as documents of that period.[61]

The Afro-modernist files of the long McCarthy era nevertheless establish Total Literary Awareness as the distinctive Cold War contribution to the stockpile of Bureau counterliteratures. Searching high and low for word of texts unimpressed by the FBI's pinnacle of popular support, these files suggest that the accelerated assimilation of postwar African American writing invited the application of post-Lowenthal techniques to imaginative literature. Heeding the upbeat future of black drama, fiction, and poetry, three cultural "shock troops of the modern civil rights movement," the Bureau moved to anticipate the course of American print culture beyond the usual journalistic suspects.[62] A new strain of criminological knowledge emerged—data on the *intent* to fantasize sedition—as G-men listened for typewriters through keyholes. By this point in the counterliterary story, the presence of TLA at the primal scene of literary invention may seem another gloomy milestone in the Bureau's serial encroachment on black authorship. In this latest installment, state police power claws at the door to composition, the first and most autonomous of the social processes (writing, editing, printing, publishing) that contemporary editorial theory claims are actually responsible for the authorizing of texts. If, as John K. Young argues, white "control of the means of production" of black books reveals the difference race makes for "apparently universal descriptions of the relationship between the author and the public," then what is revealed by Hooverism's dash to survey black manuscripts before they sought publishers of any color?[63] Under TLA, Addison Gayle Jr.'s famous figure of the "invisible censor, white power," assumed material form, incarnating the black writer's racialized self-doubt as a federal interloper, a state spook who sat beside the creative "sanctuary of [the] private room."[64] Synchronized with the indexing of African American authors for possible arrest, TLA thus dogged Afro-modernism with the prospect of cradle-to-grave supervision. This prospect was hardly ever wholly realized, of course. TLA, conceived in response to a memorable failure of Bureau preknowledge, most often conceded its imperfect origins in practice. *A Raisin in the Sun* might be insightfully pre-read, for example, but it could not be stopped in its tracks for Broadway. In fact, the play was stalked on its trial run because of the Bureau's toothless knowledge of its prestigious destination. Here, Total Literary Awareness was incompletely totalizing, and the surrounding Cold War "containment culture" was more leaky than advertised.[65] In the end, TLA's jarring extension of Bureau counterliterature to the point of literary production left tracks sufficiently deep but sufficiently pliable to inspire Afro-modernism's next generation, proudly nationalist Black Artists who burned to resist state interference by beating it to creation's starting line.

NOTES

1. See FBI.gov, 2008. Federal Bureau of Investigation (29 January 2008). Web. http://www.fbi.gov/.

2. Ibid.

3. Manning Marable, *Race, Reform, and Rebellion: The Second Reconstruction and Beyond in Black America, 1945–2006*, 3rd ed. (Jackson: University Press of Mississippi, 2007), 23.

4. "Negro FBI Agents in Action," *Ebony*, October 1947, 9–13, 9.

5. Rhodri Jeffreys-Jones, *The FBI: A History* (New Haven, CT: Yale University Press, 2007), 135.

6. "Negro FBI Agents in Action," 9.

7. Ibid., 11.

8. Ibid., 11.

9. Ibid., 13.

10. Ellen Schrecker, *Many Are the Crimes: McCarthyism in America* (Princeton, NJ: Princeton University Press, 1998), 195.

11. Quoted in Marable, *Race, Reform, and Rebellion*, 28.

12. Schrecker, *Many Are the Crimes*, 228.

13. Kenneth O'Reilly, *"Racial Matters": The FBI's Secret File on Black America, 1960–1972* (New York: Free Press, 1989), 266.

14. Quoted in Marable, *Race, Reform, and Rebellion*, 28.

15. David Caute, *The Great Fear: The Anti-Communist Purge Under Truman and Eisenhower* (New York: Simon and Schuster, 1978), 547.

16. Julia Clarice Brown, *I Testify: My Years as an F.B.I. Undercover Agent* (Boston: Western Islands, 1966), 115.

17. Kathryn S. Olmstead, *Real Enemies: Conspiracy Theories and American Democracy, World War I to 9/11* (New York: Oxford University Press, 2009), 84–85.

18. J. Edgar Hoover, "How U.S. Reds Use 'Pseudo Liberals' [*sic*] as a Front," *U.S. News and World Report*, 13 April 1956, 138–39, 139.

19. Quoted in Jeffreys-Jones, *FBI*, 141.

20. Richard Gid Powers, *Broken: The Troubled Past and Uncertain Future of the FBI* (New York: Free Press, 2004), 210.

21. Ibid., 211.

22. Olmstead, *Real Enemies*, 93.

23. See Curt Gentry's aggressively investigated biography *J. Edgar Hoover: The Man and the Secrets* (New York: W. W. Norton, 1991), in which details can be found on the care and feeding of the "FBI stable in Congress" (407). Hoover's congressional A-team at midcentury, Gentry concludes, was not composed of loyal cheerleaders (George Dondero, Roman Hruska, et cetera), quick to feed Bureau press releases into the *Congressional Record*. Instead, it featured quieter, more powerful "majority and minority leaders, Speakers, and the chairmen of the key committees," figures, like Hoover, "long on seniority" and bureaucratically shrewd

enough to keep the dollars flowing (Everett Dirksen, John McClellan, John Stennis, et cetera) (407).

24. Schrecker, *Many Are the Crimes*, 203.

25. Ibid.

26. Ibid., 212.

27. Ibid., 212.

28. Ibid., 216.

29. Quoted in Schrecker, *Many Are the Crimes*, 215.

30. Bill Adler, ed., *Kids' Letters to the F.B.I.* Illustrated by Arnold Roth (Englewood Cliffs, NJ: Prentice-Hall, 1966), unpaginated.

31. Max Lowenthal, *The Federal Bureau of Investigation* (New York: William Sloane, 1950), front matter.

32. Ibid., 465.

33. Gentry, *J. Edgar Hoover*, 387.

34. Quoted in Gentry, *J. Edgar Hoover*, 386.

35. Ibid., 386–87.

36. "The FBI Reviews a Book," *Nation*, 27 January 1951, 86.

37. Gentry, *J. Edgar Hoover*, 386.

38. Claire A. Culleton, "Extorting Henry Holt and Co.: J. Edgar Hoover and the Publishing Industry," in *Modernism on File: Writers, Artists, and the FBI, 1920–1950*, ed. Claire A. Culleton and Karen Leick (New York: Palgrave, 2008), 237–52, 237. Jon Wiener considers the more-than-archival significance of Culleton's discovery in a 2008 *Nation* column, "J. Edgar Hoover, Author," *Nation*, 22 May 2008. Web. "Today," Wiener observes, "Henry Holt publishes many writers on the left, including Noam Chomsky, Barbara Ehrenreich, Mike Davis and Chalmers Johnson—all of them bestsellers. Almost nothing like their work was published, by Holt or any other mainstream publisher, in the era of *Masters of Deceit*. The book business has changed for the worse in many ways since the 1950s, but this broadening of debate is clearly a change for the better" (Wiener, "J. Edgar Hoover, Author"). The live value of Culleton's findings nevertheless do not support her suggestion that Hoover "used his power to micromanage intellectual life in the United States by working effectively with publishing companies" (249). Her narrower thesis that "Hoover and his men cultivated an industry atmosphere grounded in anxiety and rank with panic and dread" is comparably overstated (246). On the basis of astonishing but scattered evidence, Culleton recasts midcentury U.S. publishing as a bleak existentialist novel.

39. Quoted in Culleton, "Extorting Henry Holt and Co.," 239.

40. Quoted in Culleton, "Extorting Henry Holt and Co.," 244–45.

41. Ibid., 243.

42. Ibid., 244.

43. United States Federal Bureau of Investigation, Lorraine Hansberry file obtained under provisions of the Freedom of Information Act. Assorted documents

dated 21 July 1952 to 22 January 1965. Internal case file no. 100-107297. Hereafter cited parenthetically by date of entry. I am obliged to the generosity of Kathlene McDonald, the Hansberry specialist at the City College of New York, who shared her copy of the playwright's massive file.

44. Harold Cruse, *The Crisis of the Negro Intellectual* (New York: William Morrow, 1967), 267.

45. Peniel E. Joseph, *Waiting 'Til the Midnight Hour: A Narrative History of Black Power in America* (New York: Henry Holt, 2006), 26–27.

46. See Cheryl Higashida, "To Be(come) Young, Gay, and Black: Lorraine Hansberry's Existentialist Routes to Anticolonialism," *American Quarterly* 60, no. 4 (December 2008): 899–924. In an astute pre-reading of the Hansberry file, Cheryl Higashida also notes the Bureau reviewer's disproportionate attention to Asagai. The lopsided interest in this Nigerian character, "despite the fact that he appears in far fewer scenes than Ruth, Walter, and Beneatha Younger, suggests how much Asagai's vision meant to the state" (903).

47. United States Federal Bureau of Investigation, Alice Childress file obtained under provisions of the Freedom of Information Act. Assorted documents dated 11 April 1951 to [?] 1957. Internal case file no. 100-379156. 20 March 1951.

48. United States Federal Bureau of Investigation, Lance Jeffers file obtained under provisions of the Freedom of Information Act. Assorted documents dated 8 February 1949 to 15 July 1966. Internal case file no. 100-359726. Hereafter cited parenthetically by date of entry.

49. Trudier Harris, "Lance Jeffers," in *The Oxford Companion to African American Literature*, ed. William L. Andrews, Frances Smith Foster, and Trudier Harris (New York: Oxford University Press, 1997), 397–98, 397.

50. United States Federal Bureau of Investigation, Calvin Hernton file obtained under provisions of the Freedom of Information Act. Assorted documents dated 14 March 1955 to 29 August 1969. Internal case file no. 100-417598. Subsequent quotations from this file will be cited parenthetically within the text by date of entry.

51. United States Federal Bureau of Investigation, Julian Mayfield file obtained under provisions of the Freedom of Information Act. Assorted documents dated 16 August 1954 to 6 September 1974. Internal case file no. 100-412872. Subsequent quotations from this file will be cited parenthetically within the text by date of entry.

52. Dolores M. Nelson, Information and Privacy Coordinator, Central Intelligence Agency, letter to author, 26 June 2009.

53. United States Federal Bureau of Investigation, J. Saunders Redding file obtained under provisions of the Freedom of Information Act. Assorted documents dated 13 February 1953 to 15 August 1968. Internal case file no. 123-14868. Subsequent quotations from this file will be cited parenthetically within the text by date of entry.

54. United States Federal Bureau of Investigation, Willard Motley file obtained under provisions of the Freedom of Information Act. Assorted documents dated 16 July 1951 to 12 October 1972. Internal case file no. 100-382070. Subsequent quotations from this file will be cited parenthetically within the text by date of entry.

55. Barbara Foley kindly supplemented the eight pages of the Ellison file that I originally received with dozens more—further proof that different FOIA requests for the same FBI materials can yield very different documents.

56. See United States Federal Bureau of Investigation, E. Franklin Frazier file obtained under provisions of the Freedom of Information Act. Assorted documents dated 25 June 1953 to 13 July 1961. Internal case file no. 138-825. United States Federal Bureau of Investigation, Charles S. Johnson file obtained under provisions of the Freedom of Information Act. Assorted documents dated 21 February 1952 to 1 October 1956. Internal case file no. 138-3218. United States Federal Bureau of Investigation, William Pickens file obtained under provisions of the Freedom of Information Act. Assorted documents dated 22 October 1947 to 12 May 1964. Internal case file no. 121-4978.

57. See United States Federal Bureau of Investigation, Andy Razaf [Andrea Razafkeriefo] file obtained under provisions of the Freedom of Information Act. Assorted documents dated 3 May 1949 to 19 May 1949. Internal case file no. 100-361384. United States Federal Bureau of Investigation, Shirley Graham Du Bois file obtained under provisions of the Freedom of Information Act. Assorted documents dated 8 August 1950 to 28 July 1975. Internal case file no. 100-370965. United States Federal Bureau of Investigation, Lonne Elder III [Lonnie Williams] file obtained under provisions of the Freedom of Information Act. Document dated 3 September 1954. Internal case file no. 100-116777. United States Federal Bureau of Investigation, Frank London Brown file obtained under provisions of the Freedom of Information Act. Assorted documents dated 19 December 1955 to 27 December 1957. Internal case file no. 100-30890. United States Federal Bureau of Investigation, Ollie Harrington file obtained under provisions of the Freedom of Information Act. Assorted documents dated 4 May 1951 to 22 June 2002. Internal case file no. 100-379980.

58. United States Federal Bureau of Investigation, Bob Kaufman file obtained under provisions of the Freedom of Information Act. Assorted documents dated 31 January 1950 to 18 August 1970. Internal case file no. 100-366937. 21 June 1956.

59. United States Federal Bureau of Investigation, William Gardner Smith file obtained under provisions of the Freedom of Information Act. Assorted documents dated 5 May 1951 to 7 November 1974. Internal case file no. 100-379969. 5 May 1951.

60. United States Federal Bureau of Investigation, Harold Cruse file obtained under provisions of the Freedom of Information Act. Assorted documents dated 7 August 1950 to 9 January 1969. Internal case file no. 100-370842. 26 November 1956.

61. See United States Federal Bureau of Investigation, Hoyt Fuller file obtained under provisions of the Freedom of Information Act. Assorted documents dated 27 April 1954 to 25 March 1974. Internal case file no. 157-16554. United States Federal Bureau of Investigation, Amiri Baraka file self-deposited in the Amiri Baraka Papers, Moorland-Spingarn Research Center, Howard University, Washington, D.C. Assorted documents dated 28 January 1957 to 3 March 1971. Internal case file no. 100-425307. United States Federal Bureau of Investigation, James Baldwin file obtained under provisions of the Freedom of Information Act. Assorted documents dated [?] October 1958 to 20 February 1974. Internal case file no. 62-108763.

62. John Dittmer, *Local People: The Struggle for Civil Rights in Mississippi* (Urbana: University of Illinois Press, 1994), 1.

63. John K. Young, *Black Writers, White Publishers: Marketplace Politics in Twentieth-Century African American Literature* (Jackson: University Press of Mississippi, 2006), 19.

64. Addison Gayle, Jr., introduction to *The Black Aesthetic*, ed. Addison Gayle, Jr. 1971 (Garden City, NY: Anchor-Doubleday, 1972), xv–xxiv, xx.

65. Alan Nadel, *Containment Culture: American Narratives, Postmodernism, and the Atomic Age* (Durham, NC: Duke University Press, 1995), 5.

2 REVIEWING COLD WAR CULTURE WITH EDWIN DENBY

CATHERINE GUNTHER KODAT

At his death in 1983, Edwin Denby was described in the *New York Times* as "a poet and one of the most influential dance critics in America." The phrasing seems an insinuation: Denby's poems deserve acknowledgment—he published four volumes of poetry, after all—but it is the dance writing that commands attention. However much he considered himself "a poet first," the obituary continues, Denby "achieved his greatest acclaim as a dance critic, and his criticism profoundly influenced several generations of dance writers." Eager to give readers a taste of Denby's dance writing, the obituary offers up direct quotations from reviews of Alicia Markova's performance in *Pas de Quatre* and George Balanchine's *Concerto Barocco*. The poetry, however, is left unsampled, dispatched with the briefest description: Denby's verse is "strictly formal, and he was particularly fond of the sonnet."[1] The obituary was written by Jack Anderson—like Denby, both a poet and a dance critic—and while it was likely not intended as a judgment of the relative merits of Denby's creative and critical writing, readers could be forgiven for taking it so.

But not by much. Anderson's charge in writing the obituary was not to supply a literary analysis but to provide an accurate representation of Denby's public profile, and certainly more people had read the dance reviews than the poems. To the extent that Denby is still read today, it probably remains the case that he is better known as a dance critic than a poet, which, given the high quality of his work in both genres, is a bit of a puzzle. During Denby's lifetime, Frank O'Hara, Ted Berrigan, and Anne Waldman all staked claims for the virtues of the poetry. O'Hara saw similarities between Denby's sonnets and Shelley's, Berrigan devoted an entire issue of his *C Magazine* to Denby's verse (the front cover was an Andy Warhol silkscreen of two images of Denby and Gerard Malanga: quietly posed in one, they share a passionate kiss in the other), and Waldman's Full Court Press brought out Denby's *Collected Poems* in 1975.[2] Two months after Denby's death, Lincoln Kirstein wrote an appreciation that rated Denby's poems with those of Walt Whitman, Federico García Lorca, and Hart Crane. (Denby was in fact just three years younger than Crane.) In 1986 Ron Padgett ran up the flag again with a sympathetic and incisive introduction to Denby's *Complete Poems* (now out of print) that combined biography with sensitive close readings.[3] And the efforts on Denby's behalf continue today, if in a slightly different key, as straightforward claims for the excellence of the poetry give way to appeals to history and context. In a 2007 essay in the *Yale Review*, the poet Mary Maxwell detects "indications . . . that Denby's significance is becoming more generally acknowledged," though a deepened engagement with the poetry may be more a consequence of this acknowledgment than its cause. "With the critical distance provided by fifty years since the genesis of the New York School," she writes, "there is an increasing awareness that Edwin Denby might not be, after all, a minor figure in the movement's history."[4] Maxwell is right to detect a slowly growing interest in Denby's verse. His work has been included in several poetry collections published in the last decade, among them the second volume of the Library of America anthology *American Poetry: The Twentieth Century*.[5] And she is also right to hint that his work is being revisited chiefly as part of the current scholarly reassessment of postwar American poetry. Aspects of this reassessment that would be germane to Denby's verse involve the renewed attention to once-disdained "coterie poetics" and the ongoing effort to define a gay sensibility within Cold War U.S. cultural production.[6] Knowing that Denby lived next door to (and was a close friend of) Willem and Elaine de Kooning; that he spoke at Frank O'Hara's funeral; that he had been a lover of James Schuyler's and maintained cordial relations with John Ashbery, Kenneth Koch, W. H. Auden, and Chester Kallman; that he wrote a screenplay for a Warhol film[7]—all of this may come to matter as much in raising the profile of his poetry as the fact that he wrote superbly about the work of George Balanchine and Merce Cunningham. Such a development would be welcome insofar as it brings Denby's verse to the attention of a wider audience, so long as this renewed emphasis on Denby in the context of the New York School poets retains the dance as a major aspect of that context.

Interestingly, this move toward a more thoroughly contextual understanding of Denby's life and work has not, so far, involved seeing the Cold War as a particularly salient concern. In a sense, the long neglect of Denby's poetry mirrors the general neglect of poetry within Cold War cultural studies, where (as in contemporary literary studies generally) "narrative has become the norm . . . not one possible . . . form but . . . the very condition of experience."[8] Analyses of midcentury U.S. poetry, dance, and "art" music (rather than popular or commercial genres) are the exceptions within Cold War cultural studies, despite the period's remarkable efflorescence of work in these nonnarrative lyric forms.[9] Or, to put it more exactly, the era's striking turn toward nonnarrative works becomes exemplary of Cold War culture to the extent that this turn can be recuperated to the reigning interpretive narratives of containment or American cultural imperialism. (We might think here of Serge Guilbaut's treatment of Abstract Expressionism.)[10] Works less amenable to these interpretive frames—and Denby's poetry and dance writings are equally apposite here—are either ignored or described not as aspects of Cold War culture but rather as artifacts of postwar culture or midcentury modernism (or, sometimes, postmodernism—the distinctions among *postwar*, *midcentury*, and *postmodern* often being unclear).

This chapter thus has a double aim: to make the Cold War a more pertinent aspect of the context in which Denby's work might be assessed, in part by reading the poetry and the reviews together; and to expand our understanding of Cold War culture so that Denby's writings might be seen as something other than curiosities of the period. Indeed, taking the life and work of Edwin Denby seriously involves questioning some of the assumptions underlying the dominant approach to Cold War cultural studies and its allied historicist interest in describing homologies between the era's political and economic formations and its cultural productions. The symptomatological mode characteristic of much Cold War cultural study quickly meets its match in Denby's writings, which do not readily respond to such an analysis, at least not in any way that conforms to the favored Cold War cultural hermeneutics of containment or protest. Some of the challenges Denby's case poses to the reigning paradigms of Cold War cultural study are a function of the oddly syncopated relationship between his writings and their receptions, a syncopation that is itself a Cold War phenomenon and that points to the need for a more nuanced approach to what is usually cast as a single temporality. Most of Denby's poetry and dance reviews were written in a period running from the mid-1930s to the late-1950s; the work was highly respected in its day, but it was its rediscovery during the 1960s and 1970s that brought Denby the wider measure of critical attention he enjoyed at his death. His only novel, for example, was completed in 1934 but was not published until 1972 (when it appeared under two different titles from two different publishers);[11] by the time his *Collected Poems* appeared, he had mostly stopped writing poetry. Conversely, a seminal essay on Balanchine's style that praises its formal innovation and concomitant disregard for psychology and story—aspects of modern neoclassical dance recently characterized as having "a particular appeal" in "the cold war atmosphere . . . where self-censorship was the norm"—was published in March 1945, not only well before the start of the Cold War but before the end of World War II.[12] Of course it could be (and has been) argued that the abstract, neoclassical dance values prized by Denby did not so much arise during the Cold War as come to enjoy heightened potency during it, in part by ushering in "the end of other, more obviously queer possibilities" for the ballet by rendering a "sexually suspect" art form palatable to conservative American taste.[13] But reading Denby's dance reviews alongside his poetry complicates this argument: for all its own similarly neoclassical dedication to traditional form, Denby's verse, much of it composed during the years of the homophobic "lavender scare" (to mention one aspect of Cold War self-censorship),[14] keeps its queer possibilities open. Not for nothing did Lincoln Kirstein link Denby's aesthetic to Hart Crane's.

Thus one set of received truths destabilized by a close examination of Denby's work has to do with the assumed omnipotence and omnipresence of the closet in gay Cold War cultural production. As I've already hinted, another concerns the assumed repudiation by artists of the early Cold War period of politically activist, social realist 1930s aesthetic values (most especially narrative values in literature and realistic representational values in visual art) in favor of the presumedly less politically engaged modernism of an avant-garde "aesthetic of indifference."[15] Jonathan D. Katz has recently argued that these two aspects of Cold War culture—the ubiquity of the closet and the "*performance* of silence" characteristic of the coolly abstract works of gay artists such as Cunningham, John Cage, Jasper Johns, and Robert Rauschenberg—are causally related: the seemingly apolitical cast of this early Cold War avant-garde art actually constitutes "a strategy of queer resistance to a social context of control and constraint within a culture that offered little room to maneuver, especially for gay men."[16] Katz's rereading of historical context is ingenious in its treatment of certain aspects of the work of Cage and the members of this circle, but difficulties quickly arise: are we to understand Cage's avant-garde engagements with silence as more authentically queer responses to Cold War homophobia than the somewhat traditionally conceived compositions of Samuel Barber, who hardly sought to conceal his intimate, long-standing domestic relationship with Gian-Carlo Menotti? The difficulty here lies less in the question of the relationship between sexuality and formally experimental, avant-garde artistic practices (though that is not a question easily dismissed) than in Katz's assumption—and it is an extremely common one—of a Cold War closet whose monolithic proportions dictated a limited and rigidly prescribed set of cultural responses. To question this assumption is not to deny the realities of Cold War gay life; it is rather to follow up on Michael S. Sherry's observation that:

> although [1950s] repression was frightening, it was not then imagined as creating a "closet," a term not yet used, for frightened queer inhabitants. . . . *Made retroactive, the "closet" becomes today's place to hide a complex past.* Recalling the world of arts and celebrity in 1950s New York, Alan Helms . . . stressed his fear of being spied on by authorities at Columbia, the desperation of some men to see shrinks and "go straight," the threat of "arrest or blackmail" or "a gang of fagbashers," the abuse of alcohol and drugs, and "a kind of concentration camp mentality." . . . Yet "sex was everywhere" and "remarkably out in public" . . . Helms invoked the "closet" but records no contemporary use of the term. . . . If it applies at all to this era, the "closet" had a door that swung open as often as it slammed shut.[17]

To describe Denby's poetry as an open door into the nascency of a certain style of gay artistic production in New York City during the early years of the Cold War might, perhaps, be going too far, especially given that his particular formalist bent was not widely shared. But Sherry's caveat regarding the ready invocation of the closet as a metaphor for Cold War gay life does clear a path toward an appreciation of Denby's writings as tracing the aesthetic contours of an *a-closeted* (not exactly out, but not completely masked) gay Cold War world, one whose artistic practices and forms of cultural expression have yet to receive their due. This is a world whose lived complexities and modes of expression don't plot easily onto a two-dimensional map of life before and after Stonewall (itself a Cold War politico-cultural event). As Denby put his own case:

> Summer New York, friends tonight at cottages
> I lie motionless, a single retired man
> White-haired, ferrety, feminine, religious
> I look like a priest, a detective, a con
> Nervously I step among the city crowd
> My private life of no interest and allowed[18]

Undoubtedly, a corrective refocusing on the achievements of gay artists in Cold War America is long overdue, and Denby's poetry merits a wider readership. It would be unfortunate, however, if an increased appreciation of the poetry were accomplished at the expense of the dance criticism, a genuine risk given that the dance studies community is even smaller and less institutionally secure than poetry's. Ideally one would want to raise interest in both together. This obviously is to be preferred if the aim is an enriched understanding of the relationship between Cold War sexualities and cultural production in the United States, for the dance is as much a part of that story as poetry.

Denby's advocates for the most part do acknowledge a link between the dance writings and the poetry. As Maxwell notes, "Denby's extensive dance criticism provides useful analogues for his poetics" (73).[19] However, the fact that Kirstein, Maxwell, Padgett, and O'Hara propose very different theories about the common values subtending Denby's poems and reviews makes clear that more work needs to be done. Consider, for example, the responses of these critics to the sonnets of Denby's *Mediterranean Cities*. For Maxwell, the poet-speaker "projects himself into everything he sees" (77), producing "erotic versions of the pathetic fallacy" (79); for O'Hara, Denby's sonnets do create a sense of "the poet himself [as] the place" of the poem, but "the pervading melancholy . . . reminds one of the English Romantic poets on the Continent."[20] By contrast, Padgett insists that "the expression of . . . personal feelings . . . is *not* the main thrust of the sonnets"—on the contrary, "the poet's sensibility is turned outward"[21]—while Kirstein, in an odd, unexplained gesture toward realism, declares that Denby's verse "concerns cities in history" through evocations of "atmosphere, societies, and qualities . . . [that] form an album of superpostcards, more real than any nostalgic material souvenir."[22] Tracing the connections linking Denby's dance writings, poetry, and sexuality, as well as exploring how those connections engage their Cold War context, helps us to understand how Denby's verse might inspire such disparate responses.

On the assumption that most readers know very little about Denby or his work, I preface my discussion of his writings by sketching in those aspects of his life most pertinent to understanding the relationship between his poetry and his dance writing and the connection of that relationship to the Cold War cultural landscape. I then move to an analysis that pairs a discussion of Denby's deep fascination, expressed in several essays written in the late 1940s and early 1950s, with George Balanchine's modernist approach to the ballet—an approach at once recuperative and revolutionary—with a reading of the sonnets of *Mediterranean Cities* (published in 1956, the year of Ginsberg's *Howl*, Baldwin's *Giovanni's Room*, and Ashbery's *Some Trees*). Taken together, the dance writings and the sonnets set the terms for understanding Denby's notion of modernist classicism as a way of making "the past and the present happen at the same time."[23] The Proustian aspects of this aesthetic have been deployed by other critics (Padgett and O'Hara, for example) as shorthand not only for describing Denby's particular aesthetic but also for connecting that aesthetic to his sexuality; my aim here is to draw out further connections between that aesthetic and Cold War culture.

A Private Life of Interest (and Allowed)

Denby was born in 1903 in Tientsin (now Tianjin), the third-largest city in China. His father Charles Denby Jr. was first secretary of the U.S. legation there; his grandfather Charles Denby Sr. had moved to the city in 1885 on his appointment as Grover Cleveland's minister to China.[24] When Edwin was seven, the Denbys left China for Vienna, where Charles Jr. had been named consul general. The family returned to the United States in 1915; thus, Edwin was twelve years old before he set foot in his "native" land. As Padgett writes, "From birth—an American born in China—he was out of place" (xv). As Denby himself once told a friend, "I have been scared of America all my life."[25] In his later years, Denby came to cherish his outsider status as an important aspect of his aesthetic.

After one year's schooling and private tutoring stateside, Denby entered Hotchkiss, where he graduated with honors in 1919, winning the Greek and English senior prizes and writing the class poem. He matriculated at Harvard when he was sixteen. Three semesters of stellar academic achievement followed (Denby was one of twenty members of the class of 1923 to make high honors in their first term); then, in December 1920, Denby dropped out of college and boarded a ship to England with a schoolmate, Frank Safford. The biographical essays of William MacKay and Ron Padgett, both published in 1986, describe this particular episode in fairly circumspect terms. Today's readers might be tempted to read it as something of an elopement. Working within the limits of discretion and uncertainty, both MacKay and Padgett indicate that Denby's growing recognition of his homosexuality contributed to a longing "for Europe and escape." (MacKay twice describes this interlude as an "escape" [14, 15].) Reeled in by their parents, Denby and Safford returned to the United

States after two weeks abroad. Denby stayed out of school for the rest of the academic year, spending five months working as a farmhand in New Hampshire; Safford got married. Denby returned to Harvard in the fall but dropped out again and relocated to New York, moving in with Frank Safford and his wife. After what MacKay terms a "happy but unproductive year" (15), the Saffords moved to Austria so Frank could begin medical school. In 1923, after negotiations with his parents, who wanted Denby to return to Harvard but who finally agreed that classes at the University of Vienna were an acceptable substitute, Denby joined the Saffords in Europe. He had a hazy notion of becoming a writer and a clear desire to be with Frank; he remained abroad for the next nine years. By the time he returned to America in 1935, Denby had lived most of his life outside of the United States.

Perhaps not surprisingly, Denby's Viennese reunion with the Saffords did not go well. Frank was preoccupied with his medical studies, and Denby's relations with Frank's wife—"always complicated" (MacKay 15)—deteriorated. By his own account, Denby spent his first winter in Vienna contemplating suicide; a visit to 19 Berggasse put him under the care of Paul Federn, by then one of Freud's best-known disciples. Denby ended the analysis after a few years—"too painful," he told an interviewer (MacKay 16)—but he nonetheless remained fond of Federn and grateful to him. "He saved my life," Denby maintained (MacKay 16). According to MacKay, it was Federn who urged Denby to take seriously his long-simmering interest in dance (16), and soon after beginning analysis, Denby enrolled in classes at the Hellerau-Laxenburg School. Originally founded by Emile-Jacques Dalcroze in 1919, by the time Denby arrived Hellerau-Laxenburg had become known as the school that had trained Mary Wigman, the German modern dance pioneer of *Ausdruckstanz*, or expressionist dance, a style of movement about as far from the classical ballet as Western imagination could take it. Denby's focus of study at Hellerau-Laxenburg was not dance, exactly, but *Körperbildung* (a kind of physical development that blended gymnastic and dance movement); the milieu in which his dance aesthetic took root was decidedly not a traditional one. His theatrical studies included a six-week visit to the Soviet Union in 1927. A year later, after earning his diploma from Hellerau-Laxenburg, he found employment at the Hessisches Landestheater in Darmstadt, where he performed in the dance chorus and quickly rose to the post of assistant regisseur. His theatrical work included writing as well as performance: his 1929 adaptation of Franz von Suppé's *Die schöne*

Galatea ("jazzed up" as *Die neue Galatea*) won praise from reviewers for its "scintillating dialogue and delightfully naughty lyrics" (MacKay 20). For a brief time the Hessisches Landestheater enjoyed a reputation for producing daring work, but Denby's effort to bring Gertrude Stein and Virgil Thomson's *Four Saints in Three Acts* to Darmstadt misfired so completely as to bring this period of experimentation to a close.[26] In 1930 Denby left the theater and began touring with Cläre Eckstein, a Wigman student who had been the *Ballettmeisterin* at Darmstadt. Their cabaret act specialized in comedic dance routines (*Grotesktanz*), which were well received by the public but in their worldly irreverence came to be viewed as intolerable affronts by the National Socialists. Denby soon felt compelled to leave Germany. Pausing in Paris before joining his family in Majorca, he took in the single all-Balanchine season of Les Ballets 1933 at the Théâtre des Champs-Elysées. Perhaps curious to see Balanchine's (first) treatment of Brecht and Weill's *The Seven Deadly Sins*, he was thunderstruck by *Mozartiana*. As he said later, "it wouldn't stay out of my mind" (MacKay 22).

All through this intensive period of dance and theatrical work, Denby never stopped writing. He placed three poems in Harriet Monroe's *Poetry* magazine, published essays on theater and the dance in *The Drama* and in *Theatre Guild Magazine*, and completed a psychoanalytic study titled "Über seelische Rückwirkungen der Gymnastik," which Federn helped place in the *Zeitschrift für psychoanalytische Pädagogik*.[27] He wrote his only novel during the reunion with his family in Majorca. And in his last year abroad, Denby fell in love with the Swiss photographer Rudolph Burckhardt: "he was just what I was waiting for without knowing it," Burckhardt recalled years later.[28] The two spent 1934 together in Basel before taking their leave of Europe; departing separately, they reunited in New York City, setting up house in a fourth-floor, cold-water walk-up in Chelsea. Willem and Elaine de Kooning lived next door. The apartment's address, *145 West 21st*, serves as the title of one of Denby's earliest artistic collaborations with Burckhardt, a silent, ten-minute, 16 mm film—"part screwball comedy, part home movie . . . a work utterly without pretensions"—with a cast that includes Thomson, Paul Bowles, Aaron Copland, and John La Touche (the musician and librettist who wrote the lyrics for "Ballad for Americans").[29] The Chelsea loft would be Denby's home for the rest of his life, and his artistic partnership with Burckhardt, which included acting in Burckhardt's films and producing books that combined Edwin's verse and Rudy's photographs, would last just about as long.[30]

Too old to continue making his living as a dancer (he was thirty-two in 1935), Denby rapidly found writer's work in New York's WPA arts scene. In 1936, *Horse Eats Hat*, his racy adaptation of Eugène Labiche's 1851 farce *Un chapeau de paille d'Italie*, with music by Bowles, was produced by Orson Welles and John Houseman's Federal Theatre Project. The next year he wrote the libretto for Copland's children's opera *The Second Hurricane*. Denby had become a friend of Copland's when the composer visited Darmstadt in 1929 (Copland's biographer describes Denby as one of the composer's "crushes"[31]), and Copland and Thomson suggested to Minna Lederman, the editor of the League of Composers' journal *Modern Music*, that she hire Denby as the quarterly's dance critic. As it happened, Denby's first essay in *Modern Music* was not on the dance but, reflecting his more immediate interest in putting words to music, on the art of the libretto.[32] His first dance review (of the Ballets Russes de Monte Carlo's revival of Bronislava Nijinska's *Les Noces*) was published in 1936; his earliest essays about Balanchine appeared in 1937, four years after the choreographer's arrival in the United States. When Walter Terry, the dance critic for the *New York Herald Tribune*, was called up for army service in 1942, Denby was named his replacement. After a period of adjustment, Denby was able to accommodate the rigid deadlines and length constraints of newspaper writing with an aplomb he found surprising. Upon Terry's return to his old post at the end of the war in 1945, Denby turned to other writing projects—but not easily.

In Public, In Private, his first book of poems, appeared in 1948 in "two postponed, subsidized, misprinted editions, each with its own de Kooning frontispiece" (MacKay 29). The book included photographs by Burckhardt, who by this time had married but whose devotion to Denby remained lifelong.[33] The relative ease and fluency that Denby enjoyed while reviewing for the *Herald Tribune* quickly evaporated; Padgett describes a "nervousness" in Denby's work on this collection that came to characterize his generally "skittish" approach to publication (xi). (The second edition appeared not in response to market demand but because Denby wanted to make changes in the text.) Denby's now-celebrated first collection of reviews *Looking at the Dance* appeared in 1949, its publication marked by the same anxieties that characterized the appearance of *In Public, In Private*. In the words of MacKay, the collection was "published almost against the author's will" (30).

With Guggenheim funding for a comparative study of dance styles (a book project that never moved beyond a handful of essays), Denby returned to Europe in 1948 for a four-year sojourn, spending most of his time in Italy. He met James Schuyler at Auden and Kallman's *pensione* in Ischia, saw Galina Ulanova's 1951 Western debut in Florence, and toured Sicily and Greece with Burckhardt, who came over with his wife and two-year-old son. *Mediterranean Cities*, a collection of twenty-nine sonnets on locations in Greece, Sicily, and Italy—like *In Public, In Private*, punctuated with Burckhardt's photographs—was published four years after Denby's return to the States. This handsomely produced volume seems to have been the only collection whose appearance was not marked by the anxieties and bouts of second-guessing typical of Denby's experiences with publishers. Denby's health began its long, slow decline during this period abroad (he had surgery for stomach ulcers in 1950 [Padgett xxii]), but the poems of *Mediterranean Cities* are among his most firmly conceived, confident, and challenging, their "lushness of language" tempered by "a complexity of syntax and meaning . . . almost cubistic in its displacement" (Padgett xxiii). His dance articles from this period, too, show an increased confidence. Striking declarations of a now fully developed and sophisticated appreciation of modernist classicism (an appreciation that never spoiled his interest in expressionistic, folk, or experimental dance styles), they also bespeak an experiential posture toward contemporary art that anticipates the attitude of the late 1950s and early 1960s New York City avant-garde. In retrospect, Denby's "Against Meaning in Ballet," published in Richard Buckle's *Ballet* magazine in 1949, emerges as a clear if less polemical precursor to Susan Sontag's 1964 "Against Interpretation." Some of his most important writings on the dance date from this period, among them his 1954 essay on Balanchine's *The Nutcracker* and his 1959 "Three Sides of *Agon*." His last published review appeared in 1965, the year that saw the appearance of his second collection of dance writings *Dancers, Buildings and People in the Streets*, which featured an introduction by Frank O'Hara.[34]

Denby's increasing difficulties with writer's block (expressed in a habit of "revising his new pieces out of existence" [Padgett xxv]) during the 1960s and 1970s did little to slow a growing interest in his poetry, which began with the reappearance of previously published work in the 1963 special Denby issue of Berrigan's *C Magazine* (the one with the Warhol cover). Denby's third collection of poetry, *Snoring in New York*, was published in 1974 under the now-familiar circumstances of authorial anxiety and editorial insistence; his *Collected Poems* appeared in 1975. Despite increasingly fragile health (which included eye surgery and a battle with stomach cancer), Denby maintained his connections with the dance world and the downtown New York arts scene throughout these years, attending poetry readings at St. Mark's, as well as the Spring Street loft performances of Robert Wilson's Byrd Hoffman School of Byrds. He contributed to these scenes as well, participating in a reading of his work at St. Mark's that was organized to celebrate his sixty-ninth birthday, and taking on a small role in a Wilson production in which he read aloud from Vaslav Nijinsky's diary.

In July 1983, beset by continuing health problems and increasingly worried about memory lapses, Denby died quietly from an overdose of sleeping pills at the summer home he shared with the Burckhardts in Searsmont, Maine. George Balanchine had died three months earlier.

Civilized Behavior: Ballet, the Sonnet, and *Mediterranean Cities*

In 1986, the poet Simon Pettet asked Rudy Burckhardt what he thought of a comment Edwin Denby had made in an interview published the year he died:

> SP: Let me read you something . . . Edwin said, *Well, I learned a lot from Rudy Burckhardt's photographs and movies. I got very interested in them, the way that you can study them, and know what the texture of light and air is all about. I wanted that in my poetry. Nobody really understood the films of Rudy Burckhardt because he was trying to capture that, to make you feel as if you might be able to touch the air and the light.* What is he talking about?
>
> RB: Well, this is what seems to be called "parallel poetry." In the 50s our friends, the poets—Frank O'Hara, John Ashbery, Kenneth Koch, and Jimmy Schuyler—were all writing art reviews for Thomas Hess and *Art News*. But people would object. They'd say, "he's not really criticizing the painting, he's not talking about the painting." This is parallel poetry and it's great.[35]

What Burckhardt here describes as parallel poetry is not art-inspired verse along the lines of Williams's "The Dance" or Auden's "Musée des Beaux Arts." Rather, it's writing that seeks to work the same effects (and affects) that the visual and performing arts accomplish in their quite different media: Denby wants his poetry to convey the same sense of the "texture of light and air" that he experiences in viewing Burckhardt's photographs. In his follow-up question, Pettet takes Burckhardt's explanation literally ("So is the light in the photos like the spaces in the poems?"), but Denby's sense of poetic form was never so concrete. In any event, the point that concerns us here is not whether Denby succeeds in conveying in verse the same quality of light one experiences in Burckhardt's photographs and films but rather that Denby was a poet whose strong visual sense influenced his verse formally at least as much as thematically. Understanding this aspect of his poetics makes even clearer—if there was any doubt—how important the dance was to Denby's sense of what could be accomplished in poetry.

Denby perfected his understanding of the unique qualities of Balanchine's choreography in essays published in the years immediately leading up to, during, and after the Guggenheim period that produced the sonnets of *Mediterranean Cities*. Denby's admiration for Balanchine is well known, but the grounds for that admiration are not at all obvious, especially given Denby's early training in a school of movement almost completely antithetical to ballet. *Ausdruckstanz* has much more in common with the emotive, nearly confessional movement style of Martha Graham than with the formal equanimity and emotional reserve characteristic of ballet generally and, for some, only too typical of Balanchine particularly, whose work has been criticized as excessively cold and cerebral. Denby respected Graham, but it was Balanchine he termed "the greatest choreographer of our time."[36] Why?

Reviewing Denby's writings about Balanchine turns up a habit of description that points toward an answer. For Denby, Balanchine's choreography conveys "a purity of vocabulary and cleanness of accent, qualities that belong to good manners and handsome behavior."[37] It has the "spaciousness," the "spontaneous considerateness," the "unconscious grace," of truly "civilized" behavior, and that single word, *civilized*, appears again and again in Denby's writings about Balanchine's choreography.[38] In a long meditation published in *Town & Country* in 1947, Denby developed his thesis of ballet's unique relationship to civilization—and, in turn, Balanchine's unique relationship to American ballet—in a rather unusual fashion:

> Ballet is the one form of theater where nobody speaks a foolish word all evening—nobody on the stage, at least. That's why it becomes so popular in any civilized country during a war. Its success here during the recent war surprised many people who didn't realize how civilized the country is. . . . Ballet is absurd by nature. But its absurdities are civilized ones. . . . Balanchine . . . is the man who more than any other individual created and founded our American ballet. . . . He has de-

veloped the physical qualities and the zest of our dancers as elements of style. . . . That way they learn to dance correct ballet as straightforwardly and simply as one speaks the language one is born to, and learn from their experience in his contemporary classicism to dance the nineteenth-century classics as unaffectedly. Finding out how to dance these as real dancing is a big step in a young dancer's deprovincialization. They are dances created as far away from us in time and space as ballet reaches, and an American who finds herself bringing them to life feels her power as a dancer.[39]

What Denby values in Balanchine's choreography is the assurance it gives the American dancer of her rightful place in a wider civilization that native provincialism has long kept out of reach and that the recently concluded global war has nearly destroyed. The choreography does not do this by "Europeanizing" American movement: Balanchine's ballets do not, to paraphrase William Carlos Williams's notorious dismissal of sonnet writing in America, cut New York City legs to fit a Parisian box.[40] Rather, they stress technical mastery of the movement such that its relationship to music becomes the focus of the viewer's experience. In this way the traditional steps of the dance are, as it were, lit from within by the contemporary attitude of the dancer: the pastness of the classical form and the presentness of the dancer's body "happen at the same time," with narrative intervention between the two kept to a minimum. As Denby was well aware, such an approach leaves to one side questions of characterization and "literary" drama: to "dance" the nineteenth-century classics, all of them narrative works, is not quite the same thing as to "perform" them. Denby slyly implies that, in this realm, Americans still have a way to go before attaining total "civilization":

Our current story ballets are good for giving [the dancers] practice in dance impersonation but they stress oddity of pantomime rather than expression through undistorted rhythm. So far there are not more than four or five Americans who achieve the necessary air of complete unselfconsciousness in critical situations. Most of the others seem to confuse the issue by indicating a moral approval or disapproval of the character they are acting.

"Storyless" ballets on the other hand can treat almost any situation without impropriety or moralizing. . . . For the audience to take in an exciting action without quite knowing what is going on can be an advantage over following a story self-consciously step by step. A story so easily becomes censorable at its most interesting moments; one watches it nervously. Nervousness isn't fun, it's excitement that is.[41]

A truly civilized society, Denby implies, does not confuse impersonation with moral judgment; since postwar (very soon to be Cold War) America has not yet achieved the requisite "complete unselfconsciousness" that would make such clarity possible, Balanchine's "storyless" classicism brings us as close as we are so far able to come to uncensored excitement. What to the prosaic American imagination might seem a contradiction in terms—if there's no story, what is there to censor? if there's no narrative with a moral, what's the point?—becomes something different for the more poetically inclined, those who understand lyric's gift for *telling* outside, or beyond, narrative. *Storyless* means uncensored not because lyric poetry is *more* detailed or straightforward in how it addresses its subject, but precisely because it is less so. Obliquity, elision, condensation: by the mid-twentieth century, these are the things that are seen to make verse verse. They are especially characteristic of Denby's "compressed, quirky . . . elusive [and] eccentric" poems, whose "high density of thought" emerges through their "coupling of idiomatic language and traditional form" (Padgett xx, xi). "Hard poems to read, they are not hard in the usual ways: they are not recondite, they are not high-toned, they do not make literary allusions, they do not use 'poetic' language. . . . Their difficulties lie elsewhere" (Padgett xx). For Padgett, the essential difficulty of Denby's poems is to be found in their quicksilver tonal shifts. Nimble and witty, these are poems dedicated not to the evasion of fact but, on the contrary, to its subtle exfoliation. They do not censor, but they do require readers of sophistication.

Though I can do no more here than gesture toward his work, Joseph Litvak's meticulous and convincing demonstration of the ties binding sophistication and "perversion" and his concomitant understanding of sophistication as "a process of creative interposition not so much at the level of linguistic morals, of truth versus untruth, as at the level of manners, of propriety versus impropriety" are crucial to a proper appreciation of Denby's poetry and of its parallel relationship to Balanchine's choreography.[42] Seeing how the "civilized" values of "good manners and handsome behavior" were embodied in Balanchine's revised classicism, such that audiences willingly took in exciting action without quite knowing what was going on, cleared the way for Denby to embrace as legitimate his love of the sonnet, a form that in 1952 Williams had condemned as the essence of perversion for American poets. Working within this highly traditional form, Denby developed a classically civilized poetic practice that, in its linking of public and private (recall the title of his first book of poems), deprovincializes (which is to say, demarginalizes) the gay speaking subject and assures him his place in the metropole of love's civilization. It is this sense of the classical past illuminating the contemporary present that constitutes much of the uncensored excitement of the poems of *Mediterranean Cities*.

The hoariest clichés in writing about the dance all center on its irreproducibility: the arts' perpetual child, the dance is presumed to have no past and to know no future, existing only in the moment of its passing. Of course, no event, however ephemeral, is historyless, but this in fact was precisely the view of ballet around the time Denby was writing the sonnets of *Mediterranean Cities*. It was expressed quite forcefully by Auden in an essay that appeared two years before the publication of Denby's collection. "Ballet time," Auden writes, "is a continuous present; every experience which depends on historical time lies outside its capacities. It cannot express memory."[43] This is an astonishing claim in many ways, but it is especially so considering the history of ballet itself and its highly political genesis in the court of Louis XIV, a history preserved in ballet's French lexicon. Then there is ballet's mode of transmission, in which steps and gestures hundreds of years old are in essence memorialized in the daily class, itself a kind of perpetual kinetic renewal of the past through remembered gesture. But it is not surprising that Auden would come to this view if his aim were to emphasize ballet's kinship with poetry by isolating its quality as lyric. If ballet's "represented gesture" works like lyric's "represented voice,"[44] then ballet, like the lyric, matters only on the occasion of the viewer's experience of the work, what Auden posits as "lyric seeing."[45] The evidence of his dance writings suggests that Denby may also have entertained this view; however, the evidence of the poetry, particularly the poems of *Mediterranean Cities*, reveals a more complex understanding of history and lyric, and it is here that the Cold War makes its presence felt.

Denby's Guggenheim-funded travel in Europe coincided with the entire three-and-a-half-year duration of the Marshall Plan, and he arrived in Italy in the midst of the 1948 Italian national elections, which were subjected to outrageous American and Soviet meddling. In the poems of *Mediterranean Cities*, this political scene lies embedded within portraits of the region's well-known locales of gay encounter and comfort (Ischia, Taormina) that are themselves strewn with the ruins of empire. The cities of these poems are palimpsests wherein ancient and contemporary history and politics overlay (and are overlaid by) personal and erotic investments in patterns that invite causal correlations as much as they obscure them.

The collection opens with a dedicatory sonnet to the writer Olga ("laughing Olga") Resnevic-Signorelli (MacKay 31), set in Rome's Trastevere neighborhood and mixing sardonic commentary on American efforts to buy off (and buy up) Italy with suggestive descriptions of the landscape. There, in the park across the street from Olga's apartment:

> Urchins stole the sphinx near the fence up the hill
> Where woods grow thick, sold it to a Yank I hope;
> Now young priests smoke at the basin, by blurred sea-gods
> Above them rises a hairy thicket of palms
> That males in their joint green dusk yield Rome the odds[46]

To a considerable degree, the landscape of gay desire is the most significant landscape of *Mediterranean Cities*. In "Villa Adriana," the gaze of "watchful Hadrian" (14) rests on "Antinous in the yellow water"; in "Sant'Angelo d'Ischia," "four males in a brilliant weather" drink wine on the beach (17). But there are investments in these poems other than the purely erotic, as when the ruins of ancient Rome meet "like a face unrecognized from home" "the mute wide-angle look, to Europe alien" of the camera-toting arriviste American. Whether the "stare of big men worried about their weight" belongs to the visiting American or to the ruins themselves is left ambiguous: it could be the ponderousness of ancient history or the heavy burden of an emerging new empire that informs this "gaze of bounty" ("Rome" 11). When the speaker and his companion take a bus to Thebes, the road into the ancient city brings them "past a Frankish tower, a shed / Of diggings, a clinic by American grants / Built" ("Thebes" 30). "Syracuse" ties these crosscurrents of Cold War political and sexual tensions together in almost deadpan fashion, as an encounter with Sicilian "boys" (and here it is likely—though not certain—that these are "boys" in the sense of Denby's 1950s ballet-critic lingo: young men in their early twenties) sets off on the wrong geopolitical foot and ends in ashes:

> Are you Russians the boys said seeing us strange
> Easy in grace by a poster with bicycles

Soft voices in a Baroque and Byzantine slum
Lemon pickers by swelling seas rainbow-fickle;
On the height drizzle, and among thyme and mint
A small shepherd, a large canvas umbrella
Leaps away down the crumbled ruins, timid
Where once they fought in moonlight, and Athens fell;
Up in sun, the Doric fort, stone blocks graceful
And fresh, erect as a statue in the air
Bright wind in our eyes, bright sea glittering peaceful
The dead come close trusting to embrace, and glare;
Beyond where rode an American fleet, and Pindar's
Snowy Etna, pillar of Sicily, blows cinders ("Syracuse" 21)

Describing the poems of *Mediterranean Cities* chiefly as products of the containment closet or as specimens of American cultural adventuring does considerable violence to their subtle address of the joys and vagaries of homosexual love within the rapidly emerging Cold War imperium. Clearly, the Mediterranean vistas of these poems demand a re-viewing of prevailing practices for interpreting Cold War culture, for these *are* Cold War poems, if in a manner we have yet to recognize fully. These are verses whose remarkable vision succeeds in telescoping the ruins of one empire into the foundation of another, and in doing so they predict the inevitable, if slow and sometimes painful, expansion of love's civilization within a seemingly inhospitable imperium. And it is this insistence on a traditional belief, *amor vincit omnia*, in a traditional form, the sonnet, that makes the poems of Denby's *Mediterranean Cities* true *classics* of Cold War culture.

NOTES

An early version of this chapter (titled "'A Purity of Vocabulary and Cleanness of Accent': Edwin Denby's Queer Classicism") was presented at the Choreography and Poetics II seminar held during the 2009 American Comparative Literature Association annual conference at Harvard University. I am grateful to my fellow seminar members for their interest in Denby and for comments that helped sharpen my thinking about his work. Thanks especially to Virginia W. Jackson and Jonathan Robinson-Appels, who organized the seminar, and to Michelle Clayton, Björn Kühnicke, Zoë Norridge, and Julie Townsend.

1. Jack Anderson, "Edwin Denby, Dance Critic, Dies at 80," *New York Times* (14 July 1983). Web.

2. For the cover, see http://www.specificobject.com/objects/info.cfm?inventory_id=11658. While the kiss is difficult to make out in this image, it is described in

several published accounts. For one of these, see Mary Maxwell, "Edwin Denby's New York School," *Yale Review* 95, no. 4 (October 2007): 89.

3. The 1986 appearance of *The Complete Poems* prompted publication of two additional appreciations of Denby's writings. See Richard Howard, "Luminous Paradigms," *New Republic* 196, no. 14 (6 April 1987), 37–39; and David Kauffman, "Denby on Dance," *Horizon* 30, no. 6 (July–August 1987): 38–40.

4. Maxwell, "Edwin Denby's New York School," 95, 66. Subsequent quotations will be cited parenthetically within the text.

5. *American Poetry: The Twentieth Century, Volume Two: E. E. Cummings to May Swenson* (New York: Literary Classics of the United States, 2000). Phillip Lopate's *Writing New York*, another Library of America collection, first published in 1998 and reissued in an expanded edition in 2008, also offers poetry by Denby. Other recent anthologies that include Denby's verse are Anne Waldman and Lewis Warsh, eds., *Angel Hair Sleeps With a Boy in My Head: The Angel Hair Anthology* (New York: Granary Books, 2001); Mark Ford, ed., *New York Poets II: An Anthology* (Manchester, UK: Carcanet Press, 2006); and David Lehman and John Brehm, eds., *The Oxford Book of American Poetry* (New York: Oxford University Press, 2006). Denby also appears in Terence Diggory, ed., *Encyclopedia of the New York School Poets* (New York: Facts on File, 2009).

6. See for example Lytle Shaw, *Frank O'Hara: The Poetics of Coterie* (Iowa City: University of Iowa Press, 2006); Nadine Hubbs, *The Queer Composition of America's Sound: Gay Modernisms, American Music, and National Identity* (Berkeley: University of California Press, 2004); Michael S. Sherry, *Gay Artists in Modern American Culture: An Imagined Conspiracy* (Chapel Hill: The University of North Carolina Press, 2007); and Martin Duberman, *The Worlds of Lincoln Kirstein* (New York: Alfred A. Knopf, 2007).

7. The film was never shot, but *Four Plays by Edwin Denby* was produced in 1981 by Ada Katz's Eye and Ear Theatre. The company's other productions that year were John Ashbery's *The Heroes* and James Schuyler's *Shopping and Waiting*. Web. http://dlib.nyu.edu/findingaids/html/fales/eyeandear.html.

8. Jonathan Culler, "Why Lyric?" *PMLA* 123, no. 1 (January 2008): 201.

9. Deborah Nelson's study of confessional poets Robert Lowell, Sylvia Plath, Anne Sexton, and W. D. Snodgrass, *Pursuing Privacy in Cold War America* (New York: Columbia University Press, 2002), is one of these exceptions.

10. See Serge Guilbaut, *How New York Stole the Idea of Modern Art: Abstract Expressionism, Freedom, and the Cold War*, trans. Arthur Goldhammer (Chicago: University of Chicago Press, 1983).

11. *Mrs. W's Last Sandwich* was brought out by New York's Horizon Press; the hardcover retailed for $6.95 and featured promotional flyleaf comments by Ron Padgett and Anne Waldman. By agreement with Horizon, the exact same work appeared under a different title—*Scream in a Cave*—as a ninety-five-cent paperback under the Empress Gothic imprint of Curtis Books.

12. Gay Morris, "Modernism's Role in the Theory of John Martin and Edwin Denby," *Dance Research* 22, no. 2 (Winter 2004): 176. Morris here simply repeats, with little critical examination, the received view of modernism during the Cold War: that its loose sense of narrative and embrace of abstraction made it especially appealing to government and corporate sponsors eager to avoid (or censor) potentially disruptive political commentary in art.

13. Peter Stoneley, *A Queer History of the Ballet* (New York: Routledge, 2007), 102. Stoneley later retracts this problematic assertion in his discussion of Denby's and O'Hara's responses to Balanchine's aesthetic (119–24).

14. See David K. Johnson, *The Lavender Scare: The Cold War Persecution of Gays and Lesbians in the Federal Government* (Chicago: University of Chicago Press, 2006).

15. Moira Roth, "The Aesthetic of Indifference," in *Difference/Indifference: Musings on Postmodernism, Marcel Duchamp, and John Cage*, intro. and text by Moira Roth, commentary by Jonathan D. Katz (Amsterdam: G+B Arts International, 1998), 47. Roth's essay originally appeared in *Artforum* 16, no. 3 (November 1977): 46–53. Moira Roth's "The Aesthetic of Indifference" charges artists of the Cold War avant-garde with producing work "paralyzed by the politics of the McCarthy period" that "advocated neutrality of feeling and denial of commitment in a period that otherwise might have produced an art of passion and commitment."

16. Jonathan D. Katz, "Identification," in Roth and Katz, *Difference/Indifference*, 53, 51. Emphasis original.

17. Sherry, *Gay Artists in Modern American Culture*, 96–97. Emphasis added.

18. Edwin Denby, "Snoring in New York—an Elegy," in Edwin Denby, *The Complete Poems*, ed. and intro. Ron Padgett, with essays by Frank O'Hara and Lincoln Kirstein (New York: Random House, 1986), 125.

19. See Edmund White, "The Man Who Understood Balanchine," *New York Times Book Review* (8 November 1998). Web. Prompted by the publication of Robert Cornfield's collection of Denby's reviews and poetry (Edwin Denby, *Dance Writings and Poetry* [New Haven, CT: Yale University Press, 1998]), White's essay describes Denby's "international sense of culture" and "urban insouciance" as foundational both for the poetry and for the dance writing.

20. Frank O'Hara, "The Poetry of Edwin Denby," in Denby, *Complete Poems*, 179. This is a reprint of the closing section of a longer essay in which O'Hara also reviews Chester Kallman's *Storm at Castelfranco* and John Ashbery's *Some Trees*. See Frank O'Hara, "Rare Modern," *Poetry* 89, no. 5 (February 1957): 313–16.

21. Ron Padgett, introduction to Denby, *Complete Poems*, xxii–xxiii. Emphasis added. Subsequent quotations from this introduction will be cited parenthetically within the text.

22. Lincoln Kirstein, "On Edwin Denby," in Denby, *Complete Poems*, 184. This is a revised version of a memorial essay Kirstein published in the *New York Review of Books* 30, no. 14 (29 September 1983): 3–4.

23. Edwin Denby, "Balanchine and Tchaikovsky: 'Ballet Imperial'; Carmen Amaya; Doris Humphrey," in Edwin Denby, *Dance Writings*, ed. Robert Cornfield and William MacKay (Gainesville: University Press of Florida, n.d. [1986]), 101.

24. The Denby family's history in government service includes that of Edwin's uncle and namesake, the secretary of the navy during the Harding administration who was forced to resign from office for his involvement in the Teapot Dome scandal. Some on-line sources confuse the two Edwin Denbys.

Sources for Denby's biography include Ron Padgett, introduction to Denby, *Complete Poems*; William MacKay, "Edwin Denby, 1903–1983," in Denby, *Dance Writings*; and the many recollections of Denby published in *Ballet Review*'s four-part series "Edwin Denby Remembered," 12, nos. 1–4 (Spring 1984–Winter 1985).

25. MacKay, "Edwin Denby, 1903–1983," in Denby, *Dance Writings*, 14. Subsequent quotations from this article will be cited parenthetically within the text.

26. Thomson's recollection of the contretemps in Darmstadt over Denby's efforts to produce *Four Saints* appears in the first of *Ballet Review*'s four-part homage to Edwin Denby. See "Virgil Thomson" in "Edwin Denby Remembered—Part I," *Ballet Review* 12, no. 1 (Spring 1984): 22–23.

27. Denby's three poems "Wind Song," "During Music," and "Winter" were published in *Poetry* 28, no. 3 (June 1926): 142–43; they are not included in the *Collected Poems*. His brief study of psychoanalysis and movement appeared in English translation two years after his death; see Edwin Denby, "On the Soul's Reaction to Gymnastics," trans. George Jackson and J. Michael Whitman, M.D. *Ballet Review* 13, no. 1 (Spring 1985): 44–50.

28. "Rudy Burckhardt," in "Edwin Denby Remembered—Part I," *Ballet Review* 12, no. 1 (Spring 1984): 12.

29. Doug Eklund, "The Pursuit of Happiness: Rudy Burckhardt's New York, 1935–1940," in *New York, N. Why? Photographs by Rudolf Burckhardt, Poems by Edwin Denby*. 1938 (New York: Nazraeli Press/Metropolitan Museum of Art, 2008), unpaginated.

30. Denby's roles in Burckhardt films include the mad scientist Professor Borealis ("professor of cerebral metamorphotics at Harvard") in *Lurk* (1965; 16 mm, b&w, 38 min.) and Hemlock Stinge, "the richest man in the world," in *Money* (1968; 16 mm, b&w, 45 min.). I am grateful to my colleague Scott MacDonald for screening these and other Burckhardt films for me in the fall of 2009.

31. Howard Pollack, *Aaron Copland: The Life and Work of an Uncommon Man* (New York: Henry Holt and Co., 1999), 238.

32. Edwin Denby, "A Good Libretto," *Modern Music* 13, no. 3 (March 1936): 14–21. Denby's librettos from this period were never produced and went unpublished until the 1970s. See for example *Miltie Is a Hackie* (Calais, VT: Z Press, 1973); and *The Sonntag Gang* in *Mag City* 14 (Edwin Denby issue, 1983): 2–92.

33. See "Rudy Burckhardt," in "Edwin Denby Remembered—Part I," *Ballet Review* 12, no. 1 (Spring 1984). "After the war when I married Edith and Jacob was

born, Edwin continued to be a large part of my life. It was often complicated but it seemed natural to me" (14).

34. Edwin Denby, *Dancers, Buildings and People in the Streets*, intro. Frank O'Hara (New York: Horizon Press, 1965). The dust jacket of the hardcover edition features Rudy Burckhardt photographs of Balanchine rehearsing *Agon* with Arthur Mitchell and Melissa Hayden.

35. Simon Pettet, *Conversations with Rudy Burckhardt About Everything* (New York: Vehicle Editions, 1987), unnumbered pages, last set of ellipses in original. The Denby interview that Pettet quotes was conducted by Mark Hillringhouse and published in *Mag City* 14 (Edwin Denby issue, 1983): 101–17; the quoted passage appears at the end.

36. Edwin Denby, "Serenade," in Denby, *Dance Writings*, 214.

37. Edwin Denby, "Some Thoughts About Classicism and George Balanchine," in Denby, *Dance Writings*, 435.

38. Ibid., 439.

39. Edwin Denby, "Ballet: The American Position," in Denby, *Dance Writings*, 507, 511–12.

40. See Dorothy Tooker, "The Editors Meet William Carlos Williams" (interview with the editors of *A.D.*, 1952), in *Interviews With William Carlos Williams: "Speaking Straight Ahead,"* ed. Linda Welshimer Wagner (New York: New Directions Publishing Corporation, 1976), 27–40. "Forcing twentieth-century America into a sonnet—gosh, how I hate sonnets—is like putting a crab into a square box. You've got to cut his legs off to make him fit. When you get through, you don't have a crab anymore" (30).

41. Denby, "Ballet: The American Position," in Denby, *Dance Writings*, 514.

42. Joseph Litvak, *Strange Gourmets: Sophistication, Theory, and the Novel* (Durham, NC: Duke University Press, 1997), 14.

43. W. H. Auden, "Ballet's Present Eden: Example of *The Nutcracker*," in *The Complete Works of W. H. Auden, Volume III (1949–1955): Prose*, ed. Edward Mendelson (Princeton, NJ: Princeton University Press, 2008), 393.

44. Paul de Man, "Anthropomorphism and Trope in the Lyric," in *The Rhetoric of Romanticism* (New York: Columbia University Press, 1984), 261.

45. As with Litvak's study, I can do no more here than note the importance to my argument of the new lyric studies, which seeks to trouble long-standing assumptions about the ahistorical "nature" of lyric poetry. For an example of work in this vein, see Virginia W. Jackson, *Dickinson's Misery: A Theory of Lyric Reading* (Princeton, NJ: Princeton University Press, 2005).

46. Edwin Denby, "Trastevere: A Dedication," in *Mediterranean Cities* (New York: George Wittenborn, Inc., 1956), 5. Subsequent quotations from this collection will be cited by title and page number parenthetically within the text.

3 DEMOCRACY, DECENTRALIZATION, AND FEEDBACK

DANIEL BELGRAD

Among the metaphors that Americans of the Cold War era used for thinking about their world, that of the feedback loop has proven one of the most persistent and most powerful. Once recognized, the image of a decentralized system held together by feedback loops can be identified as a key component of the democratic vista from the 1940s through the 1970s. This chapter closely examines three disparate works from the period—Gregory Bateson's anthropological *Steps to an Ecology of Mind*, Max Neuhaus's "Feed" (a realization of John Cage's musical score *Fontana Mix*), and John Updike's story "Packed Dirt, Churchgoing, a Dead Cat, a Traded Car"—in order to suggest the pervasive presence of this metaphor in Cold War American culture and to explain its history and implications. The importance of the feedback loop as an idea derives from its usefulness in modeling an alternative to the centralized authority structures that came to predominate in postwar society, profoundly reshaping American life.

The centralization of power is a defining characteristic of modernity. Whether we speak of the power of national or federal governments over regional ones, of the power of large cities over their hinterlands, or of the integration of economic processes under a single corporate entity, the organization of large-scale enterprises through the concentration of power in a hierarchical "central command" structure is one of modernity's prevailing dynamics. From the mid-nineteenth through the mid-twentieth century, the centralization of power developed in tandem with new industrial technologies and new organizational techniques such as the "scientific management" of Taylorism.[1] The culture of the Cold War was profoundly affected by this, since both the United States and the Soviet Union were transformed in the mid-twentieth century by the rapid centralization of economic power and political authority.

From the American perspective, the centralization of power in the Soviet Union and China became one of the most potent symbols of the wrongness of Communist politics. Manifested in social and economic planning as well as in cultural directives that emanated from the central authority, it epitomized the totalitarianism of the police state. Yet American society was itself undergoing a parallel, though less visible and less violent, process of economic and political centralization. According to historian George Lipsitz, America's mobilization for World War II left behind an economic landscape radically changed from what it had been in the past. More than half a million small businesses disappeared during the war, at the same time that the federal government paid a hundred billion dollars in war contracts to just thirty-three corporations. As a result, large corporations emerged from the war with oligarchic control of America's economy, and, as Lipsitz and many others have argued, of its government as well.[2]

The threat to democracy posed by this concentration of power was a source of widespread concern a good decade and a half before 1960, when Eisenhower in his presidential farewell address warned Americans against the "military-industrial complex." George Lipsitz's statistics and conclusions are themselves based on a report prepared for a special Senate investigating committee in 1946, titled *Economic Concentration and World War II*.[3] In that same year, political theorist Dwight Macdonald wrote in the journal *Politics* that fascism, Communism, and monopoly capitalism were all versions of the same social structure, which he called "bureaucratic collectivism."[4] Sociologist C. Wright Mills is now probably the best-known critic of the centralization of power in Cold War America. In his essay "The Structure of Power in American Society," Mills described "the enlargement and the centralization of the means of power—in economic, in political, and in military institutions."[5]

As the impact of centralization increasingly shaped how life was lived in the United States, however, the idea persisted that decentralized organizational structures were both more desirable and in some ineffable way more powerful than centralized ones. Thus Harvard psychologist Gordon Allport, writing on the eve of American involvement in the Second World War, insisted that "democratic morale has far greater potential strength" than the engineered social unity of totalitarianism.[6] In 1941 and 1942, Allport was among a group of social scientists recruited by the Council for Democracy to form a Committee on Public Morale: 350 expert consultants enlisted to devise ways of boosting American commitment to the war effort. The privately funded Council for Democracy had been founded in August of 1940, following the Hitler-Stalin Pact and the Soviet invasion of Finland, to counter anti-interventionist propaganda emanating from Germany and the Soviet Union. It represented a broad constituency of American interventionists, ranging from internationally minded corporate liberals such as Henry Luce to anticommunist labor leaders such as David Dubinsky. A precursor of the federal Office of War Information, its Committee on Public Morale considered how best to go about changing some habitual ways of thinking that could compromise wartime unity, such as isolationism, racism, and anti-Semitism. Its list of consultants included many distinguished social scientists, among them Ruth Benedict, Hadley Cantril, Erik Erikson, Erich Fromm, Margaret Mead, and Gregory Bateson.[7]

The wartime information campaign ultimately came to be dominated by advertising executives and social engineers who favored centralized authority structures. But anthropologists Mead and Bateson spoke out vociferously against such "social engineering" techniques, which they insisted were antithetical to democratic values.[8] "It is hardly an exaggeration to say that this war is ideologically about just this," wrote Bateson in 1942. "Could deliberate social planning be reconciled with the democratic ideal?" Deliberate social planning, he asserted, was characteristic of centralized, bureaucratic systems such as fascism and Communism. By contrast, democracy had to be embraced as the *means* as well as the end of the American war effort. As Margaret Mead argued, "If we go on defining ends as separate from means *and* apply the social sciences as crudely instrumental means, using the recipes of science to manipulate people, we shall arrive at a totalitarian rather than a democratic system of life." Bateson agreed, asserting that "a basic and fundamental discrepancy exists between 'social engineering,' manipulating people in order to achieve a planned blue-print society, and the ideals of democracy." The paradoxical solution, Bateson suggested, was that a democratic leadership must "discard purpose in order to achieve our purpose."[9]

From these beginnings, Bateson's thinking about the value of "purposelessness" in social organization developed over the next three decades into a ramified articulation of one of the most powerful principles in postwar American thought. Even as decentralized structures faded from American economic and political reality, the ideal re-emerged in American intellectual and cultural life, linked to the origins of a vision that we now call "postmodern."[10] At the core of this image of decentralized authority is the model of *autopoiesis*, or the self-adjusting network of feedback loops. This dynamic is now thought to describe the "chaotic" functioning of complex systems as diverse as human subjectivity, the global market, and the ecosystem.

On a practical level, Bateson's 1942 recommendations regarding how to encourage the development of democratic values did not so much involve "discard[ing] purpose" as focusing on "second-order" purposefulness, or, as he termed it, "deutero-learning." Deutero-learning is the process of learning how to learn, the habits of thought and perspective that are cultivated by the first-order learning experience. Bateson gave as an example the practice, in totalitarian societies, of teaching children to spy on their parents. Such a practice might be justified on the level of first-order learning (that is, in terms of its ends) by an appeal to the national good; but on the level of deutero-learning (that is, in terms of its means), it is self-defeating. For "they [the children] will build this experience into their whole philosophy of life; it will color all their future attitudes toward authority" ("Social Planning" 164). Similarly, if a man were to lecture before an audience and pronounce that "democracy is good; fascism is bad," the message on the level of first-order learning would be prodemocratic. The message on the level of second-order learning, however, would be to the contrary, because the epistemological dynamic is that of an authority figure telling others what to think. For democracy to be operative in second-order learning, the "audience" would have to become active participants in a process of examining the relative merits of democracy and fascism and arriving at their own conclusions. Then, if on the next day another lecturer (or the same one) were to return and announce that "fascism is good; it is democracy that is bad," the inculcated habits of deutero-learning would militate against the acceptance of his message.

In this sense, deutero-learning is a form of feedback: it is a learning output produced by the culture that is fed back into the system as information that affects its subsequent operation. Bateson's argument was that the real cultural work of democracy could not be achieved by focusing on the transmission of information, but could only be accomplished indirectly, through deutero-learning feedback mechanisms cultivating open habits of mind. From this perspective, cultures are decentralized, autopoietic systems of social order, sustained by self-reinforcing processes (information feedback loops) of learning and deutero-learning.[11] This vision is the link between Bateson's earlier anthropological work and his subsequent turn to the field of cybernetics, which he helped create.

Cybernetics developed from a series of eight conferences beginning in

May of 1942 and ending in 1953 on the topic of "Feedback Mechanisms and Circular Causal Systems in Biological and Social Systems."[12] Bateson and Mead were among those who participated with American mathematician Norbert Wiener in this series of conferences. In 1942, the same year that Bateson articulated his theory of deutero-learning, Wiener worked out an algorithm to enable an antiaircraft gun to predict the future location of its target. In collaboration with engineer Julian Bigelow, he devised a mechanical system with electrical circuits that measured the targeted plane's evasive maneuvers and modified the gun's position accordingly, creating an information feedback loop that made the gun self-guiding, or "intelligent."[13] Wiener then theorized that the feedback loop was the essence of all intelligent systems, whether biological or artificial. In 1948, he gave the emerging field of artificial intelligence a lasting name when he published *Cybernetics: or, Control and Communication in the Animal and the Machine*.

Yet Wiener's focus in cybernetics was electrical engineering; it was Bateson and others who developed the field in the direction of studying societies as intelligent systems.[14] Between 1942 and 1944, for example, American agronomist Aldo Leopold wrote an essay that he called "Thinking Like a Mountain"; as its title suggests, it described the system of feedback loops governing animal populations as a decentralized form of intelligence ("thinking"). Leopold was writing against the long-standing practice of killing wolves in order to eliminate their threat to deer, cattle, and sheep.

> I now suspect that just as a deer herd lives in mortal fear of its wolves, so does a mountain live in mortal fear of its deer. And perhaps with better cause, for while a buck pulled down by wolves can be replaced in two or three years, a range pulled down by too many deer may fail of replacement in as many decades. So also with cows. The cowman who cleans his range of wolves does not realize that he is taking over the wolf's job of trimming the herd to fit the range. He has not learned to think like a mountain. Hence we have dustbowls, and rivers washing the future into the sea. We all strive for safety, prosperity, comfort, long life . . . but too much safety seems to yield only danger in the long run.

The danger of unintended consequences that Leopold's essay emphasizes ("too much safety seems to yield only danger in the long run") echoes Bateson's contemporaneous argument against "purposive" intervention in favor of second-order strategies. Today Leopold is considered one of the founders of modern ecology.[15] In his later work, Bateson adopted ecology as the governing metaphor that he used to describe autopoietic systems.

Clearly, the vision of the decentralized, autopoietic network was a key image on the cutting edge of Cold War American thought. It appeared not only in sciences as diverse as computer engineering, anthropology, and ecology, but also in music, literature, and the visual and performing arts. The remainder of this essay is devoted to exploring the development of this idea through a few key texts from later in the era. Max Neuhaus's "Feed" (1963) uses feedback loops to bring harmony and form to John Cage's anarchic musical conception *Fontana Mix* (1958). John Updike's short story "Packed Dirt, Churchgoing, a Dead Cat, a Traded Car" (1961) describes a universe in which life's quotidian details are given meaning by immanent, recursive patterns. Bateson's later essays in *Steps to an Ecology of Mind* (1972) tread the same path scientifically that Updike mapped creatively, integrating ecology, psychology, and theology in a holistic view of the universe as an autopoietic network.

John Cage and Max Neuhaus: An Infinite Play of Interpenetrations

Beginning in 1963, percussionist and electronic music pioneer Max Neuhaus staged a number of musical performances featuring the structuring principle of feedback loops. Of these projects, the one that was most often performed and recorded was a realization of John Cage's score *Fontana Mix* of 1958. In keeping with Cage's philosophy, that score leaves most of the aspects of the musical performance indeterminate. Therefore, Neuhaus's realization, titled "Feed," is best understood as a collaborative work between the two men. This collaboration has a time dimension that stretches beyond the ten-minute duration of the piece itself: from the late 1950s, when Cage's score posed the question of decentralization, to the mid-1960s, when Neuhaus answered it with a network of feedback loops.

The decentralization of authority is in fact a key concept in understanding the work of John Cage, who earned a place in music history with his radical refusal of the authority of the composer. "A composer is simply someone who tells other people what to do," he wrote in *A Year from Monday* (1967). "I find this an unattractive way of getting things done."[16] Cage's alternative to the traditional model of a composer—someone who thinks up music for a listener to hear—was to promote what might be called "second-order listening," because of its parallel to what Bateson called second-order learning. That is, Cage was not interested in communicating emotions through the manipulation of a musical "message," but in changing the listener's idea of what music could be.[17] "New music: new listening," he wrote in his 1961 manifesto *Silence*.[18]

The Western musical heritage, Cage complained, represented a deeply ingrained listening habit (*Silence* 4). Cage wanted to challenge his listeners to discard their habitual expectations and value judgments and instead to adopt a frame of mind open to all experience—an aesthetic expressed in the Zen Buddhist maxim, "before the beautiful and the ugly were differentiated."[19] Cage's compositions therefore allow for no distinction between "musical" sounds and "noise." Typically they are filled with thumps, screeches, and snippets of radio broadcasts or tape recordings in addition to notes played on conventional musical instruments.

Because sounds (noises) are everywhere, if the process of deutero-listening that Cage promoted were to take hold, the listener would always be surrounded by music. But what is meant by music is radically redefined in the process. "Not an attempt to understand something that is being said . . . just an attention to the activity of sounds," Cage wrote in *Silence* (10). In a manner similar to Bateson in 1942, who had written that democratic leaders must "discard purpose in order to achieve our purpose," Cage called in 1957 for "a purposeful purposelessness" that would register as "an affirmation of life" (*Silence* 12).

For Cage, then, to eliminate the authority structure by which the composer traditionally affected the emotions of the listener through music was not to sacrifice the emotional power of music. Instead, he wrote, by "giv[ing] up the desire to control sound," he "let sounds be themselves" (*Silence* 10). Emotions would continue to arise in the listener, but not in response to sounds that the composer had commandeered as vehicles of his or her own emotion. Cage wanted his music to lead the listener instead "to the world of nature, where gradually or suddenly, one sees that humanity and nature, not separate, are in this world together" (*Silence* 8). His Zen Buddhist practice of disengaging from egoistic musical action inevitably contributed, he believed, to an ecological vision in which humans were embedded in—rather than outside of and opposed to—nature.

Cage's thinking in this respect is in keeping with what we know about the influence among the postwar avant-garde of what is often called "field theory." (As Jackson Pollock is famously said to have stated, "I *am* nature.")[20] According to field theory, all things that we perceive as discrete entities are actually interrelations. As Natalie Schmitt has explained in reference to Cage's work, "If we abandon the idea of discrete unified wholes . . . an elementary particle is . . . a *set of relationships* extending outward to other things."[21] Similarly, Cage wrote that music should bring us to realize that "an individual, having no separate soul, is a time-span, a collection of changes. Our nature's that of Nature. Nothing's fixed."[22]

This intellectual context offers insight into Cage's particular investment in decentralized structures. Paraphrasing Ananda Coomaraswamy's 1934 treatise *The Transformation of Nature in Art*, he often insisted that the purpose of art was not to present the face of nature but to present "nature's *manner of operation*" (*Silence* 9). Therefore one purpose of his work was to dispel the notion of simplistic causal relationships in favor of the more chaotic complexity of actual events. "There are an incalculable infinity of causes and effects . . . [because] in fact each and every thing in all of time and space is related to each and every other thing," he wrote in *Silence* (46–47); and "there is no need to minimize the complexity of the situation."[23] This sense of interpenetration was an important aspect of the consciousness that he hoped to encourage through second-order listening. To emphasize it, he made works that demand an attitude of "polyattentiveness" in the listener.[24] He once suggested that five simultaneous activities constituted a bare minimum for a good performance, in order to maintain a sufficient level of "perplexity" (*Silence* 173).[25] "This disharmony," he asserted, "to paraphrase Bergson's statement about disorder, is simply a harmony to which many are unaccustomed" (*Silence* 12). He compared the decentralized quality of attention that resulted to that evoked by the "allover" painting style of Abstract Expressionism pioneered by Jackson Pollock in the late 1940s. Such painting, he wrote, "carries one's attention not to a center of interest but all over the canvas."[26]

As this musical practice illustrates, Cage's commitment to the principle of decentralization extended from the role of the composer to the forms of the music itself. Instead of composing a complete musical score, for instance, he composed the parts of a piece and left indeterminate the manner in which they were to be combined, because, he insisted, "the requiring that many parts be played in a *particular* togetherness, is not an accurate representation of *how things are*" (*Silence* 10, emphasis added). Without a score to provide a centralized coordination of the musical experience, the plurality of the listeners' experiences was emphasized. "The central points where fusion occurs are many: the ears of the listeners wherever they are" (*Silence* 10).

Cage felt that such strategies of decentralization achieved an important ideological effect by means of deutero-listening: a pluralism in which every point was its own center, in lieu of having a single center that subordinated everything else. As Natalie Schmitt has explained:

> Central focus in space, like central focus in time (climax) is a system of subordination of all the rest of the space or time, controlling the audience's attention. But if the audience itself is not to be subservient to the work, the idea of getting and holding their attention must be relinquished.[27]

Instead of attempting to hold the attention of the listener, Cage's strategies of decentralization throw back to each listener the problem of what it means to listen.

One of the most famous expressions of this principle is Cage's *4′33″* from 1952, a piece in which the musicians onstage play nothing: the music is whatever sounds from other sources are heard by members of the audience.[28] In this extreme statement of Cage's musical philosophy, the implicit connection between decentralization and feedback emerges, because the output of the system (the sounds made by the listening audience) is an input of the system (the very music that the audience is listening to).

Max Neuhaus's realizations intensified the role of feedback as an organizing principle in Cage's decentralized aural field. In the early 1960s, Neuhaus pioneered the use of electronic feedback as a source of musical sounds. In his performances, he used microphones resting on drums in front of loudspeakers to create a system of feedback loops. The microphones picked up room sounds, creating electrical signals that passed through a four-track mixer and were sent out through the speakers, which converted the electrical signals back into sounds. The sound waves created by the speakers caused the drums on which the microphones were resting to vibrate, and these vibrations and sounds were once more encoded by the microphones into electrical signals, which were mixed and sent out again to the speakers, and so on.

To Neuhaus's initial surprise, the "noise" generated by these multiple feedback loops is not random but forms standing electronic wave patterns similar to conventional musical tones. As he described it:

> In 1963, while exploring ways of changing the timbre of percussion instruments through amplification, I had discovered a means of generating sound which I found fascinating—the creation of an acoustic feedback loop with a percussion instrument inserted inside it. Instead

> of the usual single screeching tones of acoustic feedback, this created a *complex multi-timbered system of oscillation.*[29]

The feedback loops functioned as an organizing mechanism for the decentralized field of sound.

The result was an autopoietic system that caused pattern, variety, and even beauty to emerge from chaotic complexity in a manner that reminded Neuhaus of natural processes. "Feed" used Cage's score *Fontana Mix* to determine the power settings of the four channels of the mixer for the duration of a ten-minute performance. Even at this level of determinacy, however, the pattern of sounds was never reproduced from one performance to the next: small differences in initial conditions (the instruments, the spatial configuration of microphones and speakers, the acoustics of the room, the ambient room noise) made each performance unique. Neuhaus compared the system in this respect to a living organism: "The factors here are so complex that even if the piece were to be performed twice in the same room with the same instruments, and the same loudspeakers, it would have completely different sound and structures each time. It seems something alive."[30]

"Feed" embodies dynamics of interaction that were being described at the same historical moment by the emerging field of chaos theory. Chaos theory developed in the early 1960s from efforts to use mathematical equations organized into feedback loops to model the behavior of complex systems like weather patterns and cotton prices. Meteorologist Edward Lorenz found by accident that small differences in initial conditions caused great disparities after a few cycles (iterations) of the feedback functions. For this reason, the behavior of the system was virtually unpredictable and therefore "chaotic." Yet Lorenz discovered that mapping multiple versions of the system's behavior on top of one another revealed a hidden pattern within the chaos. Though a specific outcome could not be predicted, an overall shape to the outcomes could be discerned.[31]

Among these larger patterns is that of "self-similarity," in which a part of the system reiterates the pattern of the whole, reproducing exact smaller copies of the larger system within it. The most famous mathematical example of self-similarity is the graph of the Mandelbrot set.[32] A related phenomenon is "bifurcation," in which the difference attributable to:

> something as small as a single photon of energy . . . is swelled by iteration to a size so great that a fork is created and the system takes off in

a new direction [leading it] . . . to stabilize a new behavior through a series of feedback loops.[33]

Neuhaus observed this phenomenon in his execution of Cage's score: "As the amplification controls are gradually changed, the feedback channels suddenly break into different modes of oscillation; sound seems to swing through the room."[34]

Neuhaus's "Feed" thus fulfills, better than many of Cage's own performances, Cage's dictum that music should imitate "nature's manner of operation." Cage worked to liberate composing, performing, and listening from the conventions of centralized planning, in favor of an anarchy of sound. Neuhaus discovered the role played by feedback loops in bringing order to such a decentralized system. "Feed" gathers every stray vibration into an "infinite play of interpenetrations" (*Silence* 14–15). These feedback loops offer an alternative method of organization to that of the centralized authority, creating an autopoietic system that seems to model ecological processes.

John Updike: The Fruit of a Single Impossible Tree

The major theme of Neuhaus's work—the emergence of pattern from chaos in a decentralized system—is shared by John Updike's short story "Packed Dirt, Churchgoing, a Dead Cat, a Traded Car." This story was written in 1961 and originally published in *Pigeon Feathers* (1962), where it had pride of place as the last story in the collection. In fact, it is not so much a short story as a collage, since, as the fragmented quality of the title suggests, there is no narrative thread tying together its four sketches. Instead, its coherence is achieved by other means. But this story is for that reason quintessential to Updike's oeuvre, for he claimed that his stories were primarily spatial rather than temporal arrangements: "the books are conceived, as objects in space, with events and persons composed within them like shapes."[35]

Updike's explanation of his method resonates with the Abstract Expressionist artist Robert Motherwell's description of his relationship to collage from 1946:

> The sensation of physically operating on the world is very strong in the medium [of collage]. . . . One cuts and chooses and shifts and pastes, and sometimes tears off and begins again. In any case, shaping and arranging such a relational structure obliterates the need [for conventional narrative representation.][36]

Motherwell's statement emphasizes the collage artist's sense of working in close contact with the world of material objects, wresting meaning from the way they are finally juxtaposed. In 1974, Updike offered a related description of his process for "work[ing] several disparate incidents or impressions into the shape of a single story." He used an anecdote from his childhood to develop a key visual metaphor:

> I would draw on one sheet of paper an assortment of objects—flowers, animals, stars, toasters, chairs, comic-strip creatures, ghosts, noses—and connect them with lines, a path of two lines, so that they all became the fruit of a single impossible tree.[37]

This is an embellishment of an image that he first introduced in his *Paris Review* interview of 1968:

> When I was little, I used to draw disparate objects on a piece of paper—toasters, baseballs, flowers, whatnot—and connect them with lines . . . *these little connections—recurrences . . . are in [my stories] as a kind of running, oblique coherence.*[38]

What gives Updike's collage "Packed Dirt" its coherence are exactly such recurrences of objects and images, the way it returns, recursively, to topics such as deacons or patches of bare earth.[39] The fabric of its reality is woven from these successive reiterations.

Updike uses writing to connect the dots of seemingly disparate objects. Therefore a characteristic feature of his prose is its evocation of concrete, circumstantial detail. This stylistic feature makes sense in relation to Updike's world view and his sense of the writer's role. Truth, he asserted, is not captured in abstractions or generalizations but "is anecdotal, narrative, the snug opaque quotidian."[40]

In the story "Packed Dirt," this motif of circumstantiality is presented through a catalog of the artifacts in a natural history museum. This far-flung assortment of objects, gathered according to the principles of an outmoded "natural history," makes a single impossible tree:

> Black swans drifted through flotillas of crumbled bread. As a child I had believed literally that bread cast upon the waters came back doubled. I remembered that within the museum there were mummies with astonished shattered faces; a tiny gilt chair for a baby Pharaoh; an elephant tusk carved into thousands of tiny Chinamen and pagodas and squat leafy trees; miniature Eskimo villages that you lit up with a switch and

peeped into like an Easter egg; cases of arrowheads; rooms of stuffed birds; and, upstairs, wooden chests decorated with hearts and pelicans and tulips by the pious "plain people" and iridescent glassware from the kilns of Baron von Steigel and slashing paintings of Pennsylvania woodland by the Shearers and bronze statuettes of wrestling Indians that stirred my first erotic dreams and, in the round skylit room at the head of the marble stairs, a black-rimmed pool in whose center a naked green lady held to her pursed lips a shell whose lucent contents forever spilled from the other side, filling this whole vast upstairs—from whose Palladian windows the swans in their bready pond could be seen trailing fan-shaped wakes—with the music and chill romance of falling water.[41]

The museum is reassuringly premodern and also suggestively postmodern in its refusal of rational ordering principles. Opposed to its benign space in the story is the hospital where the narrator goes to visit his dying father. This hospital is described as a "linoleum maze" with corridors "lined with petitioners waiting for a verdict" ("Packed Dirt" 116). As a modern space, it is characterized by rigid geometries and hierarchical relations.[42] By contrast, the natural history museum possesses a chaotic coherence, emphasized by the repeated image of the black swans that thread their way through a pond littered generously with flotsam.

The self-consciousness that is often noted as another feature of Updike's prose style (the volume of memoirs that he published in 1989 is even titled *Self-Consciousness*) derives, like his emphasis on the concrete, from his belief that truth can be captured in words only through a faithful description of how it is reiterated in the "opaque quotidian." For Updike, the great hazard of writing is always the sin of omission, the risk of sacrificing the "enigmatic concreteness" of circumstances and the "verbal and psychological accuracy" of human interactions in favor of the simple solution and the foregone conclusion.[43] For this reason, he was particularly reluctant to discuss the meanings of his stories in interviews. As he observed self-consciously to one interviewer in 1968, "My relationship to you and my linear way of coping out loud are distortive . . . everything is infinitely fine, and any opinion is somehow coarser than the texture of the real thing."[44]

Because in Updike's view truth inheres only in the "infinitely fine . . . texture of the real," slicing through it with the "rigid patternings" of a master plan or an externally imposed order is a presumptuousness akin to evil.[45] In "Packed Dirt," this error is symbolized by the construction of a new curve of highway next to the narrator's house. Like John Cage and Aldo Leopold, Updike associates this misguided purposefulness with a self-defeating alienation from nature's processes. Contrarily, the virtue of packed dirt lies in that it is "unconsciously humanized": "It seemed precious because it had been achieved accidentally, and had about it that repose of grace that is beyond willing."

> We in America have from the beginning been cleaving and baring the earth, attacking, reforming the enormity of nature we were given, which we took to be hostile. We have explored, on behalf of all mankind, this paradox: the more matter is outwardly mastered, the more it overwhelms us in our hearts. Evidence—gaping right-of-ways, acres mercilessly scraped, bleeding mountains of muddy fill—surrounds us of a war that is incapable of ceasing, and it is good to know that now there are enough of us to exert a counter-force. ("Packed Dirt" 103)

Road building is the antithesis of the process that Updike associates with packed dirt; as a result of the highway construction, he writes, "the beaten path that does for a sidewalk in front of my home was sheared diagonally by a foot-high cliff" ("Packed Dirt" 102–3).

Packed dirt offers evidence of an alternative kind of order that supersedes the conscious planning and imposed control that the highway represents. Like the subtly ordered chaos of the natural history museum, it connotes an order that inheres in the accretion of apparently random and contingent events. Updike's story explores the possibility of this kind of inherent order, implying that the microcosmic patterns connecting its quotidian details are indexical of macrocosmic patterns governing the universe.[46] As he explained in an interview, "In writing, I try to adhere to . . . the undeniable little thing. Somehow, I hope the pattern in the art will emerge, and *I guess I must have some such hope cosmically*."[47]

The decentralized authority that Updike conveys through the image of packed dirt is manifested in other aspects of his narrator's life as well: in his churchgoing, in his help for a dying cat on the night his daughter is born, and in the trip that he makes to his father's bedside in a car that he has already traded away. Decentralized authority—the vision of creation as an autopoietic network—is the underlying theme that unifies these different episodes. It is both the story's theme and its organizing formal principle, so that as the collage *becomes* a story, its form functions as second-order storytelling in Bateson's sense.[48]

Updike equates spiritual faith with a trust in the organizing power of such patterns of seemingly incidental events as his story brings together. Significantly, when defining his *vocation* as a writer–a term that connotes a religious calling—he describes it as just such a coalescence of incidents, in which "a number of personal accidents drift us toward the occupation . . . which pre-exists [our conscious choices]."[49] Ultimately Updike felt that this was the only evidence of God's presence compatible with human freedom. As he later wrote in his memoirs, "a loud and evident God would be a bully, an insecure tyrant, an all-crushing datum. . . . [Instead] his answers come in the . . . facts of our lives, strung on that thread running through all things."[50] Updike's God is an autopoietic network, as the alternative to His being a tyrant.

In a parallel to John Cage's Zen Buddhism, Updike's faith in the presence of divinely immanent patterns minimizes for him the importance of the boundaries that set each individual apart as a discrete and unified entity. The self as ego is less relevant, writes Updike, than the self as conduit or "point of focus" for larger, transpersonal processes, what the philosopher Alfred North Whitehead once called a "concrescence of prehensions."[51] In an essay in *Self-Consciousness* titled "On Being a Self Forever," Updike observes that the self is in truth neither unified nor individual:

> The frangibility and provisionality of the self is well within our modern competence to perceive. . . . Each day, we wake slightly altered, and the person we were yesterday is dead. So why, one could say, be afraid of death, when death comes all the time?[52]

Updike's characters are (as the poet Allen Ginsberg described himself in 1974) "already in eternity while . . . living on earth."[53]

In a useful critical essay written in 1970, Richard Rupp argues that "Updike's style circles relentlessly on the circumference of experience, seeking entry into its center."[54] In historical hindsight, we can assert more confidently that Updike's style circles relentlessly across the surface of an experience that has no center. Significantly, in the story "Packed Dirt," the question of God's existence is subsumed by the practice of churchgoing. Churchgoing, like packed dirt, acts as a synecdoche for the unconscious group processes that order human social behavior in a decentralized universe. "Belief builds itself unconsciously and in consciousness is spent," Updike asserts in the story ("Packed Dirt" 104). Churchgoing is a ceremony, a pattern that accrues meaning through its persistent repetition; Updike concludes, "We in America need ceremonies" ("Packed Dirt" 121).

The topological space of the closed surface is the trope by which Updike conveys his idea of a decentralized universe. When the narrator of "Packed Dirt" succumbs to existential anxiety, he imagines himself as a hollow shell: "I was dismayed to see myself, a gutted shell, appearing to [my children] as the embodiment and pledge of a safe universe" ("Packed Dirt" 111). In the course of the story's last segment, however, this negative image of a "gutted shell" is supplanted by the positive image of another closed surface: a habitable shelter. Specifically, this is represented by the narrator's first car (the "traded car" of the title). Its space is hallowed by the coalescence of personal events, similar to the process of packing dirt: "Not only sand and candy wrappers accumulate in a car's interior, but heroisms and instants of communion" ("Packed Dirt" 108).

By the story's end, the car has also become a metaphor for the human body. "My car, beginning as a mechanical assembly of molecules, evolved into something soft and organic and consciously brave . . . [that,] though its soul the driver had died, maintained steady forward motion" and arrived home ("Packed Dirt" 121).[55] This metaphor is so consistent that the reader may not at first realize that Updike has accomplished a significant inversion of the familiar idea of a religious afterlife: here it is the physical surface that persists and the inner individual essence, the "soul," that is sloughed away. The physical world's "steady forward motion" is autopoietic and maintains itself without the control of "the driver."

This is the decentralized dynamic that informs Updike's religious and social vision. The reiteration of ceremony replaces the wish for a transcendent purpose, in the same way that packed dirt clothes the raw landscape: "As our sense of God's forested legacy to us dwindles, there grows, in these worn, rubbed, and patted patches [of dirt], a sense of human legacy—like those feet of statues of saints which have lost their toes to centuries of kisses" ("Packed Dirt" 103).

Gregory Bateson: The Processes of Ecology Are Not Mocked

Gregory Bateson's work from the 1960s shares with the works of Neuhaus and Updike this vision of an autopoietic network in which systemic feedback mechanisms create an invisible net of order. "No man . . . has ever seen or experienced formless and unsorted matter; just as no man has ever seen or experienced a 'random' event," Bateson writes in the introduction to his book of collected essays *Steps to An Ecology of Mind* (1972).[56] He argues that in this sense the universe must be understood as intelligent, in keeping with the definition of intelligence formulated by the pioneers of cybernetics during the Second World War: "Wherever in the Universe we encounter that sort of complexity, we are dealing with mental phenomena. . . . Call the systemic forces 'God' if you will."[57] In his later writings, he used ecology as a universal metaphor for *autopoiesis*—hence the title of his book. "'Mind' [is] immanent in the . . . ecosystem," he asserted in a lecture that he first gave in 1970 and later included in *Steps to an Ecology of Mind*. "There is a larger Mind of which the individual mind is only a subsystem. This larger Mind is comparable to God . . . immanent in the total interconnected social system and planetary ecology."[58] Bateson envisioned human individuals (both biologically and psychologically), human societies, and the global ecosystem as cybernetic systems, one nested inside another.[59]

By the time Bateson wrote the last essays collected in *Steps to an Ecology of Mind*, America's postwar corporate-liberal culture had entered a period of crisis. Radical movements like the hippie counterculture, antiwar protests, Black Power, and radical feminism actively rejected the postwar social order and the assumptions on which it was based. In addition, many "middle Americans" were frustrated by the failure of the technocratic society to deliver on its promise of a better quality of life and withdrew their support for the liberal consensus.[60] In this context, decentralization again emerged as an explicitly political vision. Bateson's work from the late 1960s brought the idea of *autopoiesis* back into the political sphere, insisting that it offered the necessary model of social governance.

Expanding on the thoughts of his 1942 essay against propaganda, Bateson in 1968 polemicized against all social planning directed by a singleminded effort to accomplish an objective without due attention to the system of interactions through which such an effort would be inflected. Such misguided "purposiveness," he argued, typically devised actions inconsistent with ecological thinking.[61] He used as an example the effort at Prohibition, which did not end alcohol consumption but instead brought both bootlegging and policing to a higher level of organization. Predictably, he wrote, these hypertrophied criminal gangs and police forces were then united in their opposition to the repeal of Prohibition. Bateson saw the war in Vietnam as another self-perpetuating system that had originated through a similar "excessive purposiveness" and that subsequently fostered the development of interest groups that were opposed to ending it.

Because of the feedback mechanisms governing autopoietic systems, Bateson insists, "lack of systemic wisdom is always punished."[62]

Paraphrasing the biblical verse from the book of Galatians, "God is not mocked," he writes, "The processes of ecology are not mocked."[63] Pursuing the religious analogy, Bateson compares the development of purposive thinking and the discarding of ecological thinking with the loss of the Garden of Eden. But in his version, it is people who have cast God out of the garden, rather than vice versa.[64] In Bateson's opinion, the Industrial Revolution in particular led to an "increase of scientific arrogance" that has to be tempered by the understanding "that man is only a part of larger systems and that *the part can never control the whole*. . . . We do not live in the sort of universe in which simple lineal control is possible. Life is not like that." Therefore our penchant for surgical interventions and quick fixes has to give way to a slower process of "learning" by the system as a whole. The "self-maximizing" purposes of various subsystems must not be allowed to outweigh the general interest.[65]

Bateson contrasts "consciousness," the attribute that he uses to denote purposive, centrally directed planning, with "wisdom," the goal of systemic thinking. The latter, he writes, is cultivated chiefly in areas of human activity dangerously far removed from the typical policymaking apparatus of Cold War America. These include "the arts, poetry, music, and the humanities"; what Martin Buber called "I-Thou" relationships; and "contact between man and animals."[66]

As with the conclusions arrived at in John Updike's story "Packed Dirt," Bateson's thinking in the 1960s led him to imagine "a profound redefinition of the self" that challenged the individualistic ethos of liberal society.[67] As he explained in 1970:

> It is understandable that, in a civilization which separates mind from body, we should either try to forget death or to make mythologies about the survival of transcendent mind. But if mind is immanent not only in those pathways of information which are located inside the body but also in external pathways, then death takes on a different aspect. The individual nexus of pathways which I call "me" is no longer so precious because that nexus is only part of a larger mind. The ideas which seemed to be me can also become immanent in you.[68]

Bateson's own ideas were given extended life through the work of Stewart Brand, founder and editor of that counterculture bible *The Whole Earth Catalogue* (1968–71). Brand championed Bateson's ideas throughout the mid-1970s. He promoted *Steps to an Ecology of Mind* by writing extended reviews of it for *Rolling Stone* and *Harper's* magazines; the former included an account of several days that Brand spent visiting and interviewing Bateson in California.

In 1974, Brand began publication of the *CoEvolution Quarterly*, which featured Bateson's ecological thinking and related ideas. In the summer of 1975, the *CoEvolution Quarterly* was the first to introduce the American reading public to the "Gaia hypothesis," which imagines the entire biosphere as a single living intelligence.[69] Gaia, like the image of existence that recurs in John Updike's story, is a closed surface, a hollow sphere (with a thickness extending from the subsoil to the top of the atmosphere) constituted by patterns of ecological interaction.

As these few examples illustrate, from the beginning of World War II and into the 1970s, the decentralized, autopoietic system was clearly an important idea in American intellectual life. The history of this idea is part of the story of the evolving image of American democracy. It is also part of the story of the development of postmodernism, for identity in modernity is centralized and interiorized, as epitomized by the stream-of-consciousness technique of modernist writing, whereas identity in postmodernity is exteriorized in cultural constructions and generic conventions.

As a persistent metaphor, the vision of a decentralized system that governs itself through feedback loops offers us, as historians and cultural critics, a new interpretive paradigm to bring to the task of interpreting Cold War American culture. As such, it offers us a new lamp with which to look at the texts of the era, bringing with it the possibility of reassessing their social meanings. Reexamining them in its light may cause them to shine back at us with a new light of their own, casting new shapes and new shadows.

NOTES

1. See Richard Edwards, *Contested Terrain: The Transformation of the Workplace in the Twentieth Century* (New York: Basic Books, 1979). See also Samuel Haber, *Efficiency and Uplift: Scientific Management in the Progressive Era 1890–1920* (Chicago: University of Chicago Press, 1964).

2. George Lipsitz, *Rainbow at Midnight: Labor and Culture in the 1940s* (Chicago: University of Illinois Press, 1994), 57, 61.

3. John Blair et al., *Economic Concentration and World War II*, Report of the Smaller War Plants Corporation to the U.S. Senate Special Committee to Study Problems of American Small Business (Washington, D.C.: Government Printing Office, 1946).

4. Dwight Macdonald, "The Root Is Man (Part I)," *Politics* 3 (April 1946): 112.

5. C. Wright Mills, "The Structure of Power in American Society," *British Journal*

of Sociology 9, no. 1 (March 1958): 31. See also C. Wright Mills, *The Power Elite* (New York: Oxford University Press, 1956); and C. Wright Mills, "The Powerless People: The Role of the Intellectual in Society," *Politics* 1, no. 4 (April 1944): 69–71.

6. Gordon W. Allport, "Liabilities and Assets in Civilian Morale," *Annals of the American Academy of Political and Social Science* 216 (July 1941): 91.

7. Cedric Larson, "The Council for Democracy," *Public Opinion Quarterly* 6, no. 2 (Summer 1942): 284–85. See also Patti Clayton Becker, *Books and Libraries in American Society during World War II: Weapons in the War of Ideas* (New York: Routledge, 2005), 65.

8. See Margaret Mead, "The Comparative Study of Culture and the Purposive Cultivation of Democratic Values," in *Science, Philosophy, and Religion, Second Symposium*, ed. Lymon Bryson and Louis Finkelstein (New York: Conference on Science, Philosophy and Religion in their Relation to the Democratic Way of Life, Inc., 1942), 59, 66. For more on the struggle over information management during the war, see Daniel Belgrad, *The Culture of Spontaneity: Improvisation and the Arts in Postwar America* (Chicago: University of Chicago Press, 1998), 22–25.

9. David Lipset, *Gregory Bateson: The Legacy of a Scientist* (Englewood Cliffs, NJ: Prentice-Hall, 1980), 166. Gregory Bateson, "Social Planning and the Concept of Deutero-Learning," in *Steps to an Ecology of Mind* (Chicago: University of Chicago Press, 1972), 160–62. Subsequent quotations from this section of *Steps to an Ecology of Mind* will be cited parenthetically within the text as "Social Planning."

10. See Daniel R. White and Gert Hellerich, *Labyrinths of the Mind: The Self in the Postmodern Age* (Albany: State University of New York Press, 1998), 5.

11. See Gregory Bateson, "Morale and National Character," in *Steps to an Ecology of Mind*, 88–106. Bateson believed that what distinguished the members of one culture from another were exactly these habitual ways of thinking and contextualizing that were inculcated by characteristic processes of deutero-learning. See also Lipset, *Gregory Bateson*, 167.

12. Lipset, *Gregory Bateson*, 178–80.

13. See Peter Galison, "The Americanization of Unity," in *Science in Culture*, ed. Peter Galison, Stephen R. Graubard, and Everett Mendelsohn (New Brunswick, NJ: Transaction Publishers, 2001), 57–58.

14. See Lipset, *Gregory Bateson*, 219, 180. The conceptual connection between cybernetics and social governance was far from new: the Greek *cybernetes* is rendered in Latin as *gubernator*, the root of such words as *government* and *governor*. Indeed, one of the earliest mechanical feedback mechanisms, devised in the 1800s to regulate the speed of a steam engine, is called a "governor."

15. Aldo Leopold, *A Sand County Almanac* (New York: Oxford University Press, 1966), 140–41. See Susan L. Flader, *Thinking Like a Mountain: Aldo Leopold and the Evolution of an Ecological Attitude toward Deer, Wolves, and Forests* (Madison: University of Wisconsin Press, 1974); and Susan L. Flader and J. Baird Callicott, intro-

duction to *The River of the Mother of God and Other Essays by Aldo Leopold* (Madison: University of Wisconsin Press, 1991), 4–8.

16. John Cage, *A Year from Monday* (Middletown, CT: Wesleyan University Press, 1967), ix.

17. Richard Kostelanetz, "Inferential Art," in *John Cage*, ed. Richard Kostelanetz (New York: Praeger, 1970), 107–8.

18. John Cage, *Silence: Lectures and Writings* (London: Marion Boyars, 1995), 10. Subsequent quotations from this work will be cited parenthetically within the text or notes.

19. Soetsu Yanagi, *The Unknown Craftsman: A Japanese Insight into Beauty* (New York: Kodansha International, 1978), 185. See also Richard Kostelanetz, "Conversation with John Cage," in Kostelanetz, *John Cage*. In connection with this idea, Cage liked to quote the ninth-century Buddhist text *The Huang-Po Doctrine of Universal Mind*: "Imitate the sands of the Ganges who are not pleased by perfume and who are not disgusted by filth" (31).

20. Belgrad, *Culture of Spontaneity*, 104, 109.

21. Natalie Crohn Schmitt, *Actors and Onlookers: Theater and Twentieth-Century Scientific Views of Nature* (Evanston, IL: Northwestern University Press, 1990), 30, 34. Emphasis mine.

22. John Cage, *M: Writings '62–'72* (Middletown, CT: Wesleyan University Press, 1973), 3.

23. John Cage, quoted in Michael Zwerin, "A Lethal Measurement," *Village Voice* (6 January 1966), reprinted in Kostelanetz, *John Cage*, 164. Schmitt, *Actors and Onlookers*, 25.

24. See Belgrad, *Culture of Spontaneity*, 162.

25. Schmitt, *Actors and Onlookers*, 16.

26. Cage, *A Year from Monday*, 31. For more on Pollock's painting and field theory, see Belgrad, *Culture of Spontaneity*, 109–14.

27. Schmitt, *Actors and Onlookers*, 31.

28. Cage wrote, "In this new music nothing takes place but sounds. . . . Those that are not notated appear in the written music as silences, opening the doors of the music to the sounds that happen to be in the environment" (Cage, *Silence*, 7–8).

29. Max Neuhaus, liner notes for Max Neuhaus, *Fontana Mix—Feed (six realizations of John Cage)*. Alga Margnen, 2003. Emphasis mine.

30. Ibid.

31. See John Briggs and F. David Peat, *Turbulent Mirror: An Illustrated Guide to Chaos Theory and the Science of Wholeness* (New York: Harper and Row, 1989), 68–69, 74, 77.

32. Ibid., 90–91, 98–101.

33. Ibid., 143.

34. Neuhaus, liner notes for Neuhaus, *Fontana Mix—Feed*. David Ernst, *The Evolution of Electronic Music* (New York: Macmillan, 1977), 161–2.

35. John Updike, "Why Write?" in *Picked-Up Pieces* (New York: Alfred A. Knopf, 1975), 36, 35.

36. Robert Motherwell, "Beyond the Aesthetic," quoted in E. A. Carmean, Jr., *The Collages of Robert Motherwell* (Houston: Museum of Fine Arts, 1972), 91.

37. Updike, "Why Write?" 34.

38. *Conversations with John Updike*, ed. James Plath (Jackson: University Press of Mississippi, 1994), 27. Emphasis mine.

39. See Plath, ed., *Conversations with John Updike*. In the story, Updike refers to the job that he shares with his father as that of "usher," but in later interviews he identified it as "deacon" (75). See also the discussion of *exempla* in Kenneth J. Knoespel, "The Emplotment of Chaos: Instability and Narrative Order," in *Chaos and Order: Complex Dynamics in Literature and Science*, ed. N. Katherine Hayles (Chicago: University of Chicago Press, 1991), 109–11.

40. John Updike, *Self-Consciousness: Memoirs* (New York: Alfred A. Knopf, 1989), 234.

41. John Updike, "Packed Dirt, Churchgoing, a Dying Cat, a Traded Car," in *Olinger Stories* (New York: Vintage, 1964), 115–16. Subsequent quotations from this work will be cited parenthetically within the text or notes.

42. These themes are also explored in Updike's 1959 novel *The Poorhouse Fair*. In that story, a new prefect in an old-age home for the poor undertakes a campaign of rational control and discipline that is ultimately controverted by the fair. The old people themselves "look at nature sensing that there are mysteries beyond the legible regularities of man-made patterns and propositions." Tony Tanner, "A Compromised Environment," in *John Updike*, ed. Harold Bloom (New York: Chelsea House, 1987), 40–42.

43. Updike, "Why Write?" 36. See also Plath, ed., *Conversations with John Updike*. This idea is borne out by Updike's critical opinions, for example, his preference for the works of J. D. Salinger over those of Saul Bellow, whose endings, he complained, always attempt to leave the reader on a firm moral footing, "endings which would point the way." Instead, he praised Salinger as one who "made new room for shapelessness, for life as it is lived," and even Kerouac, because "maybe something can get into sloppy writing that would elude careful writing" (Plath, *Conversations*, 42–43).

44. Plath, ed., *Conversations with John Updike*, 31.

45. Tanner, "A Compromised Environment," in Bloom, *John Updike*, 42.

46. Updike, *Self-Consciousness*, 227. I take issue here with the conclusions of D. Quentin Miller in *John Updike and the Cold War: Drawing the Iron Curtain* (Columbia: University of Missouri Press, 2001), for I do not believe that existential anxiety is the main point in "Packed Dirt." I believe neither that its presence in the story is due to a "fear of nuclear annihilation" that is "suppressed," leaving the

characters psychically numbed, isolated, hedonistic, and "not able to communicate effectively or connect with one another" (25), nor that Updike's elegiac tone can be attributed to a "painful longing to return to the earlier, unfallen, innocent world of 1950s middle-class suburbia" (3). These are all well-worn clichés about Cold War culture as an age of anxiety and suburban anomie, but they fail to get at what is really going on in Updike's writing.

47. Plath, ed., *Conversations with John Updike*, 99. Emphasis mine. The comment was made in explication of some lines from "Midpoint," (John Updike, *Midpoint and Other Poems* [New York: Alfred A. Knopf, 1969]), a collage poem written by Updike in the late 1960s:

> Atomically all writers must begin, the truth arises as if by telegraph
> One dot, two dots, a silence, then—a laugh,
> The rules inhere and will not be imposed. (38)

48. See Plath, ed., *Conversations with John Updike*. Updike calls this, following Henry James, the "figure in the carpet" (184). The reference is to a James story in which the characters are themselves unknowingly participating in constructing the meaning that they seek to discover. The obstacles and rewards that the characters encounter seem to them to exist objectively but are actually feedback generated by their own behavior and assumptions.

49. Updike, "Why Write?" 33.

50. Updike is here alluding to a passage from Emerson: "a thread runs through all things: all worlds are strung on it, as beads: and men, and events, and life, come to us, only because of that thread." Updike, *Self-Consciousness*, 227–29. This world view accounts for Updike's emphasis on continuity, as opposed to the sense of apocalypse that gripped many other Cold War writers. See also Plath, ed., *Conversations with John Updike*. As Updike said in that interview, "I do see the world much more in terms of persistence. I feel that it's going to limp along" (103).

51. Updike, "Why Write?" 38. For more on Whitehead's conception of subjectivity and its influence among the postwar avant-garde, see Belgrad, *Culture of Spontaneity*, 126–33.

52. Updike, *Self-Consciousness*, 218–19, 221.

53. Allen Ginsberg, *Composed on the Tongue: Literary Conversations, 1967–1977* (San Francisco: Grey Fox Press, 1980), 95. For another example of this idea in Updike's writing, see *The Centaur* (New York: Alfred A. Knopf, 1963).

54. Richard H. Rupp, "John Updike: Style in Search of a Center," in Bloom, *John Updike*, 15.

55. In keeping with this metaphor, Updike earlier in the story refers to cars as "dreaming vehicles of unitary personhood" (Updike, "Packed Dirt," 108).

56. Gregory Bateson, introduction to *Steps to an Ecology of Mind*, xxxii.

57. Gregory Bateson, "Conscious Purpose versus Nature," in *Steps to an Ecology of Mind*, 434, 440.

58. Gregory Bateson, "Form, Substance, and Difference," in *Steps to an Ecology of Mind*, 466.

59. Bateson, "Conscious Purpose versus Nature," in *Steps to an Ecology of Mind*, 436.

60. See Bruce Schulman, *The Seventies: The Great Shift in American Culture, Society, and Politics* (New York: Free Press, 2001), 2–20.

61. Bateson, "Conscious Purpose versus Nature," in *Steps to an Ecology of Mind*, 441–42.

62. Ibid., 440.

63. Gregory Bateson, "Ecology and Flexibility in Urban Civilization," in *Steps to an Ecology of Mind*, 512.

64. Bateson, "Conscious Purpose versus Nature," in *Steps to an Ecology of Mind*, 441.

65. Ibid., 443–44; and Gregory Bateson, "Effects of Conscious Purpose on Human Adaptation," in *Steps to an Ecology of Mind*, 447–48.

66. Bateson, "Effects of Conscious Purpose on Human Adaptation," in *Steps to an Ecology of Mind*, 452–53. For more on "I-Thou," see Martin Buber, *I and Thou*, trans. Walter Kaufmann (New York: Scribner, 1970).

67. Gregory Bateson, "The Logical Categories of Learning and Communication," in *Steps to an Ecology of Mind*, 304.

68. Bateson, "Form, Substance, and Difference," in *Steps to an Ecology of Mind*, 471.

69. Lipset, *Gregory Bateson*, 285–86. This idea continues to engage the popular imagination, surfacing most recently in James Cameron's film *Avatar* (2009). Stewart Brand, "Review of *Steps to an Ecology of Mind*," *Rolling Stone*, 9 November 1972, 77. Stewart Brand, "Both Sides of the Necessary Paradox," *Harper's*, November 1973, 20–37. Lynn Margulis and James Lovelock, "The Atmosphere as Circulatory System of the Biosphere—the Gaia Hypothesis," in *News that Stayed News: Ten Years of "CoEvolution Quarterly," 1974–1984*, ed. Art Kleiner and Stewart Brand (San Francisco: North Point Press, 1986), 15–25.

II Domestic Cultures/ Global Frames

4 THE NEW FRONTIER

DUNE, THE MIDDLE CLASS, AND POST-1960 U.S. FOREIGN POLICY

ANDREW HOBEREK

In a February 24, 1957, speech to the National Conference of Christians and Jews in Cleveland, then-Senator John F. Kennedy outlined some of the factors that he believed pertinent to U.S. foreign policy in the Middle East. These included the Suez Canal crisis of the previous year, the problems of disputed boundaries and arms proliferation, and the plight of the Palestinian refugees displaced by Israel. But for his final item Kennedy turned, in a move characteristic of the foreign policy doctrine he began espousing in the Senate and carried into his brief presidency, from the political and military to the economic. Declaring "economic and resource development" crucial not only "to the Middle East alone" but also to "the entire world, and certainly the United States," Kennedy proposed the creation of "a Middle East Regional Resources fund, under the auspices of the United Nations and the World Bank, for assisting in the stimulation, initiation, and financing through loans and grants of resource development and other projects in the area."[1] As possible ventures Kennedy listed:

> harnessing the waters of the Nile for the benefit of the Sudan, Ethiopia, and Uganda as well as Egypt; coordinated development of the resources of the Jordan River Valley for the benefit of Israel and the three Arab states through which it flows; the development of arable land and irrigation projects for the resettlement of refugees; and a Middle Eastern Nuclear Center, similar to the Asian Nuclear Center already proposed, which could bring untold benefits in energy utilization to former deserts and wastelands. (*Strategy* 117)

"These projects," Kennedy noted, "would be developed and administered under the auspices and control of the nations in the region, who would also participate in their financing wherever feasible," just as U.S. "states participate in Federal grant programs which assist and stimulate them to greater action" (*Strategy* 117–18).

As Leerom Medovoi and Christina Klein have argued, we must extend our accounts of Cold War culture beyond the ramifications of anticommunist containment to the equally important phenomenon of outreach to and imagined identification with the decolonizing world. Under the influence of figures such as the MIT social scientist W. W. Rostow, Kennedy made global economic development a centerpiece of his campaign, transforming the modernization theory developed in social science departments and foundation-sponsored research projects in the late 1950s into a compelling vision of reanimated mission.[2] If modernization theory proposed that the United States take a leadership role in the decolonizing world "by accelerating the natural process through which 'traditional' societies would move toward the enlightened 'modernity' most clearly represented by America itself,"[3] Kennedy saw in this notion a means of appealing not only to the decolonizing nations but also to his own countrymen. "If we are to break the aimless drifts and deadlocks in policy," Kennedy declared in a 1958 Senate speech on U.S. policy toward India, "if we are to regain the initiative in world affairs, if we are to arouse the decent emotions of Americans, it is time again that we seek projects with the power of stirring and rallying our hopes and energies."[4] In the late 1950s, at precisely the time when Americans worried that they were becoming a nation of agencyless organization men hamstrung by bureaucracy ("the aimless drifts and deadlocks in policy"),[5] both Communism and anticolonial struggle offered competing claims, condensed in the flashpoint figures of Che Guevara and Fidel Castro, to have seized the vanguard of historical progress.[6] Kennedy, alive not just to the liabilities but to the potential of this situation, saw past modernization theory's sometimes dry formulations to its vision of foreign policy as the terrain on which Americans might reanimate their sense of historical mission and thereby reclaim their command of history's leading edge.

In what follows, I read Frank Herbert's popular 1965 science fiction novel *Dune* as dramatizing Kennedy's vision of modernization theory. *Dune* tells the story of a young man named Paul Atreides, who, stranded on a desert world following an ambush by the treacherous Harkonnen family, molds the native Fremen into a fighting force with which he not only vanquishes his rivals but also seizes the imperial throne itself. Underlying this story, however, is another, of the promised Kennedyesque transformation of the planet Dune or Arrakis, begun before Paul's arrival and sped up at novel's end by his seizure of power, into a place of "flowing water . . . open to the sky and green oases rich with good things."[7] Through these two threads, *Dune* offers a dual allegory of modernization theory as a means both of "defin[ing the United States] as a nonimperial world power in the age of decolonization" and of recovering the putatively lost agency of the U.S. middle class.[8]

My account of *Dune* suggests that the novel's status as a work of genre fiction made it particularly suited to mark the major shift in Cold War ideology that took place around 1960. Describing what he calls the "late imperial romance," John McClure argues that post-Vietnam writers such as Joan Didion, Robert Stone, and Don DeLillo take up the seemingly oppositional but in fact frequently apocalyptic and apolitical discourse of anti-imperialism pioneered by Joseph Conrad, in which imperialism portends both the final rationalization of the world and countervailing outbursts of violence and oppression. Herbert's fiction, as we shall see, likewise partakes of this "modernist 'recoil' from modernization."[9] But because *Dune* was written prior to the worst reverses of Kennedy's modernization program in Vietnam—and perhaps even more importantly, because it is finally an adventure tale—it evinces an ambivalent combination of this pessimistic strain with a more Kiplingesque sense of empire as "a space of intrigue and adventure."[10] This not entirely coherent combination is what makes Herbert's science fiction novel such a fascinating window on both modernization theory and the ways in which this theory was sold to the U.S. public.

■ In 1969, the *Whole Earth Catalog* recommended *Dune*, which it noted was "enjoying currency in Berkeley and saltier communities such as Libre," as "a rich re-readable fantasy" whose "metaphor is ecology" and "theme revolution."[11] Since then, accounts of Herbert's novel have with good reason stressed its relationship to the late-twentieth-century rebirth of the U.S. environmental movement.[12] But while such readings capture a crucial dimension of the book, which Herbert himself in 1984 retroactively declared "an ecological novel,"[13] they risk oversimplifying both its environmental politics and its politics more generally. *Dune*, set on a world whose scarcity of water shapes human society at every level, addresses questions of ecology both within the narrative and in didactic set pieces delivered by its characters. But if *Dune* draws on the ecological principles Herbert encountered in the late 1950s while writing a magazine article about a USDA project to stop the spread of sand dunes along the

Oregon coast,[14] it also accesses the very different model of man-made environmental transformation exemplified by Kennedy's vision of the desert in bloom.

As Kennedy's invocations of irrigation and electrification and his analogy between Middle Eastern nations and U.S. states suggests, his development policies were among other things attempts to transpose the principles of New Deal projects such as the Tennessee Valley Authority and the Columbia Basin Project onto the world stage. In this respect it can be no coincidence that Herbert names the Imperial Planetologist who attempts to transform Dune Pardot Kynes. In doing so, he evokes John Maynard Keynes, the architect of the statist economic policies implemented domestically by the New Deal and officially integrated into U.S.-led international development policy at the 1944 Bretton Woods conference.[15] Kynes's terraforming project, moreover, suggests the Green Revolution through which the United States sought to modernize agriculture in developing nations by introducing "new high-yielding crop varieties grown by methods specifically suited to them."[16] The Green Revolution officially sought, in the words of its chief proponent Norman Borlaug's 1970 Nobel Prize acceptance speech, to advance the cause of peace and "social justice" by ensuring "adequate food for all mankind."[17] But to the extent that it became intertwined with U.S. development policy, it partook of modernization theory's characteristic blend of disinterested concern for the developing world and Cold War maneuvering. *Dune* invokes the Green Revolution in its concern with Arrakis's chief product, the life-extending and precognition-inducing drug, spice. Highly prized for its ability to bring about the future sight that enables members of a group known as the Guild to navigate through interstellar space, spice is—as a scarce commodity that is found in a desert environment inhabited by pseudo-Islamic tribesmen and that is necessary for transport—an obvious "analogue for oil."[18] But, having discovered that spice is a byproduct of the life cycle of the giant sand worms native to Arrakis, Kynes and his son and successor Liet-Kynes view the spice economy not as extractive but as a form of "agriculture" (*Dune* 271). This shift resonates with Kennedy's desire to supplant at least partly the oil economy at the center of colonialism in the Middle East with an economy driven by irrigation and electrification, when he recognized quite rightly that "the increase in outside capital poured into the area to exploit its oil and other resources has only aggravated the problems of unequal distribution of wealth and inadequate development of human resources" (*Strategy* 111).

In this respect it is crucial that the Kyneses' plans for developing Dune contrast sharply with the exploitative rule of the Harkonnens, under whose rule Dune is a "one-crop planet" whose output "supports a ruling class that lives as ruling classes have lived in all times while, beneath them, a semihuman mass of semislaves exists on the leavings" (275). The Kyneses' approach thus resonates with Kennedy's vision of modernization as a form of governance superior to that of the European colonial powers whose "policies of repression have only fanned the flames of discontent" (*Strategy* 111) and thereby abetted Communist propaganda efforts. During the Suez Canal crisis, Britain, France, and Israel invaded Egypt in response to Gamal Abdel Nasser's nationalization of the strategically vital canal but eventually withdrew under pressure from the United States and the Soviet Union. The lesson of this event was not lost on Kennedy, who understood that appeals to the decolonizing nations required the United States to distinguish itself not only from the Communist world but also from the old European empires. As he noted in a 1956 speech to the Histadrut Zionist Organization, "the close ties between this nation, home of the Declaration of Independence, and the great colonial powers have caused Arab spokesmen to warn our State Department that the nations of the Middle East were beginning to regard America as a supporter of colonialism" (*Strategy* 111). "The Economic Gap," a 1959 Senate speech heavily influenced by Rostow's developmental theories,[19] offered a solution to this problem in Kennedy's assertion that helping other nations to modernize could both replace "the pageantry of imperialism [with] the pride of new states freshly risen to independence" and "give to a doubting world the realization that we, and not Russia and China, can help them achieve stability and growth" (*Strategy* 53). If "the Harkonnen policy with planetary populations" is to "spend as little as possible to maintain them" (*Dune* 45), the Kyneses seek instead to work with the Fremen to transform Dune, albeit while making sure that "spice wealth [does not] end" (*Dune* 499).

But Pardot Kynes's story literally serves as a backdrop to *Dune*'s main narrative, relegated as it is to a seven-page appendix at the end of the novel (493–500). By the time the Atreides arrive on Dune, Pardot Kynes has already been killed in an accident, and Liet-Kynes dies about halfway through the novel while helping Paul and his mother escape the Harkonnen attack. In one respect, we might read the shift from the first father-son pair to the second as exemplifying a shift within modernization theory in the early 1960s. As María Josefina Saldaña-Portillo notes, modernization theory in this period "responded to the failure of Keynesian economics to produce immediate results in the decolonizing world" by "attempt[ing] to provide sociological, psychological, and cultural explanations for the failure of development economics to take hold in any given Third World society."[20] Thus, Pardot Kynes, with his "enormous single-mindedness" (*Dune* 494), is a scientist above all: his loyalties lie neither with Arrakis's then-Harkonnen rulers (three of whose soldiers he kills when he sees them about to kill Fremen) nor with the Fremen (whom he sees as "a tool" [*Dune* 493]), but with the ecological transformation of Dune. Paul's father Leto, by contrast, respects Fremen practices. In one scene, for instance, he ignores his men's simmering resentment and allows the Fremen chieftain Stilgar to instruct him in the etiquette surrounding a Fremen blade, responding "If it is your custom that this knife remain sheathed here, then it is so ordered—by *me*" (*Dune* 92–93, emphasis original). And Paul goes even further, immersing himself in Fremen culture, including completing the Fremen coming-of-age ritual of learning how to ride one of Dune's giant sandworms. Pardot Kynes, by contrast, travels "in a palanquin like a wounded man or Reverend Mother because he never became a sandrider" (*Dune* 499).

Even more importantly, however, Herbert's shift from the Kyneses to the Atreides allows him to address modernization as a form of outreach to the middle class of the already developed—in standard accounts, overdeveloped—United States, a way for the U.S. middle class to regain its putatively lost agency. In part, this narrative of recovery is a story of remasculinization through going native that borrows heavily from David Lean's 1962 movie *Lawrence of Arabia*.[21] But Lean's Lawrence was himself already modeled on Kennedy, whose "appeal to the Third World," Medovoi argues, united his otherwise seemingly contradictory roles as fervent Cold Warrior and icon of youthful rebellion:

> Kennedy's youth, his off-white ethnicity as an Irish Catholic, and his self-presentation as an independent leader resembled in noticeable ways . . . the "young," largely non-white, newly independent nations of the globe. . . . Weighed by voters as a potential President of America on the world stage, Kennedy's personal appeal in the months leading up to his election involved not only his presumed willingness to meet the Soviet challenge, but also his capacity to serve as a charismatic role model and mentor for the former colonized regions which he hoped to draw into an American orbit.[22]

Herbert's depictions of Liet-Kynes and Paul Atreides likewise draw on these associations surrounding Kennedy, although the two characters again differ in significant ways. Like Paul, who joins the Fremen and acquires the name Paul Muad'Dib, Liet-Kynes also lives as a Fremen. Indeed, to the extent that Liet-Kynes is born to a Fremen mother, whereas Paul learns Fremen ways after being adopted into a *sietch* (the basic Fremen social organization), the former would seem to have the more authentic claim to native status. But it is precisely Paul's ability to transcend his birth that makes him the central figure of the novel. Unlike Paul, who loses his family and must make his own way in the world, Liet-Kynes succeeds his father as Imperial Planetologist "as a matter of course. The rigid class structure of the faufreluches had its well-ordered purpose here. The son had been trained to follow the father" (*Dune* 500). Paul, who elevates himself from a wealthy but socially marginal family to the most powerful office in his society by promoting national self-determination for a colonized people, is clearly the more Kennedyesque figure. But he is also, beyond this, a figure for the heroic age of the Western middle class itself. Whereas Kynes's trajectory exemplifies the feudal system that mythically preceded U.S. modernity and individualism—what the novel elsewhere refers to as the "feudal trade culture" (*Dune* 23) of the Imperium—Paul travels to a literal new world where he seizes the opportunity to transcend his origins and make something wholly new of himself.

What Paul's story makes clear in the process is the way in which Kennedy-era modernization theory transposed the New World of American middle-class self-mythology onto the third world of decolonizing nations. In this regard, Kennedy's program of outreach to what he called "the uncommitted world"[23] did not simply function as a counterargument to the "alternative modernity"[24] through which the Soviet Union likewise sought to exercise stewardship in the developing world, or as a means of integrating newly independent nations into the global capitalist economy.[25] It also spoke to the mood of national malaise, and particularly middle-class malaise, articulated by postwar social critics. As Kennedy asserted in a 1963 speech, "I do not want it said of us what T. S. Eliot said of others some years ago: 'These were a decent people. Their only monument: the asphalt road and a thousand lost golf balls.'"[26] Here Kennedy repeats a crucial but underrecognized move of modernization theory: its transformation of the postwar middle class's frequently described plight of deindividualization and conformity into the engine driving an activist U.S. foreign policy. Rostow's 1960 treatise *The Stages of Economic Growth:*

A Non-Communist Manifesto, for instance, concurs with postwar social critics such as C. Wright Mills, David Riesman, and William H. Whyte in worrying that the completion of Americans' own modernizing revolution has raised "the question of whether or not secular spiritual stagnation will arise, and if it does, how man might fend it off."[27] But, unlike these critics, Rostow—who subsequently became a member of Kennedy's and Johnson's inner policy circles—offers a solution in "the dilemmas and worries of the men in Djakarta, Rangoon, New Delhi, and Karachi; the men in Tehran, Baghdad, and Cairo; the men south of the desert too, in Accra, Lagos, and Salisbury," whose problems require precisely the "creative imagination" that the middle class has supposedly lost.[28] With his well-known calls to service to the nation, Kennedy likewise proposed the international arena as the site where members of the middle class would regain their lost agency. In transforming the decolonizing world into a very specific instance of what either Rostow or Kennedy's speechwriter Ted Sorensen famously dubbed "The New Frontier,"[29] Kennedy provided a way of replacing the alienated organization man of the 1950s with a range of new, more appealing middle-class icons: the selfless Peace Corps volunteer, the dedicated but still socially conscious scientist of the Green Revolution, and (at least until the failures of Vietnam and the Great Society) the heroic technocrat.

If Kennedy's rhetoric was on the one hand intended to appeal to inhabitants of the decolonizing world who desired to become modern, it was on the other addressed to inhabitants of the United States who feared that they were postmodern in a specific sense: they had arrived on the scene after their own heroic age. At a 1961 state dinner in Bogotá, for instance, Kennedy promoted the Alliance for Progress by asserting the shared revolutionary heritage of the Americas and then declaring:

> We are a young and strong people. Our doctrines—the doctrines lit by the leaders of your country and mine—now burn brightly in Africa and Asia and wherever men struggle to be free. And here in our own hemisphere we have successfully resisted efforts to impose the despotisms of the Old World on the nations of the New.[30]

Here Kennedy not only proposes the United States as the proper model for decolonization—the birthplace of a revolutionary spirit of resistance to European rule that spreads first to Latin America and later to Africa and Asia—but also implicitly counters the ironic deployment of this revolutionary heritage in contemporaneous U.S. novels such as Kurt

Vonnegut's *Player Piano* (1952) and Richard Yates's *Revolutionary Road* (1961). Whereas Vonnegut and Yates invoke the American Revolution to suggest how far contemporary Americans have fallen, Kennedy treats it as an identity that may be misplaced but is not completely lost—and if misplaced, it can be recovered by helping other nations who are themselves now struggling free of Old World tyranny. The idea that the decolonizing nations are reproducing the American break with European monarchy is central to this discourse and makes clear the way in which it both imposes an American model of modernization on other parts of the world and celebrates a particular liberal, middle-class narrative of revolution.[31]

Dune presents a vision of American renewal abroad strikingly similar to Kennedy's. The novel begins with the Atreides family preparing to move from their moist, fertile home world of Caladan to dry, forbidding Dune, which the Emperor has transferred to them from their enemies the Harkonnens, an apparent victory that was in fact orchestrated by the Harkonnens to saddle the Atreides with an ungovernable, unremunerative planet. The Atreides, like their enemies, are feudal rulers whose power stems from the system of "faufreluches," which the novel's glossary defines as "the rigid rule of class distinction enforced by the Imperium" (*Dune* 518). Castle Caladan, which they are preparing to depart, has "served the . . . family as home for twenty-six generations" (*Dune* 3), and they have run the planet—as they will now run Dune—as their personal demesne. Initially, then, *Dune* seems invested in the same romanticized vision of premodern Europe central to the other great science fiction and fantasy epic of the late 1960s, *The Lord of the Rings*.[32] In fact, however, the Atreides' departure in the opening chapters sets up a very different narrative of removal to a new world where—as the name *Fremen* unsubtly emphasizes—the structure of society is more flexible: while still in Castle Caladan, Paul hears intimations that "the faufreluches class system was not rigidly guarded on Arrakis" (4). Arrakis, like America in the nation's self-mythology, is a place where people can go to make their own way, freed from the confines of a rigid social structure.

Hence the overdetermined nature of the novel's desert setting, which not only establishes a concern with the ecology of resource scarcity but also resonates with American exceptionalist mythology. Brian Edwards notes that, with the United States' entry into the North African campaigns of World War II, American journalists and filmmakers turned to the tropes of the Western as a way of:

> mak[ing] sense of an otherwise foreign setting and confusing military action. The foreignness of North Africa and the complexity of the political landscape—with Free French and Fighting French, the ambiguous position of the French colonial administration, and Italian, German, Spanish, and British colonial holdings and ambitions in the region—could be made understandable if reduced to a frontier tale. Indeed, the images that were arguably the most successful in depicting the campaign—and have lasted the longest in the popular imagination—were those in a spate of Hollywood combat films and melodramas that adopted the Western motif to a desert terrain.[33]

But *Dune* turns to the Western for far more than an overlay of familiarity. As a print version of what we might call "the Eastern"—a mixed genre that deploys the tropes of the Western in Middle Eastern settings[34]—*Dune* suggests how Cold War–era versions of the genre, like traditional Westerns of the same period, represented the frontier as a site of "heroic individualism" implicitly opposed to the denatured world of the reader or viewer.[35] As R. J. Ellis notes, Paul's story perfectly recapitulates Frederick Jackson Turner's 1893 account of "the frontier" as "the line of most rapid and effective Americanization." Paul begins the book "a [symbolic] European in dress, industries, tools, modes of travel, and thought"; Arrakis's "wilderness masters" him; "He must accept the conditions which it furnishes, or perish," a task he accomplishes by adopting the manners of the native inhabitants; "Little by little he transforms the wilderness"; but he is transformed in his turn into the "new product that is [symbolically] American."[36] In an important way, *Dune*'s environmental imagination derives not from Rachel Carson but from Teddy Roosevelt: the novel evokes scarcity less as an ecological problem than as a solution to the dilemma of overcivilization.

Herbert updates this Rooseveltian rhetoric for the mid-twentieth century United States, invoking Caladan in ways consonant with postwar social critics' accounts of middle-class decline. Echoing Whyte's claim in *The Organization Man* that "it is not the evils of organization life that puzzle [the organization man], *but its very beneficence*,"[37] the epigraph to one of *Dune*'s chapters reads:

> We came from Caladan—a paradise world for our form of life. There existed no need on Caladan to build a physical paradise or a paradise of the mind—we could see the actuality all around us. And the price

we paid was the price men have always paid for achieving a paradise in this life—we went soft, we lost our edge. (255, italicized in the original)

Similarly, Paul's father Leto claims that "most of the houses have grown fat by taking few risks. One cannot truly blame them for this; one can only despise them" (87). These aristocrats, that is, are like the organization men who, according to Whyte, have traded their ambition for the false fetish of security. By contrast, Leto asserts elsewhere, "Arrakis makes us moral and ethical" (104). Here he refers specifically to the factors that inhibit the use of poison on the planet, but his comment clearly evokes the more general dynamic through which Arrakis's harsh environment transforms Paul from the pampered scion he might have been into a distinctly modern risk-taker. This transformation becomes evident when, in the novel's climactic final battle, Paul defeats the Emperor's forces not only by taking advantage of the Fremen's skill at guerrilla warfare but also by making an innovative tactical decision: defying the long-standing injunction against the use of nuclear weapons, he employs an atomic bomb to punch a hole in the Shield Wall sheltering the Emperor's troops from the desert. Like an early modern merchant, or a nineteenth-century entrepreneur—but unlike an organization man—Paul profits from his willingness to defy dogma. He has learned to make such decisions, *Dune* makes clear, through the experience of living in the harsh frontier environment of Arrakis. "Arrakis," one of the novel's chapter epigraphs notes, "teaches the attitude of the knife—chopping off what's incomplete and saying: 'Now, it's complete because it's ended here'" (172, italicized in the original).

In this way, the Eastern's desert setting emblematizes its hybrid blend of Western and imperial romance: on the one hand, it proposes the decolonizing world as a new frontier, while on the other it invokes the tropes of imperial adventure in a distinctly American framework that is critical of (European) empire. Unlike traditional Westerns that take place in the past and thus share the elegiac quality of Turner's lament for the passing of the frontier,[38] *Dune* follows post-Kennedy foreign policy in imagining new frontiers not in time but in space, in particular the space of the developing world that modernization theory transforms, to borrow Dipesh Chakrabarty's elegant phrase, into "an imaginary waiting room of history."[39] In doing so it conflates the American break with European feudalism with the postcolonial break with European imperialism. In contrast to Baron Vladimir Harkonnen, whose first name identifies his cruel and decadent leadership with the United States' Cold War enemy and whose title aligns him with the feudal aristocracy of Europe,[40] Leto hopes to win the Fremen over as allies through his more egalitarian and meritocratic leadership. He regrets the more brutal necessities of his position, and at one point, in response to the Emperor's "disdainful" description of the Fremen as "barbarians whose dearest dream is to live outside of the ordered security of the faufreluches," he thinks that "his own dearest dream was to end all class distinctions and never again think of deadly order" (78). In *Dune* as in Kennedy-era foreign policy, this contrast becomes a selling point for the advantages of Atreidean—and by extension, U.S.—methods of governance over those of old-style imperialism. The Fremen leader Liet-Kynes, upon seeing Leto abandon property and risk both his life and Paul's to save some Fremen caught in the desert, notes "the fanatic loyalty" that such a man "would command" (126). Earlier Stilgar, the Fremen chieftain who subsequently becomes Paul's second-in-command, concisely identified the basis of such loyalty when he challenged Leto by declaring, "It is said that the Duke Leto Atreides rules with the consent of the governed" (92).

Like Kennedy, Leto promises revolution not in the Marxist but in the American sense, and he does so in ways capable of appealing as much to Americans as to the citizens of decolonizing nations. *Dune*'s conflation of the third world with the New World is also apparent in Herbert's depiction of the Fremen as possessing the putative traits not only of Middle Easterners and sub-Saharan Africans (that is, potential subjects of postwar modernization) but also of various Native American tribes.[41] In this way he aligns the Fremen with the Indians, who, in Turner's account of the frontier, teach the proto-American how to clothe, shelter, and feed himself—and, not incidentally, how to make war—in the wilderness.[42] Of course, Turner inherits a long-standing liberal and American exceptionalist tradition of contrasting the Indians' primitive individualism with European submission to arbitrary authority. In the *Second Treatise on Civil Government* (1690), for instance, John Locke cites the Jesuit missionary Josephus Acosta to the effect "that in many parts of America there was no government at all. . . . So that their politic societies all began from a voluntary union, and the mutual agreement of men freely acting in the choice of their governors and forms of government."[43] And in *Notes on the State of Virginia* (1784) Thomas Jefferson asserts:

> that were it made a question, whether no law, as among the savage Americans, or too much law, as among the civilized Europeans, sub-

mits man to the greatest evil, one who has seen both conditions of existence would pronounce it to be the last: and that the sheep are happier of themselves, than under care of the wolves. It will be said, that great societies cannot exist without government. The Savages therefore break them into small ones.[44]

For both Locke and Jefferson, the contrast between Indians and Europeans opens up a space for a privileged third term—civil government for Locke, America for Jefferson—that both implicitly and explicitly mediates between the two. As Richard Slotkin notes, this mediating position is foundational to the transhistorical model of American identity formed on the frontier: "The compleat 'American' of the Myth was one who had defeated and freed himself from both the 'savage' of the western wilderness and the metropolitan regime of authoritarian politics and class privilege."[45]

Carrying on this tradition, *Dune*'s frontier narrative not only promises the initially effete Paul Atreides an opportunity for what Slotkin famously termed regeneration through violence—although it surely does that—but also restages the mythical formation of American identity in the middle-class revolt from European class society. The preeminent post–World War II formulation of this idea is Louis Hartz's *The Liberal Tradition in America*, which takes as its starting point "what might be called the storybook truth about American history: that America was settled by men who fled from the feudal and clerical oppressions of the Old World," and for this reason it "skipp[ed] the feudal stage of history as Russia presumably skipped the liberal stage."[46] According to this version of history, not only are Americans fundamentally middle-class, but the middle class is fundamentally American, born in the opportunity afforded by the New World to break with European feudalism. That this account ignores the emergence of modernity and the middle class within Europe is beside the point, or rather all too much to the point, insofar as this elision allows Kennedy and other Cold War polemicists to describe colonialism as a latter-day version of feudalism, the solution to which is the same form of revolution that worked for the United States. This makes Americans the first postcolonial people and the ideal tutors to their brothers around the globe. But if this version of history transforms decolonizing or recently postcolonial nations into new Americas, it thereby not only promotes U.S. interests in the Cold War but also promises a new lease on life to a U.S. middle class increasingly convinced of its belatedness. Leto, as we have seen, desires "to end all class distinctions," not because such distinctions represent uneven privilege but because they embody "deadly order" (78), a form of stifling regularity that links the premodern feudal system with the postmodern world of the Organization.

In this respect Chakrabarty's concept of the "waiting room of history" is perhaps even more relevant to U.S.-style development policy than to earlier modes of European imperialism,[47] insofar as modernization theory understands the decolonizing world not only as a premodern space requiring American assistance but also, somewhat paradoxically, as the site of modernity itself: modernity as the process of breaking free from "deadly order" that the U.S. middle class enacted at its birth and can, by helping others through the same transition, experience once again. Hence, the third resonance of the Fremen, who are not only members of the third world and Native Americans but also, in brief moments, proto-Americans. At one point, for instance, Stilgar declares to Paul's mother Jessica that "we carry no paper for contracts. We make no evening promises to be broken at dawn. When a man says a thing, that's the contract" (283). Stilgar here invokes the language of contract that is central to the middle-class revolt against feudalism (quite directly central in the United States, if we follow the Federalists' reading of the Constitution as a form of contract that enables government in the absence of a king). But his preference for oral versus written contract goes beyond simply evoking the notion of contract to suggest the temporal evanescence of modernization theory's displacement of U.S.-style modernity onto the developing world.

We can tease out this distinction if we compare Stilgar's words here with the notion of "comity" evoked by Kennedy in the 1957 Cleveland speech with which I opened this chapter. In that speech Kennedy poses comity, which he declares "the basis of law and order among free equals" (*Strategy* 113), as a more lasting solution than "sanctions and hostilities" (*Strategy* 113) to the tensions raised by decolonization:

> Brotherhood, tolerance, enlightened relations between members of different ethnic groups—these are, after all, simply an extension of the concept upon which all free organized society is based. Some call this concept comity. Some find it in the Golden Rule, others in Rousseau's "social contract." Our Declaration of Independence calls it "the consent of the governed." The ancient Romans called it "*civitatis filia*," or civic friendship. (*Strategy* 112–13)

The seemingly transhistorical character of comity in this passage cannot obscure the way in which Kennedy employs it as a structuring concept for the birth of Western modernity (via Rousseau) and, more specifically, for the birth of U.S. modernity (via Jefferson). (Of course, both Rousseau and Jefferson, like other Enlightenment figures, drew upon biblical and classical precedents themselves.) In this light, we might note two things about Stilgar's invocation of contract. First, contract is not something imposed upon the non-Western world but rather an already existing potential. And second, Stilgar's simultaneous celebration of contract and denigration of its written form suggests that the Fremen possess contract in both an underdeveloped way (requiring outside assistance to realize its full potential) and a purer form (from which outsiders who have fallen into the pitfalls of bureaucracy might learn). Stilgar's brief outburst perfectly captures the temporal ambiguity of modernization theory. "The wars of independence which dot colonial history," Rostow puts it in a stunning conflation, "from 1776 in America to 1959 in Algeria, are thus, to a degree, related to the stages-of-growth. Specifically, they are related to the dynamics of the preconditions period" (112). By placing the American experience at the outset of a new universal history, modernization theory rewrites the decolonizing world as the place where the U.S. middle class's past becomes its future, again and again, but only temporarily each time.

From comments that he made in the early 1980s, it is evident that Herbert saw *Dune*'s solution to the problem of middle-class belatedness as merely temporary and that he framed this problem in relation to the Kennedy presidency. In a 1981 interview for *Mother Earth News*, for instance, Herbert contended—somewhat surprisingly, given what I have been arguing about *Dune*—that Kennedy was "one of the most dangerous presidents this country ever had" because:

> People didn't question him. And whenever citizens are willing to give unreined [*sic*] power to a charismatic leader, such as Kennedy, they tend to end up creating a kind of demigod . . . or a leader who covers up mistakes—instead of admitting them—and makes matters worse instead of better.[48]

In an essay that appeared in *Omni* magazine the year before this interview, Herbert proclaimed that it is in "the power arena of politics/economics and in their logical consequence, war," that "people tend to give over every decision-making capacity to any leader who can wrap himself in the myth fabric of the society."[49] He also described *Dune* and its two sequels in his original trilogy as extrapolations of what he called "the superhero concept,"[50] arguing that "superheroes are disastrous for humankind" because they induce people to surrender their "critical faculties."[51] And indeed the *Dune* series, as I have suggested, plays this out, charting Paul's transition from literal superhero—the product of a centuries-long breeding program who gains precognitive powers from the combination of his genes with the life-extending spice—to increasingly despotic ruler.

Consider for instance a prototypical expression of Paul's authoritarianism from the second book in the trilogy, *Dune Messiah* (1969). Responding to a request from some of his subjects for a constitution, Paul declares:

> "Constitutions become the ultimate tyranny." . . . "They're organized power on such a scale as to be overwhelming. The constitution is social power mobilized and it has no conscience. It can crush the highest and the lowest, removing all dignity and individuality. It has an unstable balance point and no limitations. I, however, have limitations. In my desire to provide an ultimate protection for my people, I forbid a constitution. Order in Council, this date, etcetera, etcetera."[52]

In its character as an official declaration, this statement partakes less of philosophical analysis than of instrumental rhetoric. Yet it comes close to exemplifying—even as it enacts—what I have been suggesting is the fundamental fear at the heart of Herbert's trilogy. It is as though, as soon as the principle of contract—in the form here of the political contract at the heart of American identity—loses its status as potential and becomes actual, it hardens into both a collection of inflexible rules and a series of cant phrases, the *et cetera* of bureaucratic language. And in anticipation of McClure's post-Vietnam heirs of Conrad, Herbert shows us the tyranny of the strong leader waiting to emerge from the wings as the dialectical product of this Weberian nightmare.

■ Here the *Dune* trilogy seems to depart from its mythologization of modernization theory and to offer instead a critical gloss on the fantasy of renewed agency underlying that theory, a fantasy that received its canonical formulation in Norman Mailer's essays on Kennedy. In his fittingly titled 1960 essay "Superman Comes to the Supermart," for instance, Mailer describes the presidential candidate as a charismatic figure capable of shattering the liberal somnolence of the United States in the 1950s. Mailer's account of Kennedy's struggle to survive following the sinking of his PT boat, like Paul's desert odyssey in *Dune*, celebrates what Mailer calls the "lonely terrain of experience, of loss and gain, of nearness to death, which leaves [the hero] isolated from the mass of others."[53] In contrast to the "mass man" and his spokesmen who "would brick-in modern life with hygiene upon sanity, and middle-brow homily over platitude," Kennedy embodies the "message in the labyrinth of the genes [that] would insist that violence was locked with creativity, and adventure was the secret of love."[54]

We might, with this in mind, see Paul's trajectory as anticipating what Sean McCann has described as the devolution of Mailer's initially individualist critique of liberalism into forms of "political mysticism" invested in "the authority of tradition," "patriarchal and hierarchical order," and "a belief in the unifying force of war."[55] Near *Dune*'s end, crucially, Paul experiences a vision of "the unborn jihad" that will stem from his actions, and over which he has no control:

> And Paul saw how futile were any efforts of his to change any smallest bit of this. He had thought to oppose the jihad within himself, but the jihad would be. His legions would rage out from Arrakis even without him. They needed only the legend he already had become. He had shown them the way, given them mastery over the Guild which must have the spice to exist. (482)

From the perspective of 1965, when the situation in Vietnam had begun to spin beyond the rational guidance of decolonization promised by modernization theory (Congress had just passed the Gulf of Tonkin Resolution granting the president authority to escalate the war without prior legislative approval), the jihad might also seem like a figure for the real-world consequences of Kennedy's existentialist image writ into foreign policy.

But Herbert's version of Mailer's version of Kennedy is, as I have suggested, only partly critical, and in the end it may be less critical than simply pessimistic about the potential even of revivifying violence to escape the enveloping constraints of the system. In *Dune* Herbert himself describes the jihad in evolutionary terms: "The race of humans had felt its own dormancy, sensed itself grown stale and knew now only the need to experience turmoil in which the genes would mingle and the strong new mixtures survive" (482). Here, like Mailer contrasting evolutionary violence and creativity with the world of mass man, Herbert depicts the jihad as the genetically programmed antithesis of what William H. Whyte in *The Organization Man* calls "the enervating effect of security."[56]

As Timothy O'Reilly suggests, there is an ecological logic through which we can understand Herbert's investment in such upheaval: "Any system or method of control neglects certain factors, and gradually the pressure of what has been neglected increases sufficiently to topple the system. Only by leaving room for the unknown and for change is there a chance for success."[57] From this perspective the problem with the jihad is that it is ultimately not violent enough. In *Dune Messiah* a veteran of the jihad living on "a cul-de-sac" in "a suburb" built for him and his fellow returnees bitterly tells a visitor, "We were a noble people."[58] Paul had announced the plan for his imperial seat at the end of the first novel:

> "The Fremen have the word of Muad'Dib," Paul said. "There will be flowing water here open to the sky and green oases rich with good things. But we have the spice to think of, too. Thus, there will always be desert on Arrakis . . . and fierce winds, and trials to toughen a man. We Fremen have a saying: 'God created Arrakis to train the faithful.' One cannot go against the word of God." (*Dune* 488)

But the plan has clearly not worked out. Instead, Arrakis seems on its way to becoming a place like Caladan, where the Atreides "went soft" and lost their "edge" (*Dune* 225), or like the "garden world, full of gentle things" (*Dune* 488) that Paul strategically promises to make of the harsh planet where the deposed Emperor had trained his own dreaded Sardaukar troops.

Moreover, neither the jihad nor the exercise of imperial power confers agency upon Paul; quite the opposite is the case. "I'm a figurehead," he tells his consort Chani in *Dune Messiah*: "When godhead's given, that's the one thing the so-called god no longer controls."[59] Hence Herbert's seemingly self-contradictory claim, in his 1981 essay on the dangers of charismatic leadership, that it is not individuals but "the systems themselves that I see as dangerous."[60] Herbert here understands systems in Emersonian terms as the ossified legacies of individuals: "Systems originate with human creators, with people who employ them. Systems take over and grind on and on. They are like a flood tide that picks up everything in its path."[61] Note here the displacement of the nature metaphor from jihad to bureaucracy, a revision that reveals the logic behind Herbert's original insight into modernization theory (even as it makes clear the problem with reading *Dune* as a proleptic critique of the Vietnam War). Simply put, if Paul's leadership devolves into violence, this is bad not because of the violence itself but because it undermines the individuality that Paul's actions were intended to affirm. In the end, the narrative of frontier Americanization that was to secure Paul's individuality becomes a narrative of apocalyptic disintegration that traps him as surely as it does everyone else in the universe.

What *Dune*, read as a text of the Kennedy-era revision of U.S. foreign policy, ultimately shows us therefore is twofold. First, it demonstrates how the charismatic revolt against the Organization imagined by someone such as Mailer receives its fullest expression in, and indeed may be impossible to imagine without, the decolonizing world as the site where the U.S. middle class seeks to recover its historical agency. What Paul recognizes and the Emperor does not, we might suggest, is that the harsh training ground must be employed to harden not simply the leader's troops but the leader himself. In imparting this lesson, however, *Dune* makes clear why the rebirth of middle-class agency can never be permanent, insofar as this agency is tied not so much to the achievement of Western-style modernity as to the inherently evanescent process of modernization. To the extent that Herbert's novel tries to imagine a social system capable of perpetuating endless renewal, the novel's fantasy is not Locke's normative description of liberalism but on the contrary one of his asides on "the Indians in America," in which he suggests that kings in the Americas:

> are little more than generals of their armies; and though they command absolutely in war, yet at home, and in time of peace, they exercise very little dominion, and have but a very moderate sovereignty, the resolutions of peace and war being ordinarily either in the people or in a council, though the war itself, which admits not of pluralities of governors, naturally devolves the command into the king's sole authority.[62]

Dune's fantasy, therefore, is the frontier, the place where absolute authority on the field of battle balances with untrammeled liberty off it; where violent renewal breeds rough democracy; where the New World, in the process of being born, has not yet calcified into another deindividualizing system. Like Kennedy and the modernization theorists, Herbert projects this fantasy outward onto the putatively modernizing regions of the world, which he envisions as a site for the recovery of lost American agency. Given much of the rhetoric underlying both the recent war in Iraq and the establishment of something like a permanent theater of combat in Afghanistan, it is tempting to see this fantasy as the Cold War's most enduring legacy.

NOTES

1. John F. Kennedy, *The Strategy of Peace*, ed. Allan Nevins (New York: Harper and Row, 1960), 117. Subsequent quotations from this work will be cited parenthetically within the text and abbreviated *Strategy*.

2. For overviews of modernization theory, see Nils Gilman, *Mandarins of the Future: Modernization Theory in Cold War America* (Baltimore: Johns Hopkins University Press, 2003); Michael E. Latham, *Modernization as Ideology: American Social Science and "Nation Building" in the Kennedy Era* (Chapel Hill: University of North Carolina Press, 2000); and Kimber Charles Pearce, *Rostow, Kennedy, and the Rhetoric of Foreign Aid* (East Lansing: Michigan State University Press, 2001).

3. Latham, *Modernization as Ideology*, 6.

4. John F. Kennedy, *"Let the Word Go Forth": The Speeches, Statements, and Writings of John F. Kennedy*, ed. Theodore C. Sorensen (New York: Delacorte, 1988), 339–40.

5. On postwar fears of middle-class decline, see Andrew Hoberek, *The Twilight of the Middle Class: Post–World War II American Fiction and White-Collar Work* (Princeton, NJ: Princeton University Press, 2005).

6. On third-world revolutionaries as icons of modernity, see John A. McClure, *Late Imperial Romance* (New York: Verso, 1994), 33–40; and María Josefina Saldaña-Portillo, *The Revolutionary Imagination in the Americas and the Age of Development* (Durham, NC: Duke University Press, 2003), 63–108.

7. Frank Herbert, *Dune*. 1965 (New York: Ace, 1990), 488. Subsequent quotations from this work will be cited parenthetically within the text.

8. Christina Klein, *Cold War Orientalism: Asia in the Middlebrow Imagination, 1945–1961* (Berkeley: University of California Press, 2003), 9.

9. McClure, *Late Imperial Romance*, 50.

10. Ibid., 24.

11. *Whole Earth Catalog*, Fall 1969, 95.

12. See William F. Touponce, *Frank Herbert* (Boston: Twayne, 1988). Touponce asserts that "the primary theme of *Dune* is . . . ecology," arguing that ecological principles provide not simply the intellectual content of the novel but its formal structure (13, 12–33 passim). See R. J. Ellis, "Frank Herbert's *Dune* and the Discourse of Apocalyptic Ecologism in the United States," in *Science Fiction Roots and Branches: Contemporary Critical Approaches*, ed. Rhys Garnett and R. J. Ellis (New York: St. Martin's, 1990), 104–24. Ellis reads the novel against the backdrop of shifting U.S. discourses of ecology, contending that it reflects (and to a limited extent criticizes) the strain of "apocalyptic ecologism" that Ellis locates in the writing of figures such as Paul Bigelow Sears and Rachel Carson (104, 104–24 passim). See Susan Stratton, "The Messiah and the Greens: The Shape of Environmental Action in *Dune* and *Pacific Edge*," *Extrapolation* 42, no. 4 (Winter 2001): 303–16. While she compares *Dune*'s environmental politics unfavorably with those of Kim Stanley Robinson's 1988 *Pacific Edge*, Stratton acknowledges that "Herbert's novel

was an important first step for a generation of SF readers who needed to learn the fundamentals of ecology" (313). See Dave Itzkoff, "Dune Babies," *New York Times* (24 September 2006): sec. 7, col. 2: 20. As the *New York Times*' Itzkoff puts it in his recent critique of the profitable franchise spun off of Herbert's original series by his son Brian and Kevin J. Anderson, the original novel provided "a metaphor for the environmentally conscious age it was written in," offering readers "a powerful ecological message and a reminder . . . that their actions will have profound consequences for generations yet unborn" (sec. 7, col. 2: 20).

13. Frank Herbert, "When I Was Writing Dune," in *Heretics of Dune*. 1984 (New York: Ace, 1987), v–vi.

14. Touponce, *Frank Herbert*, 12; Stratton, "The Messiah and the Greens," 307; Timothy O'Reilly, *Frank Herbert* (New York: Frederick Ungar, 1981), 39.

15. Gilman, *Mandarins of the Future*, 36–40.

16. Eric Hobsbawm, *The Age of Extremes: A History of the World, 1914–1991* (New York: Pantheon, 1994), 292.

17. Norman Borlaug, "The Green Revolution, Peace, and Humanity" (Nobel Lecture, 11 December 1970), in *Nobel Lectures in Peace (1951–1970)*, ed. Frederick W. Haberman (Hackensack, NJ: World Scientific Publishing Co., 1999), 456.

18. Kevin Williams, "Imperialism and Globalization: Lessons from Frank Herbert's *Dune*," *Reconstruction: Studies in Contemporary Culture* 3, no. 3 (Summer 2002). Web. Paragraph 10. See Frank Herbert, "Dune Genesis," *Omni*, July 1980: 72–74. Herbert, whose first novel *The Dragon in the Sea* (1956) unfolds against the backdrop of a competition in the near future for scarce underwater oil supplies, declares in "Dune Genesis": "The scarce water of *Dune* is an exact analog of oil scarcity" (74).

19. Pearce, *Rostow, Kennedy, and the Rhetoric of Foreign Aid*, 20.

20. Saldaña-Portillo, *Revolutionary Imagination in the Americas and the Age of Development*, 26. See also Bret Benjamin, *Invested Interests: Capital, Culture, and the World Bank* (Minneapolis: University of Minnesota Press, 2007). Benjamin identifies a similar distinction already present in embryo at the Bretton Woods conference, constrasting Keynes's "economistic" relegation of "production to the commodification of resources and the generation of wealth" (14) and his related "dismissive approach to the Global South" (16) with the American delegates' strategic commitment to "the value of cultivating a sense of mutual investment and participation in international systems of financial management" that could "serve for establishing a sustainable postcolonial framework for global capitalist expansion" (17).

21. *Lawrence of Arabia*, VHS, directed by David Lean. 1962 (Sony Pictures, 2001). See O'Reilly, *Frank Herbert*, 43–44, for a discussion of how the novel borrows from the film.

22. Leerom Medovoi, "Cold War American Culture as the Age of Three Worlds," *minnesota review*, nos. 55–57 (Fall 2000 and Spring–Fall 2001): 167–86, 168–69.

Midway through Lean's film, Jackson Bentley, the Chicago reporter played by Arthur Kennedy, warns Alec Guinness's Prince Feisal not to trust the British, telling him, "we Americans were once a colonial people. We naturally sympathize with any people anywhere who are struggling for their freedom." This line almost directly quotes a 1954 speech by Eisenhower's secretary of state John Foster Dulles. See "International Unity: Address by Secretary Dulles," *Department of State Bulletin* 30, no. 782 (21 June 1954): 935–39. Dulles declared, "We ourselves are the first colony in modern times to have won independence. We have a natural sympathy with those everywhere who would follow our example" (936), quoted in Thomas G. Paterson, J. Garry Clifford, and Kenneth J. Hagan, *American Foreign Policy: A History since 1900*, 2nd ed. (Lexington, MA: D. C. Heath and Co., 1983), 504; and in Medovoi, "Cold War American Culture as the Age of Three Worlds," 176. Dulles of course played a major role in the CIA-led overthrow of the democratically elected governments of Mohammed Mossadegh in Iran and Jacobo Arbenz in Guatemala, the second of which coups was ongoing when Dulles made his speech, and which generated "loud protest" abroad, at a time when Lean was working in Europe and Asia. Paterson, Clifford, and Hagan, *American Foreign Policy*, 509; see also Stephen Schlesinger and Stephen Kinzer, *Bitter Fruit: The Story of the American Coup in Guatemala* (Cambridge, MA: Harvard University Press, 1999), 219–20. The cynical spin that the scene gives this line—Bentley is clearly mouthing an encomium, and Feisal remains doubtful—thus seems readable as an ironic reminder, from the position of British imperial experience (and perhaps, more proximally, post-Suez resentment), of the political realities subtending Kennedy's extension of Dulles's rhetoric.

23. Kennedy, *"Let the Word Go Forth,"* 338.

24. Odd Arne Westad, *The Global Cold War: Third World Interventions and the Making of Our Times* (Cambridge: Cambridge University Press, 2005), 17.

25. Klein, *Cold War Orientalism*, 24–28.

26. Kennedy, *"Let the Word Go Forth,"* 350.

27. W. W. Rostow, *The Stages of Economic Growth: A Non-Communist Manifesto*. 1960 (New York: Cambridge University Press, 1965), 12.

28. Ibid., 166.

29. See Elizabeth Cobbs Hoffman, *All You Need Is Love: The Peace Corps and the Spirit of the 1960s* (Cambridge, MA: Harvard University Press, 1998); Stanley Corkin, *Cowboys as Cold Warriors: The Western and U.S. History* (Philadelphia: Temple University Press, 2004); Gilman, *Mandarins of the Future*; and Pearce, *Rostow, Kennedy, and the Rhetoric of Foreign Aid*. Hoffman (17) and Corkin (247) attribute the phrase "the New Frontier" to Sorensen. Gilman (198) credits it to Rostow, and Pearce (125, n. 12) says Rostow may "possibly" have been responsible for it. For an extended discussion of the ways in which Kennedy deployed the languages of the frontier tale and European imperial romance to recast the essentially reformist, capitalist narrative of development as a site of revolutionary endeavor, see McClure, *Late Imperial Romance*, 40–49.

30. Kennedy, *"Let the Word Go Forth,"* 359.

31. For Rostow, this imposition is explicit: as the most successful form of modernization, the U.S. version must be shared with other parts of the world to enable them to resist the flawed form of modernization represented by Communism, "one particularly inhumane form of political organization capable of launching and sustaining the growth process" in nations lacking, crucially, "a substantial and enterprising commercial middle class and an adequate political consensus among the leaders of society" (*Stages of Economic Growth* 164). Whereas Rostow, though describing Communism as "a kind of disease which can befall a transitional society" (*Stages of Economic Growth* 164), at least acknowledges it as a competing model for nations attempting to become modern, Kennedy instead characterizes it as a residual form of Old World, indeed, older-than–Old World, tyranny. See Kennedy, *"Let the Word Go Forth"*: "They come with banners proclaiming they have new doctrines; that history is on their side. But, in reality, they bring a doctrine which is as old as the pharaohs of Egypt, and like the pharaohs of Egypt, doomed by history" (358). For another instance of this anachronistic, Judeo-Christian reading of Communism, see Alan Nadel, *Containment Culture: American Narratives, Postmodernism, and the Atomic Age* (Durham, NC: Duke University Press, 1995), 90–116.

32. Joseph Ripp, "Middle America Meets Middle Earth: American Discussion and Readership of J. R. R. Tolkien's *The Lord of the Rings*, 1965–1969," *Book History* 8 (2005): 245–86. Tolkien's trilogy was published in 1954–55, but it first achieved major success in the United States with the publication of an inexpensive paperback edition of questionable legality in 1965, the same year that *Dune* appeared.

33. Brian Edwards, *Morocco Bound: Disorienting America's Maghreb, from Casablanca to the Marrakech Express* (Durham, NC: Duke University Press, 2005), 32.

34. See John Eisele, "The Wild East: Deconstructing the Language of Genre in the Hollywood Eastern," *Cinema Journal* 41, no. 4 (Summer 2002): 68–94. Even as I depart from his use of it, I borrow this label from John C. Eisele, who invokes it in the context of a generic taxonomy of different kinds of films set in the Middle East: the sheik subgenre, the Arabian nights subgenre, the foreign legion subgenre, the foreign intrigue subgenre, and the terrorist subgenre. Some of what Eisele describes intersects with the Eastern as I define it. His structural account, however, largely ignores historical shifts and trends in films with Middle Eastern settings, and he posits too sharp a divide between the Western and the Eastern, largely on the basis of an overly schematic contrast between their respective portrayals of Native Americans and Middle Easterners.

35. Corkin, *Cowboys as Cold Warriors*, 239.

36. These quotations are from Frederick Jackson Turner, *The Frontier in American History* (New York: Holt, Rinehart and Winston, 1962), 3–4. Ellis makes the same claim using a slightly different set of citations. Ellis, "Frank Herbert's *Dune* and the Discourse of Apocalyptic Ecologism in the United States," 117.

37. William H. Whyte, Jr., *The Organization Man* (New York: Simon and Schuster, 1957), 12. Emphasis original.

38. Corkin, *Cowboys as Cold Warriors*, 230, passim.

39. Dipesh Chakrabarty, *Provincializing Europe: Postcolonial Thought and Historical Difference* (Princeton, NJ: Princeton University Press, 2000), 8.

40. O'Reilly, *Frank Herbert*, 55.

41. Ibid., 41–42.

42. Ellis, "Frank Herbert's *Dune* and the Discourse of Apocalyptic Ecologism in the United States," 117.

43. John Locke, *Two Treatises on Civil Government, Preceded by Sir Robert Filmer's "Patriarcha"* (London: G. Routledge, 1884), bk. 2, par. 102: 243–44.

44. Thomas Jefferson, *Notes on the State of Virginia*, ed. and intro. Frank Shuffleton (New York: Penguin, 1999), Query 9: 99.

45. Richard Slotkin, *Gunfighter Nation: The Myth of the Frontier in Twentieth-Century America* (New York: Atheneum, 1992), 11.

46. Louis Hartz, *The Liberal Tradition in America*. 1955 (New York: Harvest, 1991), 3.

47. Chakrabarty employs this phrase in a discussion of John Stuart Mill, although he elsewhere asserts that U.S. global dominance takes up many of the tropes of European imperialism.

48. "The Plowboy Interview: Frank Herbert. Science Fiction's Yellow Journalist Is a Homesteading 'Technopeasant,'" *Mother Earth News* 69 (May–June 1981): 17–23, 20. Ellipsis original.

49. Herbert, "Dune Genesis," 72.

50. Ibid., 74.

51. Ibid., 72; "critical faculties" italicized in original. The other novels in the trilogy are *Dune Messiah* (1969) and *Children of Dune* (1976). Herbert subsequently continued the series with *God Emperor of Dune* (1981), *Heretics of Dune* (1984), and *Chapterhouse: Dune* (1985).

52. Frank Herbert, *Dune Messiah* (New York: G. P. Putnam's Sons, 1969), 54.

53. Norman Mailer, "Superman Comes to the Supermart," *Esquire*, November 1960, 119–27, 124.

54. Ibid., 122.

55. Sean McCann, "The Imperiled Republic: Norman Mailer and the Poetics of Anti-Liberalism," *English Literary History* 67, no. 1 (Spring 2000): 293–336, 298.

56. Whyte, *Organization Man*, 5.

57. O'Reilly, *Frank Herbert*, 66.

58. Herbert, *Dune Messiah*, 37, 38, 39.

59. Ibid., 33.

60. Herbert, "Dune Genesis," 74.

61. Ibid.

62. Locke, *Two Treatises on Civil Government*, bk. 2, par. 108: 247.

5

COLD WAR INTIMACIES

JOAN DIDION AND THE CRITIQUE OF POSTCOLONIAL REASON

KAREN STEIGMAN

In her *A Critique of Postcolonial Reason* (1999), Gayatri Spivak, the preeminent founder of the field of postcolonial studies, challenged the contemporary postcolonial academy to rethink strategy.[1] Tracking how the postcolonial critique had come to establish itself as academic truth—and at what costs—Spivak traced the philosophical, anthropological, and historical underpinnings of postcolonial thought to its uneasy alliance with Cold War area studies and the emergence of transnational cultural studies in the present-day academy. The central aim of her book was to show that the postcolonial critic had become liable to reproducing the same imperialist legacy of inequality and violence between first and third worlds that she ostensibly sought to undo, indeed that certain reflexive and retrograde proofs and platitudes of imperialism had persisted in postcolonial criticism, even as the postcolonial project proposed to challenge those very postulates. Likening postcolonial practice to the same operative "information-retrieval approach" of imperialist discourse, Spivak underscored a particularly persistent Cold War motif, in which first-world literary agents repeat a foundational, imperialist trope of discovery, uncovering third-world documents in complicity with a native informant, and data-mining and decoding those documents in order to render them legible to the imperialist subjects of the first-world academy. Spivak's complaint was that the postcolonial ratification of the emergent South by way of the ubiquitous category of "Third World literature" had in fact failed to realize anything like intimate knowledge of the other.[2] Rather, postcolonial studies, still imprinted with Cold War area studies, repeated the same uneven exchanges and failed intimacies between the first world and the third world that it sought to replace. As Spivak depicted it, the academic method that was in vogue operated somewhat like a Cold War spy mission, an informant's project conceived in order to "deliver the emergence of a 'South' to provide proof of transnational cultural exchange," but where little exchange took place save that self-congratulatory proof. Not a little unsettled to find her own work imbricated in this neocolonial, neo–Cold War method of literary espionage, Spivak noted that "it seems particularly unfortunate when the emergent perspective of feminist criticism reproduces the axioms of imperialism," and she noted a particular irony when her own words appeared to inform and secure that feminism's "facts with a certain narcissism" (113–14).

A Critique of Postcolonial Reason is thus part of Spivak's ongoing effort to rethink the forms of intimacy and exchange at postcolonialism's base; the book reanimates her recurrent question, how does the postcolonial feminist negotiate with the metropolitan feminist? It also renews her call for a strategic practice of intimacy. Rereading imperialism's foundational texts with "critical intimacy," as Spivak has suggested, offers the "challenge of deconstruction": it is "not to excuse, but to suspend accusation . . . to examine if the protocols of [a] text can produce something that will generate a new and useful reading" of it (98). She continues, "Such a reading, as I have pointed out, is a 'mistake,' inappropriate to the text. Yet deconstructive approaches have suggested that every reading may be an upheaval parasitical to the text. Here I use the resources of deconstruction 'in the service of reading' to develop a strategy (rather than a theory) of reading matching the situation of reading that might lead to a literary critique of imperialism . . . a reading that, in a certain way, falls prey to its own critique, perhaps" (153). In other words, intimacy for Spivak produces upheaval, if not deliberate error; we might say that reading with critical intimacy produces a reading estranged from itself. In *A Critique of Postcolonial Reason*, for example, Spivak subjects her own foundational essays in postcolonial criticism to critical intimacy's disfiguring and estranging practice: each chapter of that book rereads an earlier piece, re-elaborating and reframing it in order to resist the false intimacy that is the "condition and effect of received ideas," even—or especially—if they are her own. Indeed, Spivak's impatience with the calcified logic of postwar truths, what she calls the "done deal forever" of Cold War critique (113), instigated her strategy of intimacy as estrangement in *A Critique of Postcolonial Reason*; in *Death of a Discipline*, she extended the concept of reading with critical intimacy to produce a series of retakes on the originary imperialist reason of Cold War area studies discourse,[3] renegotiating with and repurposing its canonical texts.

This chapter takes Spivak at her word, bringing the strategy of critical intimacy to bear on a rereading of the canonical Cold War writer Joan Didion. I might say from the outset that, at least from their usual reading and reputation, this pair is not one of immediate or obvious intimates. Counted "among the most fundamentally conservative writers in America,"[4] and a preeminent Cold War author of first-world anxiety, Didion's literary and political investments typically run to the neo-Conradian tropes of alienation, isolation, and romanticism in Cold War discourse that of course Spivak typically works against. Indeed, Spivak herself might describe their pairing here as one of unlikely accomplices (*A Critique* 119). But if the work of critical intimacy is precisely in forging and reading misalliance, reading Didion with Spivak follows in critical intimacy's strategic unease. In fact, there is also some shared critical ground between them. That is, we can find in Spivak's cutting characterization of the re-emergence of imperialist philosophical and anthropological discourses in the neoliberal discourse of the Cold War academy—"yesterday's imperialism, today's Development" (*A Critique* 124)[5]—a striking echo of Didion's own earlier condemnation of the guise of intimacy in Cold War internationalism. Writing of the 1950s Santa Monica Jaycees in an essay from *The White Album* entitled "Good Citizens," for instance, Didion describes the Jaycees' project for "improving one's world and one's self simultaneously" in a particularly cutting line of her own. She notes the Jaycees' "boosterism and pancake breakfasts," their "belief in business success as a transcendent ideal," and, with particular irony, their "approach to international problems which construed the underdeveloped world as a temporarily depressed area in need mainly of People-to-People programs."[6] Didion's irritated critique of the specious Cold War rhetoric of "development" and "People-to-People" programs that undergirds the international intimacy of the Jaycees anticipates Spivak's critique of an academy that has made literary studies into something like a People-to-People Program of friendly literary agents doing fieldwork for national defense and development. Both take exception to the gloss of intimacy in neoliberal humanism that reifies imperialism's foundational inequities.[7] In fact, Didion reads the Jaycees' creed of "brotherhood in action" as an "astonishing" program of institutionalized and self-congratulatory intimacy, and she sardonically quotes the group commending its own work in a program report: "'Word of Operation Brotherhood swept through the teeming masses of Asia like a fresh wind from the sea'" (*White Album* 94).

In contrast to the Jaycees, Didion offers a critique of Cold War intimacy that is distinctly, if somewhat surprisingly, in the mode of Spivak's deconstructive strategy of critical intimacy. Her novels, especially *A Book of Common Prayer* (1977), *Democracy* (1984), and *The Last Thing He Wanted*

(1996),[8] are themselves transgressive and parasitical reworkings of canonical texts of imperialism. Indeed, now "it is *women* who have obscure crises of spirit in seedy hotel rooms and die forlorn and solitary deaths in warm climates."[9] This chapter will thus read *A Book of Common Prayer* as a Cold War novel that exemplifies what Spivak calls the "scrupulous travesty" (*A Critique* 9) of postcolonial critical intimacy.[10] In fact, Didion coins the "impossible intimacy" (*A Book of Common Prayer* 39) of the postcolonial encounter using the very formulation that Spivak has continued to rework. If, as Spivak writes, the "hardest lesson" for the postcolonial feminist to learn is precisely "the impossible intimacy of the ethical,"[11] the project I am proposing here accords with that lesson of impossible intimacy as a postwar literary studies strategy that operates "without guarantees" (*Discipline* 31).[12] This is a project of intimacy forged, or forced, in difference. In the context of a collection focused on rethinking Cold War literature and culture, I am thus attempting, in Spivak's words, to "force a reading" (*Discipline* 91).

Joan Didion, Cold Warrior?

We might begin by noting that Joan Didion is herself something of an impossible figure in Cold War literature and culture, standing, with an odd intimacy, at once inside and outside the Cold War literary academy. On the one hand, Didion is a Cold War icon, a legendary if not metonymic figure of the anxiety, instability, and debauched political and cultural moods of the postwar American era. Over the past five decades, she has garnered steady acclaim for her portraits of American Cold War "atomization," for deconstructing the promises of twentieth-century American imperialism, and for exposing its failures in a trenchant series of exposés of U.S. Cold War "frontier" expansionism and its aftermath, from the essays of the louche 1960s and 1970s in *Slouching Towards Bethlehem* and *The White Album*, to the paranoid political fictions of America's interventions abroad in *A Book of Common Prayer*, *Democracy*, and *The Last Thing He Wanted*, to a retrospective, post-9/11 analysis of U.S. Cold War foreign and domestic policy in *Fixed Ideas: America Since 9.11* (2003). As her era's "foremost practitioner of the literature of permanent nervous collapse,"[13] her essays are regularly mined for their famously epigrammatic phrases on the anomie, alienation, and turmoil of the postwar period. Her novels of disintegration are dutifully name-checked alongside major writers of postwar paranoia such as Mailer, Updike, Roth, Pynchon, and DeLillo, and her work is integral to the Cold War criticism of Alan Nadel and John McClure. As Nadel argues in his seminal reading of *Democracy*, for example, if "*democracy* has been the name we have given to a narrative of American global politics," Didion "exposes the personal and national costs of propagating that colonialist narrative" by deconstructing both the alibi (democracy for containment) and our own ability to believe in it, too."[14] Elizabeth Hardwick similarly observes that Didion's world emerges in "an obsessive attraction to the disjunctive and paradoxical in American national policy and the somnolent, careless decisions made in private life."[15] Even Didion's recent and ostensibly most personal narratives, of her California childhood in *Where I Was From*, and of the death of her husband in *The Year of Magical Thinking* (which garnered renewed if sentimental readerly attention, along with a 2005 National Book Award and a Broadway show starring Vanessa Redgrave), are also incisive investigations of the American political and cultural scene over the past fifty years. Indeed, in all of her work, Didion has relentlessly tracked and critiqued the narratives that underwrite the American century's foundational imperialist ideologies of progress and security (its "redemptive romances of development and liberation," as McClure describes them); she has produced instead a counternarrative of insecurity—an evasive rhetoric of reticence, parataxis, aphasia, and magical thinking that both picks apart the intelligibility of late imperialist discourse and registers her famous, ironic detachment from it.[16]

Emily Apter's recent suggestion that Didion "warrants inclusion in the canon of American writers" of paranoid fiction that extends from Poe and Hawthorne to Heller and Pynchon is thus something of a superfluous assertion about this apparently already crucial, or at least shorthand, figure of the Cold War literary scene.[17] Didion's signature portraits of American insecurity are undoubtedly hallmarks. But Apter's suggestion also points up an interesting paradox of Didion's iconicity. Hers may be the stuff of the classic Cold War thriller—chaotic U.S. foreign policy, national in/security, and the uncertain relation of truth to appearance—but by the time the critics came to review her last novel *The Last Thing He Wanted*, Didion herself admitted in the *Guardian* that "a lot of people didn't really get it." In fact Didion's famously arch cynicism, the ironic "central narrative principle [to depict] the disintegration of the times,"[18] has precluded her inclusion in the Poe-to-Pynchon political-literary canon; her critics resort instead to a kind of biological criticism, conflating, in Ross Posnock's line, the allegedly "chilly narcissism" of a frigid sexual persona with an empty, hollow prose, and thus discounting her politics altogether.[19] She is “almost too skillful” in wielding her “inescapably alarmed fragility,” wrote Alfred Kazin of her early novels *Run River* (1963) and *Play It As It Lays* (1970).[20] A less circumspect reviewer of *The Last Thing He Wanted* deemed it “women’s paranoia. Whereas the male paranoiac truly does hate and fear the secret Establishment,” Didion’s “typical paranoid female has a crush on it.”[21] No doubt readers are troubled by an apparently unknowable figure of woman in her texts; her “female way of being serious”[22] results in “thinness, a sense of things missing” in “even her best writing”; her prose is “as resonant as a pop-gun.”[23] The critical misogyny extends even to the pages of *Ms.*, where Catharine Stimpson dismissed her outright: “I once had an image of Joan Didion: slick novelist, fine reporter, a woman who critics said told men and women what the modern woman’s experience was. . . . She now seems a curious creature, whose sense of literature and of life is common, disappointingly conventional, and always problematical. Her attitudes pose a problem for us all.”[24] Even the influential and nuanced readings of Nadel and McClure to some extent follow this convention: Nadel construes his allegory of containment in the withholding narrator-journalist “Joan Didion” of *Democracy*, while McClure finds the embodiment of his thesis of late imperial romance in her prototypical “spacey and sometimes promiscuous”[25] Didion-Women.[26] In short, such critics find in Didion a “profoundly conservative message”[27] and a “sneering dismissal of liberal and leftist narratives.”[28]

Of course part of the difficulty with Didion, to continue the refrain, has come in the very figure of impossible intimacy that she crafted for herself early on. As Joyce Carol Oates notes, Didion “has never been easy on her heroines”; “her art has always been one of understatement and indirection, of emotion withheld.”[29] Didion might say the same. “My only advantage as a reporter,” run the famously antagonistic lines in *Slouching Towards Bethlehem*, “is that I am so physically small, so temperamentally unobtrusive, and so neurotically inarticulate that people tend to forget that my presence runs counter to their best interests.”[30] Much later, the unnamed narrator-journalist of *The Last Thing He Wanted* reiterates the taunt: “For the record this is me talking. You know me, or think you do” (5). In a typical move, the essay “In the Islands” in fact begins with a presumptive invitation to intimacy: “I want you to know, as you read me, precisely who I am and where I am and what is on my mind. I want you to understand exactly what you are getting.” But the possibility of understanding exactly this “I” is immediately put into question: “You are getting a woman who for some time now has felt radically separated from most of the ideas that seem to interest other people. You are getting a woman who somewhere along the line misplaced whatever slight faith she ever had in the social contract" (*White Album* 133–34). Here Didion puts the reader and narrator in a precarious relation, in uneasy intimacy, in which a lack of faith in contractual relations, common interests, and even the narrative record is paramount. Narrative itself runs counter to intimacy with Didion; instead, her writing is, as Hardwick describes, "a structure for the fadings and erasures of experience" designed to "express a peculiar restlessness and unease. . . . You read that something did or did not happen; something was or was not thought" in a narrative pattern of "willful obfuscation, a purposeful blackout of what was promised or not promised."[31] In the example of *Democracy*, the narrator asks the reader to "call me the author," and requests, "let the reader be introduced to Joan Didion," but this "Joan Didion" comes across as a radically ambivalent narrative figure, an "I" who says, "I lack" (certainty, conviction, patience, interest, "even faith in my own narrative technique"), and who finally admits that the high-wire act of the novelist has dispersed into "shards" of a novel that "I am no longer writing." Any understanding promised by *Democracy*'s narrative, by a "tacit contract between writer and reader," is misplaced and eventually fails, and intimacy comes only in "fitful glimpses. [This] has not been the novel I set out to write, nor am I exactly the person who set out to write it" (16–17, 108, 162, 232). Or, as Nancy K. Miller puts it, an "invitation to intimacy" is one "we do not associate with Didion."[32]

Didion's famous technique of "calculated ellipses" (*Democracy* 162) produces, therefore, a crisis of intimacy and narrative authority that, as Nadel has importantly argued, imbricates the reader as well.[33] Her uneasy intimacy with her Cold War readers—and her peripheral, if not sexually diminutive status in relation to the big books of her contemporaries—came to the fore when she seemed to turn from her ubiquitous, inward concerns about her own place as a feminized subject in postwar America to outward, overtly political examinations of the place of the United States on the Cold War world stage. Particularly, her dissections of U.S. policy relations in Central America and the Pacific Rim in the 1970s and 1980s troubled her position on the Cold War political spectrum, and critics generally accustomed themselves to a contradictory figure who, as Ellen Willis describes, writes on politics while remaining "leery of the very category of 'the political' as a mode of human engagement."[34] But when Everyman's Library brought out her collected nonfiction in 2006,

John Leonard faulted readers for misunderstanding Didion's politics in the first place. Critics made her into the postwar "poster girl for anomie" by focusing on her "intuition and anxiety" and on "every syllable on rattlesnakes and mesquite," but in fact it was inevitable that the quintessential American Cold War writer (always fascinated, Leonard recalled, by Huey Newton, the Hoover Dam, and nuclear reactors) would end up "going left and going south," to Hawaii and El Salvador and Costa Rica, in order to write "postcolonial NAFTA novels."[35] I find Leonard's line instructive for rethinking the Cold War novel within an international framework. Indeed, Didion's investigation of the postcolonial crisis of engagement, of the figures of intimacy (and enmity) at "the far frontiers of the Monroe Doctrine" (*Last Thing* 7), is exemplified in her construal of *A Book of Common Prayer*'s Charlotte Douglas, her first turn to the postcolonial NAFTA novel, and her central figure of impossible intimacy.

Impossible Intimacy

"Obviously the book finds her at a crisis," Didion has remarked of Charlotte.[36] *A Book of Common Prayer*'s crisis of "impossible intimacy" (39) comes in Charlotte's radical separation from her family—she has left two husbands and lost two daughters, one "to 'history' and another to 'complications'" (12)—and in her mysterious arrival in Boca Grande, the novel's fictional, postcolonial Central American country. Charlotte has traced a "blind course south" (144) to Boca Grande, from a middle-class childhood in Hollister, California, two desultory years at Berkeley, and a house in San Francisco where she was the wife of Leonard Douglas, a famous and also corrupt international rights lawyer. And then she makes an abrupt departure from all of that, leaving San Francisco (and her second husband) to travel through the American Southeast (with the first), and to leave him, again, after her newborn child dies, to await the appearance of her other missing daughter Marin (a Patty Hearst–styled American terrorist who is on the run from the FBI). Marin never arrives in Boca Grande, but Charlotte refuses to leave. She becomes involved with Victor and Gerardo, the two main figures of the ruling family's political insurgency, and is eventually killed in the inevitable October violence, shot in the back at the national stadium by the militia of one or the other of her lovers (which side, it is not clear), her body tossed on the lawn of the American embassy. Funeral arrangements are left to Grace Strasser-Mendana, the novel's narrator, another American expatriate, and a member by marriage of Boca Grande's ruling elite; she is the widowed sister-in-law of Victor and the mother of Gerardo. She has also been left in putative control of the family's wealth. *A Book of Common Prayer* is framed as Grace's attempt to piece together the sequence of events that led to Charlotte's "death," or "murder," or "previous engagement"—but "neither word works" (56). Grace sends Charlotte's body back to San Francisco (after draping the coffin in a child's T-shirt printed with an erroneous facsimile of the American flag), noting, "I think this T-shirt did not have the correct number of stars and stripes but it did have the appearance of stars and stripes and it was red and it was white and it was blue" (270). She returns to living out her last days (she is dying of cancer) as Boca Grande's overseer: "You will notice my use of the colonial pronoun, the overseer's 'we.' I see now that I have no business in this place but I have been here too long to change. I mean 'we'" (271). Imperialist intimacy in the novel is thus circumscribed by the neo-Conradian encounter of these two American female figures abroad in Cold War Central America, and intimacy is made its central narrative concern in the ambivalent character of Charlotte, and in Grace's ambivalent role.

Grace describes her narrative trouble early on: "We are uneasy about a story until we know who is telling it. In no other sense does it matter who 'I' am: 'the narrator' plays no motive role in this narrative, nor would I want to" (21). In effacing her, Grace's narrative is thus structured as a series of retakes as she attempts to reconstruct Charlotte's story. Opening with a minimalist biographical sketch of Charlotte's life—"She left one man, she left a second man, she traveled again with the first; she let him die alone. She lost one child to 'history' and another to 'complications.'... In summary. So you know the story" (11)—each chapter retells, reframes, and adds details of events. But the book ends with Grace's admission of her inability to understand Charlotte and thus of an unrealized narrative project, an unrealized project of intimacy. In the novel's oft-noted failed frame, which begins with Grace's opening declaration, "I will be her witness" (11), and which ends with the admission that "I have not been the witness I wanted to be" (272),[37] Grace effaces herself and negates her narrative gesture of intimacy. Already by page one, "you know the story," and the promise of its witness notwithstanding, there will be no narrative involvement in *A Book of Common Prayer* beyond the minimal biographical facts set out in its first lines. These facts themselves are set off in quotations ("history" and "complications") and are offered as the secondhand "evaluation of others" (11).

When Grace's proclamation "In summary. So you know the story" reappears verbatim in the final chapter, its reiteration deepens the irony of a text that has, with its failed witness and impossible subject, offered a record of "extenuating circumstances" (11) that is no more reliable at the end than at the beginning. In other words, the novel's crisis (of narrative reliability, testimony, evidence, and the narrative record) is rendered as a problem of intimacy, a problem of reading constructed on the uncertainty of intimacy, on the problem of pronouns and relations (*I* versus *we*; the intricacies of kinship), and on the question of appropriate words or figures themselves (the mistaken facsimile of the flag). Grace after all is a failed student of intimacy, an anthropologist who once "worked with Lévi-Strauss at São Paulo" but who has "lost faith in her own method, who stopped believing that observable activity defined anthropos" (12). Even more, if the anthropological discourse of kinship has failed, Grace's new discipline of biochemistry, "in which demonstrable answers are commonplace and 'personality' absent" (12), fails as well: "I am less and less convinced that the word 'unstable' has any useful meaning except insofar as it describes a chemical compound" (105); "I try to make a model of Charlotte's 'character' and I see only a shimmer" (215); "I recognize the equivocal nature of even the most empirical evidence" (271). The intimacy of investigative journalism fails too. Grace instructs herself to "look at the visas. Track back the course" (145) of Charlotte's itinerary, but evidence has been deliberately lost or "mislaid" (31). There are "no visible distinguishing marks" other than "*madre*" and "*turista*" (22) on her documents in the first place. Other evidence is second- or thirdhand rumor: "Some of what Charlotte said about the months which followed Marin's disappearance she did not even say to me. She said it to Gerardo. I would call that the least reliable part of what I know" (59).

Instead, Grace recounts Charlotte's time in Boca Grande as a series of strange encounters and inexplicable relations, moments of the opposite of intimacy. There is Charlotte's strangely absent-minded appearance, the "extreme and volatile thinness of the woman," with her overly heavy hair, pale skin, and expensive clothes in "just perceptible disrepair" (26). There is her self-imposed isolation at the Caribe, the shabby hotel where she breakfasts and dines alone, types alone in her room, walks the terraces after dinner alone, and where encounters with other Americans, "the occasional mineral geologist," OAS field worker, and "CIA man traveling on one or another incorporeal AID mission," all tend to "end in obscurely sexual misunderstandings and bewilderment" (26). There are her appearances in the airport café with the Spanish-language *Revista Boca*

Grande, when she sits by herself, "reading the classified as attentively as she read[s] the front page" and appearing "entirely absorbed by what she read[s]." Only later do we learn that she is rereading the same newspaper copy day after day, that she has no apparent interest in the cultivation of vanilla, the reform of the tax structure, or the contradictions of the common market that are the current topics of Boca Grande's political economy, and that she cannot read Spanish anyway. In an exchange with the girl at the airport coffee counter, we see Charlotte questioning the girl about flights, speaking in English but not looking at her, and we see the girl refusing to respond but silently "plung[ing] her index finger into the sugar bowl at the counter" and then, "still gazing at Charlotte, lick[ing] the sugar from her finger" (28). Didion makes the moment a key point of failed exchange: "In another country," Grace notes, the girl "might have gone the extra step, made her point explicit, jammed her grimy finger between *la norteamericana*'s teeth, but the expression of proletarian resentment in Boca Grande remains largely symbolic. The *guerrilleros* here would have nothing to say to this girl in the airport. The *guerrilleros* here spend their time theorizing in the interior, and are covertly encouraged to emerge from time to time as foils to the actual politics of the country."

A series of such symbolic exchanges ensues. We see Charlotte failing to explain her dysentery symptoms to an uncomprehending pharmacist (41); asking for her messages at the Caribe desk "in a halting but flawlessly memorized Castilian Spanish which the night clerk [finds] difficult to understand" (27); or sitting in detached silence at the dinner parties that she hosts for "what passe[s] for the intelligentsia in Boca Grande," the "'poets' who [publish] verses in anthologies with titles like *Fresh Wind in the Caribbean*, and the usual complement of translators and teachers and film critics who [support] themselves stringing for newspapers and playing at politics." She "smil[es] vaguely" at these dinners and ignores the desultory political arguments between Victor and Gerardo, the ironic "men of action" (226–27) in Boca Grande's "notoriously frequent revolutions" (29). And she is "like someone dreaming," as her guests pontificate on Fanon and Debray and "what they always called 'the truly existential situation of Central America.'" Grace recalls a particularly offensive guest reading aloud a paper at the dinner table on "The Singular Position of Intellectuals with Respect to the Crisis of the Underdeveloped World," while Charlotte brushes away moths (225–28). When Grace warns Charlotte that the authorities in Boca Grande suspect her of ties to the revolution, given her evenings and her sexual involvements with Victor and

Gerardo, Charlotte in turn brushes her off in the text's key line: "Actually I'm not 'political' in the least. I mean my mind doesn't run that way" (199).

In Charlotte's failed engagements and in Grace's failed narrative reconstruction of her story, Didion thus underscores the novel's central concern, intimacy: the question of American involvement or engagement in Boca Grande, the question of the "actual politics of the country." But the actual politics are in fact not clear. When Charlotte reiterates her creed of noninvolvement and tells Grace, "I'm simply not interested in any causes or issues," the novel's political aporia comes to the fore in Grace's reply: "*Neither is anyone here*" (235). Political interest in Boca Grande is a vacuum. Charlotte's interests remain obscure when she suggests to the governing elite at a U.S. Embassy party that what will really turn Boca Grande's collapsed economy around is a film festival (the only response she gets is a sexual proposition), or when she brings Grace to a shabby storefront that she is considering for a boutique and planning to decorate with lattice and hemp baskets and with "masses of cymbidiums," to give it "the illusion of the tropics" (an "odd effect to strive for in a city rotting on the equator," as Grace puts it). Charlotte is apparently "oblivious" to the storefront's cache of sleeping bags, hot plates, and military guns, and to its current inhabitants, the itinerant revolutionary Bebe Chicago, a self-promoter who has turned up in Boca Grande after some years at the London School of Economics and "a few more organizing Caribbean 'liberation fronts' out of Mexico," and the pseudonymous "Mr. Sanchez," who sits at a card table "translating a United States Army arms manual into Spanish." Bebe Chicago himself "was said to have connections" with the revolutionaries, but his only relations seem to be with the people hired to follow him and tap his telephones (78–79). Grace notes, "one could not be certain of knowing the right people in Boca Grande" (244). Here again no one speaks to Charlotte, instead staring "as if she were a moth . . . never before observed" as she muses over paint colors (218–19).

Indeed, Charlotte "talked as if she had no specific history of her own" (46), appearing in the text as one "immaculate of history, innocent of politics" (60). For all Charlotte's difficulty, Grace repeatedly describes the comfortable, temperate life of this "child of the western United States," with her "faith in the value of certain frontiers on which her family had lived, in the virtues of cleared and irrigated land, of high-yield crops, of thrift, industry and the judicial system, of progress and education, and in the generally upward spiral of history." By the time Charlotte reached Boca

Grande, Grace adds, she "had absorbed a passing fluency in Third World power, had learned what the initials meant in Algeria and Indochina and the Caribbean, but on a blank map of the world she could not actually place the countries where the initials were in conflict. She considered the conflict dubious in any case. She understood that something was always going on in the world but believed that it would turn out all right. She believed the world to be peopled with others like herself" (59–60). In other words, Charlotte, with her first-world sense of (the world like) herself, remains outside in Boca Grande; she is variously "*una turista*" (11), an "outsider of romantic sensibility" (29), "*la bonne bourgeoise*" (240), and most damningly, the "*norteamericana* cunt" (204). "She tried to read a book about illiteracy in Latin America, but in lieu of finishing it she wrote a letter to *Prensa Latina* offering her services as author of a daily 'literacy lesson.' She tried to read Alberto Masferrer's *El Mínimum Vital* but she still had difficulty reading Spanish, and she had read a hundred pages . . . before she learned from Gerardo it was about the progressive tax." In a "CIA-sponsored 'handbook' on Boca Grande," that distinctly Cold War, American-style guide to practices of international intimacy, Charlotte takes literally its invitation to send "her suggestions 'for factual or interpretive or other changes'" to Washington (220–21).

Charlotte does volunteer in Boca Grande, dispensing birth control and cholera inoculations, and she is rumored to be working up her own series of "Letters" from Boca Grande to sell to the *New Yorker*. But she receives no response from *Prensa* or the CIA, nor does she publish her "impenetrably euphemistic" letters either. When Charlotte describes Boca Grande as "the economic fulcrum of the Americas," Grace must remind her that Boca Grande's main source of revenue is garnered "from an airport landing fee and eighteen slot machines": capital from planes flying from "Los Angeles to Bogotá, or New York to Quito," which "did not seem to me to constitute, in the classical sense, an economic fulcrum." Boca Grande exports copra, parrots, anaconda skins, and macramé shawls, but Charlotte again dismisses Grace's objection. "Another of Charlotte's Letters cover[s] the 'spirit of hope' she divine[s] in the *favelas*," which is another mistake, because "Boca Grande has no *favelas*, even the word is Portuguese." In fact, Grace and Charlotte dispute what constitutes the narrative style of the letter itself. "A 'Letter' from a city or country, I suggested," says Grace, "was conventionally understood to be a factual report on that city or country, not as it 'could become' but as it 'was.' . . . Not necessarily, Charlotte said. . . . What I was overlooking entirely, Charlotte said, was what Boca Grande 'could become'" (14–15).

The "verb form ma[kes] a difference," but Charlotte "[cannot] get it straight": her attempted intimacy with Boca Grande as it is fails repeatedly (160). The women's clinic is bombed, and one of Victor's colonels shoots up the crates of vaccine so that it runs into the streets. These instances of intimacy's infelicities jibe rhetorically with Charlotte's own "bizarrely arresting stories" that according to Grace come "out of some deep vacuum of nervous exhaustion." The "absence of the banyan trees at the American Embassy remind[s] Charlotte" of a story (about her absent daughter), but it devolves into nonsense in the telling.[38] Charlotte begins a story with a non sequitur, loses her place, and then loses "her interest in telling it" (38). Grace notes that she "used words as a seven-year-old might, as if she had heard them and liked their adult sound but had only the haziest idea of their meaning, and she also mentioned names as a seven-year-old might, with a bewildering disregard for who was listening" (35–36). Speaking at the U.S. Embassy party in typically paratactic and apparently oblivious fashion of her second husband Leonard Douglas (the corrupt human rights lawyer), she says, "He runs guns. I wish they had caviar" (38).[39] She is at once inviting and off-putting, "aware of nothing she was doing" and "reflexively seductive" (40). At the party, Grace notes the "odd intimate laughs that seemed simultaneously to include everyone within hearing and to exclude all possibility of inquiry" (37), the "ambiguous signals that [she] tended to transmit" (61), "that way she had of physically touching strangers, of reaching out unconsciously and then drawing back as if she just realized the gesture's sexual freight; that mannerism, that tic, that way of barely suggesting impossible intimacy" (39).

"To intimate," Lauren Berlant suggests, is to:

> communicate with the sparest of signs and gestures, and at its root intimacy has the quality of eloquence and brevity. But intimacy also involves an aspiration for a narrative about something shared, a story about both oneself and others that will turn out in a particular way. . . . People consent to trust their desire for "a life" to institutions of intimacy; and it is hoped that the relations formed within those frames will turn out beautifully, lasting over the long duration, perhaps across generations. [But] this view of "a life" that unfolds intact within the intimate sphere represses, of course, another fact about it: the unavoidable troubles, the distractions and disruptions that make things

turn out in unpredictable scenarios . . . the instabilities of sexuality, money, expectation and exhaustion . . . the dramas of estrangement and betrayal . . . the spectacles of neglect and violence.[40]

In Berlant's terms, a narrative of intimacy is also a narrative of repressed violence; the concept of intimacy is itself counterintuitive. On the one hand, intimacy promises an invitation, a union, something shared, generative, in common. But that very invitation is also an injunction to a violent collision between public and private realms. Intimacy for Berlant is a corrupted, even impossible, concept: precisely, a gesture of intimacy is its own undoing, because to make a gesture of intimacy is to make intimacy public, and in that instant to destroy it. Even more, as Berlant argues, the very institutions of intimacy that support relations in common (the nuclear family, et cetera) also repress intimacy's inherent and internal violence.

In *A Book of Common Prayer*'s circumscription, Grace locates the "marriage bed as the true tropic of fever and disquiet" (84), and Charlotte dreams of intimate violence and sexual punishment, of "sexual surrender and infant death, commonplaces of the female obsessional life" (57). Grace has "never known anyone who regarded the sexual connection as quite so unamusing a contract"; Charlotte's sense of intimacy's freighted gestures makes her "incapable of walking normally across a room in the presence of two men with whom she ha[s] slept." Grace, a scholar of kinship structures and intimate relations across cultures, recalls "once telling Charlotte about a village in the Orinoco where female children were ritually cut on the inner thigh by their first sexual partners, the point being to scar the female with the male's totem. Charlotte saw nothing extraordinary in this. 'I mean that's pretty much what happens everywhere, isn't it,' she said. 'Somebody cuts you? Where it doesn't show?'" Grace is "not even certain if she is talking figuratively" (85–86). Instead, we have Charlotte's "rather demented account" of her past intimacies, in which she claims that she and her daughter Marin "are inseparable" (48), even though Marin has vanished after committing a series of attacks on American soil and Charlotte has not heard from her in over a year. The utterly severed connection between Marin and Charlotte is emphasized by a litany of intimate ironies, as Charlotte insists on her "inseparability" with others and represses the violence of intimacy's institutional frames. In fact, her "inseparability"—in ironic quotation marks in the text—is repeatedly violated: with Warren Bogart, her sexually abusive, twice-abandoned, and now-dying first husband; with Leonard Douglas, her emotionally abusive and similarly abandoned second husband; and with Dickie, her estranged and taunting brother (111). And at the same time that she pretends to have immutable connections that do not exist, Charlotte's own sense of the sexual connection has her telling one lover that "I wasn't connected to you actually" (265), and another that "I think I fucked you one Easter. I think I did that and forgot it" (235). But in either case, Grace says, "Of course it had not been exactly that way at all" (111).

Charlotte's stories too, therefore, are a continuous series of retakes—Grace calls them her "revisions and erasures" (62)—that refigure the connections of intimacy. According to Grace, she reworks her story of intimacy, at once severing connections and reshaping events "to coincide with her own view of human behavior" (62). She "could make no connection between the pitiless revolutionary" the FBI men describe to her and her memories of the "sweet, soft" candy-striper daughter "who at seven had stood on a chair to make her own breakfast and wept helplessly when asked to clean her closet" (58). She deliberately misreads the conjunction—the connecting word—in the slogan of Marin's Episcopal school by reading their Good Citizens approach, "the development of a realistic but optimistic attitude," as instead "realistic and optimistic" (68). When Marin's terrorist group sends out a tape, she transcribes its slogan "word for word" but cannot parse the connection of the circular rhetoric: "The fact that our organization is revolutionary in character is due above all to the fact that all our activity is defined as revolutionary." That is, she "could parse the sentence but she could make no sense of it, could find no way to rephrase it. . . . She wondered if she had misheard Marin, or missed an important clause" (82). Her own answers to Marin's childhood questions are also rhetorically confused, and confusing; they "strike the child as weird and unsettling, cheerful but not quite responsive. 'Do you think I'll get braces in fourth grade,' Marin would ask. 'You're going to love fourth grade,' Charlotte would answer" (112). Charlotte's language of disconnection and mistaken intimacy thus recalls the grammar of her letters. Grace describes Charlotte's reading one letter aloud: "'The outlook is not at all bright . . . Nor is the outlook all black.' Paragraph. 'Nonetheless—' and then breaking off. 'That's where I seem to be blocked,'" she says. Grace tries to explain to Charlotte the impossible grammar of her sentences, the linguistic insensibility that arises when a neither/nor construction is followed by "nevertheless," that "it can't possibly mean anything." But Charlotte ignores Grace's instruction or misses her point, insisting on her paratactic shift even if it is meaningless, even if it means she will never complete her letter. "'Anyway,' she says, creasing her paper in half as a schoolgirl would and putting it away, 'It's not just a new sentence. It's a new paragraph.'" Grace considers this a "graphic illustration of how the consciousness of the human organism is carried in its grammar" (233–34), in that Charlotte's very grammatical style forms her impossible intimacy.[41] Enduring generational connections (pace Berlant) are thus severed too. Charlotte tries to forget her past altogether ("remembering is shit," Charlotte's brother tells her [134]). She has come to Boca Grande precisely in order to "avoid the backward glance" (96).

The critics Victor Strandberg, Leonard Wilcox, and John McClure have read such moments in the novel as exemplifying a central narrative contest between passion and delusion, with Charlotte as the spiritual martyr of Grace's "sacred biography" or "saint's tale."[42] Such accounts hold *A Book of Common Prayer* to be emblematic of Didion's essentially conservative, romantic, frontier imagination. Charlotte is a martyr to Boca Grande who signifies the novel's Conradian pessimism, a damnation of the third world as evil and beyond hope.[43] McClure does grant that Didion "give[s] the lie to all simply celebratory rhetorics of development or liberation or progress," but he reads the ending of the novel as a sign of Didion's "trademark blanket contempt for political struggle," a failure of engagement and a retreat from politics that "we cannot afford."[44]

To construe the text's conservative politics as emerging in this series of scenes—Charlotte's ignored suggestions to change the putative facts of the CIA handbook; her unanswered letters to Washington, New York, and Cuba to promote international aid programs; her misreading of Latin American economics textbooks; her boutique and her volunteerism—seems to miss the point, however. Certainly Didion sees a failure of international exchange between the United States and its others. But as to the inconclusive narrative of Charlotte's story, it is not entirely clear that Grace is interested in telling Charlotte's story at all: "I am interested in Charlotte Douglas . . . only insofar as the meaning of [her] sojourn continues to elude me" (21). As it happens, there is something at stake in erasing herself from the narrative, because Grace's story of Charlotte is an alibi for her own story of delusion and discovery; even as Grace asserts her narrative authority—"Charlotte would call her story one of passion. I believe I would call it one of delusion" (12)—by the end of the story she finds herself "less and less certain that this story has been one of delusion. Unless the delusion was mine" (272). "It occurred to me," she remarked earlier, looking at her spindly roses being sprayed by a perpetual haze of DDT, "that my attempt to grow roses and a lawn at the equator was a delusion worthy of Charlotte Douglas" (206). What in fact occurs to Grace is that she and Charlotte are not so different after all, and this becomes both the central insight of her witness account and also the realization that she would repress. When describing Charlotte "talk[ing] as if she had no specific history of her own," Grace signals Charlotte's problem with intimacy, but when we are told that the apparent absent-mindedness of Charlotte's "reflexive monologues she tended to initiate at the instant of distraction" also has "the same protective function that ink has for a squid" (203), we can read a model for Grace's own strategy too, in the ink that she spills in her text, the reflexive monologues that cover over or distract from the narrative she wants to avoid, the stories that she would "prefer not to know" or tell (69). Grace insists on not knowing, on the undecidable quality of empirical evidence, on the failure of intimacy, because to admit her certainty or her own motive role in the narrative is also to admit her culpability in the political chaos of Boca Grande, in the security of her own position, and in Charlotte's death. Thus she refuses narrative certainty precisely at the moment when she finds out that her husband Edgar earlier obtained the hardware for a guerrilla insurgency via Charlotte's second husband Leonard, the lawyer-cum–gun runner. As Leonard Wilcox points out, these are the same guns, the same hardware, used by the guerrilla insurgency in the October violence when Charlotte is killed.[45] In other words, Leonard Douglas, Grace, and Charlotte are all implicated in a certain kind of impossible intimacy that structures the geopolitical context of relations between North, Central, and South America. And in order for Grace not to admit the violent relations of international intimacy that she is implicated in, she must remain a failed witness to the terror and intrigue in Boca Grande.

It is critical that the setting for the novel is postcolonial Boca Grande, with its fevers, bacteria, termites, rust, and parasitical insects (155), and its morbid, "opaque equatorial light" (14). "Boca Grande is relentlessly 'the same,'" Grace says. Poverty and wealth are "obdurately indistinguishable" (15), and while "the politics of the country first appear to offer contrast, involving as they do the 'colorful' Latin juxtaposition of *guerrilleros* and colonels, when the tanks are put away and the airport reopens nothing has actually changed in Boca Grande" (13). The narrative imagination fails in Boca Grande: "Boca Grande is the name of the country and Boca Grande is also the name of the city, as if the place defeated the imagination of even its first settler," as does the historical imagination: "Information is missing here. Evidence goes unrecorded. Every time the sun falls on a day in Boca Grande that day seems to vanish from local memory, to be reinvented if necessary but never recalled. I once asked the librarian at the Intellectual Union to recommend for Charlotte a history of Boca Grande. 'Boca Grande has no history,' the librarian said, as if we had together hit upon a catechistic point of national pride" (14). But if it is Charlotte who initially fails to see "the point" of Boca Grande, by the end it is Grace who "no longer know[s] where the real points are" (268). Indeed the question of the point recurs throughout the text, but the im/possibility of recovering *A Book of Common Prayer*'s point remains a political irony. Recalling the revenue-generating planes that stop in Boca Grande on their way to Bogotá or Quito is not, as it happens, an offhand geographical point of interest at all, as it is in fact in one of those places that Leonard Douglas went to "meet the man" who financed the Tupamaros. That is, he met Edgar, Grace's husband. Charlotte apparently cannot remember in which city they met, and Grace only obliquely hints, but she eventually comes to understand that Boca Grande is indeed the economic fulcrum at the center of her narrative: Leonard and Edgar met for their hardware deal in Bogotá. In fact, Charlotte is only seemingly oblivious. It is she who sends Grace the emerald ring that she always wore in place of a wedding ring—"a memento from the man who financed the Tupamaros" (271).

The geopolitics of the text thus emerges via an ironic figure of intimacy, a spatial-temporal narrative frame in which past, present, and future events and places are not coincidental or singular moments but deeply relational events-in-common that imbricate one another. Yet these relations and imbrications are also intimated but denied, violated, and undone. Indeed, the irony of intimacy in *A Book of Common Prayer* comes to the fore in the embassy party scene, in which Charlotte regales others with her stories of guns and caviar, and in which we have the text's explicit suggestion of her "impossible intimacy." There the U.S. ambassador in Boca Grande remarks that "we're making great headway with the People-to-People program . . . Leaps and bounds" (39). The ambassador's remark, which of course recalls the Jaycees' astonishingly erroneous brand of People-to-People intimacy in "Good Citizens," thus augurs the ironic operative rhetoric of the novel. In a later scene, Didion underscores that rhetorical operation as "solecism" when she describes a violent argument between Leonard and Warren about the ethics of involvements in international affairs (94). In fact, *solecism* is a rhetorical figure of violence referring precisely to impossible intimacy, what the second edition of the *Oxford English Dictionary* defines as "a faulty concord."[46] *A Book of Common Prayer* thus seeks to account for that solecism, to apprehend intimacy that is not only "in common" but also (pace Spivak and Berlant) inextricably linked with insecurity and violence. In plotting postcolonial intimacy's "faulty concord," in other words, Didion offers her Cold War reading lesson.

NOTES

1. Gayatri Chakravorty Spivak, *A Critique of Postcolonial Reason: Toward a History of the Vanishing Present* (Cambridge, MA: Harvard University Press, 1999). Subsequent quotations from this work will be cited parenthetically within the text and notes.

2. As Spivak writes, the postcolonial critic gained traction by "foster[ing] the consideration of the old Third World as distant cultures, exploited but with rich literary heritages waiting to be recovered, interpreted, and curricularized" into the first-world academy (*A Critique* 113).

3. Gayatri Chakravorty Spivak, *Death of a Discipline* (New York: Columbia University Press, 2003). Subsequent quotations from this work will be cited parenthetically within the text and notes. See John Mowitt, *Re-takes: Postcoloniality and Foreign Film Languages* (Minneapolis: University of Minnesota Press, 2005) for his reading of the cinematic retake as a critical strategy for postcolonial critique. Although outside the purview of this chapter, Didion's signature narrative technique as a cinematic novelist operates via the retake as well.

4. Thomas Mallon, "Joan Didion: Trail's End," in *In Fact: Essays on Writers and Writing* (New York: Pantheon, 2001), 31–34, 31.

5. Spivak's line from *A Critique of Postcolonial Reason* reads: "[travestied philosophy] can justify the imperialist project by producing the following formula: make the heathen into a human so that he can be treated as an end in himself; in the interest of admitting the raw man into the noumenon; yesterday's imperialism, today's 'Development'" (123–24).

6. Joan Didion, *The White Album.* 1979 (New York: Farrar, Straus and Giroux, 1990), 93. Subsequent quotations from this work will be cited parenthetically within the text.

7. My argument is that Didion refuses to traffic in the kind of neoliberal discourse that makes the work of someone such as Martha Nussbaum so particularly irritating to Spivak. In fact, Spivak describes her impatience with this failure of exchange in a long footnote on Nussbaum in a 2004 essay that elaborates on the concerns in *A Critique of Postcolonial Reason* and *Death of a Discipline*. Gayatri Chakravorty Spivak, "Righting Wrongs," *SAQ* 103, nos. 2 and 3 (2004): 523–81. Nussbaum's

concept of the literary imagination, Spivak argues, construes the same "sympathetic identification, a bringing of the other into the self" of humanist discourse (self-identification, trained emotion, ethical judgment) that she is allegedly trying to critique (566–68). The figure of Nussbaum appears again in Cathy Caruth, "Interview with Gayatri Spivak," *PMLA* 125, no. 4 (October 2010): 1020–25. That interview refers to "the legacy of the eighteenth century, Martha Nussbaum et al. The European eighteenth century did not finally work in the interest of a just world" (1023).

8. Joan Didion, *A Book of Common Prayer*. 1977 (New York: Vintage, 1995); Joan Didion, *Democracy*. 1984 (New York: Vintage, 1995); and Joan Didion, *The Last Thing He Wanted* (New York: Vintage, 1996). Subsequent quotations from these works will be cited parenthetically within the text.

9. Diane Johnson, *Terrorists and Novelists* (New York: Alfred A. Knopf, 1982), 131, my emphasis. Critics frequently note the influence of imperial and neoimperial fictions in Didion's work. See John McClure, *Late Imperial Romance* (New York: Verso, 1994). McClure reads *A Book of Common Prayer* "as a reverent rewriting of *Heart of Darkness*, which it echoes in any number of ways: in the structure of its plot, with its drama of descent, disorientation, illumination, and death, and in its narrative structure as a survivor's tale complicated by the survivor's uncertainty as to what she has seen" (78). See also Peter S. Prescott, "Didion's Grace," in *The Critical Response to Joan Didion*, ed. Sharon Felton (Westport, CT: Greenwood, 1994), 97–98. Prescott notes Joseph Conrad in the novel's "morally obtuse narration" and Graham Greene in its "rotting ambience" (98). Patricia Merivale in "Through Greene-Land in Drag: Joan Didion's *A Book of Common Prayer*," *Pacific Coast Philology* 15 (1980): 45–52, has traced *A Book of Common Prayer*'s debts particularly to Greene's *The Quiet American*, in its "strange blend . . . of shabby-exotic tropical setting, topical reference, political content, and random explosions almost as inept as the inadvertent acts of heroism" (46–47).

10. See Elizabeth Hardwick, "In the Wasteland: Joan Didion," in *Sight-Readings: American Fictions* (New York: Random House, 1998), 147–57. Hardwick describes the novel's title as "a daring title, a risk, even, some would name a presumption" (153).

11. Gayatri Chakravorty Spivak, *Outside in the Teaching Machine* (New York: Routledge, 1993), 171.

12. Spivak writes that "we stand outside, but not as anthropologists; we stand rather as reader with imagination ready for the effort of othering, however imperfectly, as an end in itself" (*Death of a Discipline* 13).

13. Prescott, "Didion's Grace," 97.

14. Alan Nadel, *Containment Culture: American Narratives, Postmodernism, and the Atomic Age* (Durham, NC: Duke University Press, 1995), 276–78.

15. Hardwick, "In the Wasteland," 147–48.

16. McClure, *Late Imperial Romance*, 56. Discussions of such narrative strategies can be found in Samuel Chase Coale, *In Hawthorne's Shadow: American Romance from Melville to Mailer* (Lexington: University of Kentucky Press, 1985); Carol Hult, "Metonymy and Metaphor in Joan Didion: A Personal Grammar of Style," in *The Peirce Seminar Papers* vol. 3, ed. Michael Shapiro (New York: Peter Lang, 1998): 59–73; Janis P. Stout, *Strategies of Reticence: Silence and Meaning in the Works of Jane Austen, Willa Cather, Katherine Anne Porter and Joan Didion* (Charlottesville: University Press of Virginia, 1990); and Gordon O. Taylor, *Studies in Modern American Autobiography* (New York: Macmillan, 1983).

17. Emily Apter, "On Oneworldedness: Or Paranoia as a World System," *American Literary History* 18, no. 2 (2006): 365–89, 387.

18. Taylor, *Studies in Modern American Autobiography*, 139.

19. Ross Posnock, "A Great Memoir! At Last!" *New Republic*, 19 February 2010. Web. See John Lahr, "Entrepreneurs of Anxiety," *Horizon*, January 1981, 36–37. She is "alienation in a twin set," declared Lahr (36).

20. Alfred Kazin, *The Bright Book of Life* (Notre Dame, IN: University of Notre Dame Press, 1980), 191–95.

21. David Klinghoffer, "Putting Down Didion Thriller is the Last Thing Reader Will Do," *Washington Times* (15 September 1996): 15. Web.

22. Susanna Rustin, "Legends of the Fall," *Guardian* (21 May 2005). Web.

23. Martin Amis, *The Moronic Inferno and Other Visits to America* (New York: Viking, 1987), 167.

24. Catharine Stimpson, "The Case of Miss Joan Didion," *Ms.*, January 1973, 36–41, 36.

25. McClure, *Late Imperial Romance*, 63–64.

26. Michiko Kakutani, "Joan Didion: Staking Out California," *New York Times* (10 June 1979). Web. Kakutani argues that the "'Didion woman' has by now become a recognizable literary figure. . . . Women who have misunderstood the promises of the past, they are habitués of a clearly personal wasteland, wandering along highways or through countries in an effort to blot out the pain of consciousness."

27. Leonard Wilcox, "Narrative Technique and the Theme of Historical Continuity in the Novels of Joan Didion," in *Joan Didion: Essays and Conversations*, ed. Ellen G. Friedman (Princeton, NJ: Ontario Review Press, 1984), 68–80, 71.

28. McClure, *Late Imperial Romance*, 56.

29. Joyce Carol Oates, "A Taut Novel of Disorder," *New York Times Book Review* (3 April 1977). Web.

30. Joan Didion, *Slouching Towards Bethlehem*. 1968 (New York: Farrar, Straus and Giroux, 1990), xvi.

31. Hardwick, "In the Wasteland," 147–48.

32. Nancy K. Miller, "The Entangled Self: Genre Bondage in the Age of the Memoir," *PMLA* 122, no. 2 (March 2007): 537–48, 545.

33. See Nadel, *Containment Culture*. In his reading of *Democracy*, Nadel argues that Didion's "attack" on the "conventional boundaries between reader and text, fact and fiction" implicates the reader in a central narrative "crisis of authorial authority" that intensifies the novel's deconstruction of the national allegory itself (102–4).

34. Ellen Willis, "From Democracy to Demagogy," *Women's Review of Books* 19, no. 2 (November 2001): 7–8, 7. See also Vivian Gornick, "The Prose of Nothingness," *Women's Review of Books* 14, no. 3 (December 1996): 6–7. Gornick writes, "To some readers she appeared a conservative writer turning liberal; others, like myself, thought her a conservative turning libertarian" (6).

35. John Leonard, introduction to Joan Didion's *We Tell Ourselves Stories in Order to Live: Collected Nonfiction* (New York: Everyman's Library, 2006), xv.

36. Sara Davidson, "A Visit with Joan Didion," in Friedman, *Joan Didion*, 13–21, 20.

37. See Judith Kegan Gardiner, "Evil, Apocalypse and Feminist Fiction," *Frontiers: A Journal of Women Studies* 7, no. 2 (1983): 74–80. Gardiner notes that the failed witness in *A Book of Common Prayer* reflects Didion's "epistemological insecurity about what one can and cannot know" (78). See also John Hollowell, "Against Interpretation: Narrative Strategy in *A Book of Common Prayer*," in Friedman, *Joan Didion*, 164–76. Hollowell argues that the novel's narrative structure of the failed promise promotes Didion's theory of fiction as "an illusive surface without a final meaning" (164).

38. See Stout, *Strategies of Reticence*. Janis Stout reads Charlotte as a figure of blankness whose stories are "inspired by absences" (173).

39. Didion regards this as the key line. See Linda Kuehl, "Joan Didion: The Art of Fiction No. 71," *Paris Review* (Fall–Winter 1978). Web. "When I heard Charlotte say this," Didion tells *Paris Review*, "I had a very clear fix on who she was" (13).

40. Lauren Berlant, "Intimacy: A Special Issue," *Critical Inquiry* 24 (1998): 281–88, 281.

41. Later Grace describes Marin's grammar as, like her mother's, the rhetoric of "a daughter who never had much use for words but had finally learned to string them together so that they sounded almost like sentences" (*A Book of Common Prayer* 214). In Didion's dictum, "*Style is character*" (*White Album* 127).

42. See McClure, *Late Imperial Romance*; Victor Strandberg, "Passion and Delusion in *A Book of Common Prayer*," in Friedman, *Joan Didion*, 147–63; and Wilcox, "Narrative Technique and the Theme of Historical Continuity in the Novels of Joan Didion," in Friedman, *Joan Didion*, 68–80.

43. Jane Harred makes a similar claim in her reading of *Salvador*. See Jane Harred, "The Heart of Darkness in Joan Didion's *Salvador*," *College Literature* 25, no. 2 (1998): 1–16.

44. McClure, *Late Imperial Romance*, 86.

45. Wilcox, "Narrative Technique and the Theme of Historical Continuity in the Novels of Joan Didion," 78.

46. *Solecism* is both a grammatical error ("an impropriety or irregularity in speech or diction; a violation of the rules of grammar or syntax; a faulty concord") and a violation of manners ("a breach or violation of good manners or etiquette; a blunder or impropriety; an error, incongruity, inconsistency, or impropriety of any kind").

III The Global Cold War

6 PYONGYANG LOST

COUNTERINTELLIGENCE AND OTHER FICTIONS OF THE FORGOTTEN WAR

CHRISTINE HONG

The task of intelligence is thus to penetrate into the forbidden and protected space, cross borders, and investigate the enemy's territory. This space is by definition an uncharted, secret-filled, necessarily dangerous zone.—Eva Horn, "Knowing the Enemy"

Ruse de guerre

In his preface to *The Hidden History of the Korean War* (1952), an investigative report published when "truce talks [were being] dragged out" and the prospect of peace was serially deferred, American journalist I. F. Stone likened writing the Korean War's "hidden history" to "writing a novel, with suspense and with three-dimensionality."[1] After a series of plot twists and turns, Stone, whose initial investigative pieces on the war were titled "The Korean Mystery" and "The Origins of the Korean War," arrived at a military-Keynesian explanation for U.S. involvement in the Cold War's first hot war. Presaging a permanent war economy with "new Koreas in the making" (348), the war—which Stone described as a "deadly stimulant"—was seized upon by an "American leadership . . . gripped by dread of the consequences of peace upon the economy" (346, 347). That the war sparked an "economic boom" domestically and "legitimated the unprecedented, worldwide garrisoning of large numbers of American troops in a network of bases"—in essence furnishing the occasion for a militarized remapping of the globe that in turn enabled the "reconstruction of a world market under American auspices"—is an argument that has since been more intricately theorized and elaborated.[2] What Stone's account strikingly modeled, however, was a hermeneutics for reading the Korean War that exploited the narrative method of U.S. war planners and politicians while taking inspiration from detective fiction. Seeking to challenge the fictitiousness of U.S. war propaganda with truth told in a novelistic spirit, Stone strategically mobilized narrative as a mode of speaking truth to power. Beyond simply borrowing its structuring logic from the official proclamations he subjected to scrutiny, *The Hidden History of the Korean War* wielded narrative as a malleable form whose very instrumentality derived from and therefore must be understood within the context of war.

Offering what he called "a case study in the Cold War" (xvi), Stone's report pointed damningly to the role of narrative pretext in the instigation of U.S. military interventionism abroad, thereby calling attention to the lethal instrumentalization of information in U.S. and South Korean etiological accounts of the Korean War. That the war was triggered on June 25, 1950, by a "North Korean invasion" across the thirty-eighth parallel, belligerence that U.S. Army intelligence failed to anticipate, is not just a commonplace in U.S. and South Korean historiography of the war.[3] As the casus belli at the core of the U.S.–South Korean alliance, it has served as the rationale for the unleashing of massive U.S. military might in defense of its ally and for the expanding of its garrison state to the Korean peninsula. In a July 19, 1950, radio address to a national audience estimated at 130 million, President Truman, deploring North Korea's "sneak attack," argued along ideological "free world" lines that "what [was] happening" in Korea was vital to every American "detesting communist slavery." Aimed at building consensus for armed U.S. intervention, Truman's speech called for government subsidies for "private industry to increase defense production."[4] Although the Korean Liaison Offices (KLO), which had four times as many operatives in North Korea as the CIA, who "filed a total of 1,195 reports" in the lead-up to June 25, 1950, the question "as to why the U.S. apparently did not exploit this information to better prepare itself" remains to be reckoned with. Was "U.S. 'failure' to act on this intelligence," as Mark Caprio asks, "truly a result of problems of communication or outright incompetence, or was it a planned 'failure' consistent with a calculated strategy?"[5]

In briefly returning focus to the original emplotments of the war, accounts that turn on North Korea's violation of the thirty-eighth parallel and that historically legitimized the UN march northward, I do not mean to rehearse debates over which side "started" the war. Rather, adapting Hayden White, I wish to consider how intelligence, as a narrative-generating logic of war, conditions "the 'meaning' of a story."[6] Relative to boundary-crossing accounts of the Korean War, in particular, how do we theorize the correspondence of text to context when the latter is fundamentally distorted by ideological warfare? Identified with an antitriumphalist image of a startled United States reluctantly drawn into freedom's defense in a godforsaken corner of the globe, "first shot" emplotments of the war, it must be noted, are inadequate to the task of explaining why the last shot has not been assuredly fired; relative to the war's remarkable perdurance, they function as something of a red herring. Although they might have justified U.S. entry into the war, narratives of unprovoked North Korean aggression have been marshaled to perpetuate an unyielding state of hostilities on the Korean peninsula and to defer the publication of "restorative truths" with regard to the war.[7] The question that I wish to consider is how incursionary war narratives, including those insisting upon U.S. and South Korean intelligence failure, are instrumentalized within a fraught discursive field conditioned by counterintelligence, by an epistemology of war that paradoxically militates against knowledge. How has counterintelligence, as a critical subset of intelligence directed toward neutralizing the enemy on a politicized terrain of information, destabilized the category of truth as an end unto itself? If the Korean War reportedly began with intelligence failure, to what degree can its irresolution be attributed to the effectiveness of counterintelligence?

At midcentury, journalist Claude Bourdet hailed Stone's Korean War reports as exposing "the greatest swindle in the whole of military history," a "terrible maneuver in which deception is being consciously utilized to block peace at a time when it is possible."[8] For Stone, disinformation could not be reduced to "simplistic" salvos launched by one side or the other, much less to plain "lying" (xvi). Nor for that matter were clandestine policies or intelligence work the overt focus of his study, even as these hovered as untheorized context in the margins of his analysis. Instead, Stone contended that deception must be understood in terms of the official U.S. fixation on surface details of who, what, where, and how—details that distracted from the more inculpatory question of why. Taking the form of obfuscation and narrative misdirection, the official position on "the outbreak of the Korean War," Stone implied, was a *ruse de guerre*:

> The White Paper issued by the American State Department spoke of it as a "surprise attack." The United Nations Commission on Korea reported that South Korean forces "were taken completely by surprise as they had no reason to believe from intelligence sources that invasion was imminent." General Douglas MacArthur's biographer . . . wrote that "the South Koreans and Americans in Korea, to say nothing of SCAP [MacArthur Headquarters] in Tokyo, were taken utterly by surprise." (1)

Reading these official statements of total U.S. "surprise" against the grain, Stone conceded that "who started the war and how" might have been something of "a mystery" (345). In contrast, answers to the question *why* relative to U.S. involvement and the deferral of peace could be arrived at by discerning readers of "United Nations documents," "respected American and British newspaper sources," "the North Korean Blue Book," and "Vishinsky's speeches at the United Nations" (xv)—in short, publicly accessible materials.

Conducting his investigation when NSC-68 and other Cold War policy documents were still classified and "writing in an atmosphere much like that of a full war" (xv), Stone asserted that "'inside stuff' or keyhole revelations" (xvi) would not be had within the pages of his report. Strategically limiting himself to "material which could not be challenged by those who accept the official American government point of view," Stone, seeking to "put the people of the United States and the United Nations on guard," alerted his readers to the narrative dimensions of ideological warfare: "Emphasis, omission, and distortion rather than outright lying are the tools of the war propagandists" (xv, xvi). Maintaining that the war's "hidden history" could be gleaned from "facts to be found in the official accounts themselves" (xvi), he closed his report with the words of General James Van Fleet, the commander of the Eighth Army, who in early 1952 guilelessly stated: "'Korea has been a blessing. There had to be a Korea either here or some place in the world'" (quoted 348). Echoes of Van Fleet's "simpleminded confession" (*Hidden History* 348) resonated in the transparency of Dean Acheson, Truman's secretary of state, who "was clearly not exaggerating when he stated in 1954 that 'Korea came along and saved us.'"[9] If U.S. liberation of South Korea from the forces of global Communism was driven by efforts to engineer economic salvation at home, the truth of this rationale, Stone argued, was hidden in plain sight.

Stone's exposé paradoxically helped to inaugurate a paradigm whereby the Korean War would be negatively registered as hidden, forgotten, unknown. With its unremarkable character ironically its most salient feature within a U.S. context, the Korean War corresponds to an intransigent historiographical problematic. As a "structured absence," an "ellipsis" wrought by the Cold War's disjunctional geopolitics, the Korean War "masks a reality in which we [in the United States] are all a product of Korea whether we know it or not":

> It was the Korean War, not Greece or Turkey or the Marshall Plan or Vietnam, that inaugurated big defense budgets and the national security state, that transformed a limited containment doctrine into a global crusade, that ignited McCarthyism just as it seemed to fizzle, and thereby gave the Cold War its long run.[10]

Although Stone did not anticipate the Korean War's ensuing legacy of obscurity in his midcentury analysis of its "hidden history," we might extrapolate the basis of a Cold War "cognitive mapping" from his fledgling discussion of military Keynesianism as a world-ordering system.[11] If World War II's total-war economy was associated with visible icons, slogans, and campaigns of a victory culture, the Korean War's limited-war economy by contrast gave rise to "structural coordinates" that obscured the war's impact domestically and internationally.[12] Immeasurably accelerating the militarization of American society, the war represented "a watershed for American involvement in Asia."[13] Yet it often appears as a hot sideshow in U.S. Cold War cultural studies.[14] Relative to the United States, the war may have been "limited, both geographically and in weapons employed," its political, ideological, and economic transformation of the domestic landscape notwithstanding. For Koreans, however, the war was "the most devastating they had ever experienced."[15] As Allan Millett states, the war "does not look the same to Koreans as it does to all the other participants."[16]

The unevenness of the Korean War's phenomenological, epistemological, and mnemonic terrain goes some distance toward explaining its negative registration on the American historical consciousness. If "official memories and knowledge of the war" have been reified as "pillars of both [the northern and southern] regimes and guarantors of their existence," as South Korean sociologist Kim Dong-Choon states, conversely, forgettableness has been enshrined as the war's characteristic feature within the United States.[17] Of the Cold War's riven memory politics, Asian studies scholars remark that "the U.S.–South Korea security relationship" remains "one of the longest-standing restraints" on the articulation and integration of war memory.[18] It is perhaps no stretch to say that few Americans know the scope and scale of the ruin that Korea experienced, that "the number of people killed, wounded, and missing approached three million, a tenth of the entire population," "ten million Koreans saw their families divided," and "five million became refugees."[19] Noted Korean

War historian Bruce Cumings writes that North Koreans were subjected to a "bombing holocaust" by the United States: "they suffered one of the most appalling, unrestrained, genocidal bombing campaigns in our genocidal twentieth century" and ever since have been "shouting themselves hoarse at a nation of amnesiacs, who aren't listening."[20] However much the Korean War might once have been regarded as the defining conflict of the classic Cold War era, it now complicates narrow "truths" about the Cold War, be they naïve definitions of the latter as "the absence of outright war," or universalizing assumptions regarding its end around the globe.[21] Never resolved by a peace treaty, the Korean War did not "end with the breaching of the Berlin Wall in 1989 and the collapse of the Soviet Union in 1991."[22] Far from it: the United States still stations nearly thirty thousand troops in South Korea, and war remains the volatile substrate of U.S.–North Korean and intra-Korean relations. Although it might therefore be tempting to conclude that the Korean War has become the exception to the Cold War norm, what if it were considered as precedent and paradigm? What are the broader implications of the apparent contradiction that it poses? As the first hot war of the Cold War, a brutally indiscriminate intervention into the third world in which the United States placed the nuclear option on the table, and an unended conflict that resists triumphalist periodizations of the Cold War's close, the Korean War points to permanent war as the discomfiting "long-run" truth of the Cold War.

Persistently "treated by many Western commentators as though it were a black hole in outer space, where a war just happened to happen . . . in June 1950," the Korean War is structured by "near-complete ignorance."[23] Though superficially explained by an infelicitous "sandwich[ing] between 'the good war' and the 'bad war,'" the absence or erasure of the war from U.S. historical consciousness demands careful theorization, particularly in light of the war's irresolution.[24] Scholars are "trained to trust only the verifiable printed word," yet the war's "ulterior history," as Cumings suggests in his landmark study *The Origins of the Korean War*, is resistant to traditional evidentiary recovery.[25] As he writes, "ultimately a dogged empiricism becomes a kind of misguided zealotry" (*Origins* 11). Though his aim is not to contest the methodology of I. F. Stone, whom he lauds as "almost alone in his spirit of principled dissent" (*Origins* 106), Cumings implicitly questions Stone's proposition that the war's "hidden history" can be empirically recovered from "the official accounts themselves." In 1952, Stone acknowledged the limitations of his investigation when he surmised as likely an "unsavory secret history no outsider yet knows" (*Hid-*

den History 21). Some four decades following the publication of Stone's investigative report, Cumings updated the assessment: "at the empirical level we have much that remains to be explained about the mysterious realm of intelligence politics" (*Origins* 123). Operating during the Cold War with little scrutiny, U.S. intelligence agencies, by their nature largely impervious to scholarly methods of research and inquiry, have posed a challenge to Korean War historiography. As an intentionally opaque arena of U.S. national security infrastructure where "formal and informal action meet," the world of intelligence, as Cumings puts it, has little "respect for [the historical record], consigning facts to a never-to-be-opened dustbin of history" (*Origins* 122).

Not merely a feature of the war, what Cumings calls "hidden intelligence politics" is essential context for "the rollback impulse and the beginning of the Korean War," which are otherwise "inexplicable" (*Origins* 122). Military historians readily concede that the war signaled "a major milestone in the development of Army Intelligence," giving rise to counterintelligence as a signature Cold War weapon, with applications on and off the battlefield and operations abroad and at home.[26] Indeed, there is a vast expository literature devoted to this globally far-reaching arena of Cold War power politics, "the newest of the proliferating bureaucracies of the national security state," endowed with "munificent budgets" (*Origins* 124) and great discretionary authority. Relative to the Korean War, however, histories of battlefield intelligence typically train their focus on U.S., South Korean, and British exploits.[27] Few if any analyze intelligence as a structuring logic of the war, much less its role in the war's continuation. As the "'*fourth dimension of war*' in addition to the famous 'communication, control, command,'" intelligence may be the least recoverable in terms of documents, yet this does not mean that it is beyond analysis.[28] We might ask, To what extent does the miasma of ignorance about the Korean War stem from an active "epistemology of enmity" ("Knowing the Enemy" 64), namely, the governing logic of intelligence? How does narrative misdirection, what Stone called "emphasis, omission, and distortion," figure into this unorthodox epistemology? Taking the enemy rather than knowledge as its object, intelligence, which compasses counterintelligence, is dually structured, "includ[ing] not only information retrieval but also disinformation" ("Knowing the Enemy" 62). Not limited to what field operatives call "positive" intelligence, or "the gathering of dependable information on the enemy," intelligence extends into the art of deception, the "misleading of the enemy" ("Knowing the Enemy" 62) and of the public. In any case directionally aimed against the enemy, intelligence is justified by its ends and has little to do with the pursuit of verifiable truth. Valued insofar as it is tactically or strategically useful, intelligence thus destabilizes the category of knowledge itself. It is, moreover, precisely this irreducibility of information to evidence that renders fiction, as I contend, a potent instrument of political warfare.

Espionage through Other Means

Near the end of *The Martyred* (1964), Richard Kim's critically acclaimed, best-selling Korean War novel, the narrator Captain Lee pauses to cast a final glance upon Pyongyang as the bridge he has just crossed over is blasted by the rear guard.[29] As the convoy of trucks evacuating U.S. and South Korean units to the South comes to a standstill, Lee "look[s] back toward Pyongyang," only to see the "doomed city" consumed "in flames."[30] This haunting image of ruin, with its evocation of Sodom and Gomorrah, marks a point of no return for the young South Korean, who henceforth is cut off from the North Korean capital. Ablaze in the distance, the Pyongyang that has hitherto furnished the novel's location effectively no longer exists. Yet if the "doomed city" is from this moment forward off-limits to U.S. and South Korean forces beating a retreat below the thirty-eighth parallel, Lee, by violating the biblical injunction not to look back, reveals a lingering orientation to and preoccupation with the city. As an officer with South Korea's Counterintelligence Corps (CIC), the "investigative arm of the Occupation Army" responsible in the novel for inquiring into and reconstructing Pyongyang's brutal history prior to its UN capture, Lee understands that possession of geographic terrain corresponds to narrative opportunity.[31] The UN withdrawal from the city and its imminent possession by Chinese and North Korean forces notwithstanding, the battle over the *story* of occupied Pyongyang in late 1950—as staged on the level of *The Martyred*'s narrative and demonstrated by the novel's publication—is bound to continue.[32] In Kim's self-reflexive account of the Korean War, which posits the first hot war of the Cold War as a strategic fiction and locates its ongoing contestation on discursive terrain, the exit of U.S. and South Korean forces thus comes with a weighty narrative charge. In particular, Lee's tormented rearward gaze raises the question of his accountability, not only in terms of his complicity in the devastation and suffering behind him, with the city's Christian population deserted, but also in terms of his future fidelity to the truth of what he, in the course of investigating the fate of the city's Christian leaders, has uncovered. With Pyongyang now lost and its fate ceded to the "enemy," how will the story of the occupation of the city early in the war be told, according to whose perspective, and to what ends?

Pointing to the quandary of geographic and temporal remove for exilic writers, novelist Salman Rushdie observes that "writers in [his] position, exiles or emigrants or expatriates, are haunted by some sense of loss, some urge to reclaim, to look back, even at the risk of being mutated into pillars of salt."[33] He adds, "But if we do look back, we must also do so in the knowledge—which gives rise to profound uncertainties—that our physical alienation . . . means that we will not be capable of reclaiming precisely the thing that was lost; that we will, in short, *create fictions*."[34] By approximating "the thing that was lost," fictionalization, for the exilic writer, stands in uneasy compensatory relation to the country of origin that has been left behind and is time-warped in memory. Yet a distinction must be drawn between the nostalgic reclamations that Rushdie identifies with postcolonial fiction of exile, on the one hand, and boundary-crossing acts of literary trespass, which can be encountered in Korean American and South Korean fiction of the Korean War, on the other. Although the retrospective gaze onto the North in novels such as *The Martyred* implicitly posits the prosecution of the war as a process of the past, literary preoccupation with and imaginative recoveries of the North, particularly in internationally marketed fiction on the war, demand theorization against the latter's ongoing irresolution. When it comes to the Korean War, collusion between war and letters cannot be neatly explained by the formulation that each is "a subset of the other," as some scholars assert.[35] Nor is it my intention to cast aspersions on the Korean American and South Korean authors of Korean War fiction, much less to imply that their literary ventures north of the thirty-eighth parallel stem from willful collaboration with the secret intelligence apparatuses of the U.S. or South Korean governments. My aim is rather to examine the destabilizing consequences of fiction of the war and in so doing to inquire into the latter's homology—in Raymond Williams's definition, a "correspondence of *forms* or *structures*"—with counterintelligence as an active operation of the unended Korean War.[36]

The backward gaze, I therefore submit, cannot be construed solely as a sign of engagement with a painful past, much less as a long-awaited thawing orientation within the realm of culture toward a Cold War conflict whose origins, historiography, and legacies have been the subject of much scholarly and political debate. However much it may be the case that "over time, it becomes possible to speak the hitherto unspeakable, to question official shibboleths, to probe the painful heart of memory" relative to the Korean War, and in so doing to open "forbidden zones," access to the North in boundary-crossing fiction must be understood against the war's temporality.[37] Narrative encroachment on the North in fiction of the Korean War does not simply mirror but rather draws its epistemic basis from the geospatial realities of the unending war on and the enduring national division of the peninsula. Such fiction is inextricably if inadvertently bound up with the deterritorializing logic of a war that has yet to come to an end.[38] Less an "imaginary homeland," to use Rushdie's phrase, than a forfeited site whose failed "liberation" at the hands of UN forces has long haunted U.S. and South Korean accounts of the war, North Korea, via the device of fiction, is regained, and we as readers are permitted access to terrain otherwise off-limits. Never an innocent or neutral practice, the imagination of enemy territory in Korean War fiction is a performative infringement and possessive articulation that cannot be dismissed as the stuff of mere fantasy. As Arjun Appadurai argues, "the image, the imagined, the imaginary—these are all terms that direct us to something critical and new in global cultural processes: *the imagination as a social practice*."[39] Intimately implicated in "the terror and coercion of states and their competitors,"[40] the distinctively literary processes of scenario, enactment, and reenactment are crucial to war's geospatial imaginary. In "Knowing the Enemy," a theoretical account of secret intelligence, Eva Horn contends that the "real spatial fantasies of the intelligence world are to be found in literary scenarios. Space is rendered intelligible and structured by its representation"; provocatively riffing on Clausewitz's war dictum, she argues that novels, as a "'continuation of espionage through other means,' develop spaces as semiotic structures" (74).

When, however, the extraliterary context is one of unresolved war, how should questions of space—or, for that matter, nation—be understood relative to the literature of that war? If war denotes less a state of affairs than a restructuring violence with shattering political and geographic consequences, then what are the organizing principles, spatial and national, of Korean War fiction? Drawing upon the insight that novelistic space operates according to a semiotic logic, we might further ask: if the thirty-eighth parallel, relative to the major national literatures of the Korean War (North Korean, South Korean, Chinese, American), functions as a defining "third term"—not just a "limiting situation," pace Fredric Jameson, but rather a deforming, if not destabilizing, situation—then to what degree must the utility of the rote interpretive concepts of setting, scene, and context be fundamentally rethought and the assumed stability of national literary categories challenged?[41] Of U.S. authorship of Korea's division into Soviet and U.S. occupation zones at the Pacific war's end by junior U.S. Army officers Dean Rusk and Charles Bonesteel, Bruce Cumings states, "from partition forward, war was predictable if not inevitable" (*Origins* 9), and he identifies the 1945 drafting of the thirty-eighth parallel without Korean input as one of the war's triggers. Given that "what started out as a temporary line" hardened as the Cold War intensified "into an impermeable wall" that "blocked the free movement of people and ideology," a civil war aimed at unifying the peninsula was sure to follow.[42] Not an international border, to be clear, but an imposed division that has lethally polarized the peninsula, the line bisecting the Koreas, neither of which constitutionally recognizes the other, has engendered an antagonistic topography, political economy, and cultural imaginary of war. As a Cold War structure of deferral (sovereignty, reunification, reconciliation, decolonization, peace), displacement (separated families, refugees), and disavowal (ongoing war, militarization, foreign military occupation, continued Cold War), the thirty-eighth parallel does not just shape narratives of the Korean War and international reception of such literature. By nullifying the basis of "true political independence" on which "national literary space" is predicated, it renders fiction an overdetermined arena of competing deterritorializing desires, with some narratives in what Pascale Casanova calls "the world republic of letters" more politically legible and potent than others.[43] Whether originally written in or translated into English or specifically marketed to an American readership, the various "national" literatures of the Korean War must be understood, in terms of their geospatial imaginaries, as mapped according to the U.S. hegemonic design that carved the Korean peninsula into contiguous zones of hostility. In light of the Korean War's ongoing irresolution, these literatures are unavoidably implicated, I argue, within a geopolitical structure of enmity.

Set for the most part north of the thirty-eighth parallel in the autumn interval between UN rollback northward toward the Yalu River and UN bugout southward, *The Martyred* offers an on-the-ground portrait of counterintelligence operations as the war rages at midcentury. Exhibiting, however, little fascination with the arcane or technical minutiae of covert warfare and in this regard departing from the detail-fetish of Cold War spy thrillers, *The Martyred* approaches the world of wartime counterintelligence specifically through a focus on the latter's fictionalizing strategies. If counterintelligence traditionally designates a range of operations aimed at deflecting enemy access to information and neutralizing "sabotage, subversion, and espionage," in Kim's novel, by contrast, it takes the form of anticommunist fabrications and political dramaturgy aimed at manipulating the Christian population of the North Korean capital and garnering sympathy from the Western world.[44] Offering a metafictional account of CIC activities as narrative operations aimed at swaying local and international popular opinion as well as at sabotaging the North Korean Communist regime, *The Martyred* highlights the strategic value of fiction in the ideological remapping of terrain deemed, in the novel's language, "Red." Not reducible to propaganda even as it churns propaganda out, counterintelligence in the novel corresponds to rollback's ideological and epistemological dimensions, with Pyongyang's ruins furnishing compositional grounds for the rearguard machinery of narrative. Neither an epiphenomenon of war, then, nor for that matter a rarefied question of aesthetics in the wake of world-shattering violence, fiction in *The Martyred* is a procedure of war vital to the success of rollback, which cannot secure territory through tanks and aerial strafing alone.

Described as forbidden turf, as "an enemy city that our victorious army occupied" (*Martyred* 12), Pyongyang is viewed through the retrospective lens of its loss and is limned, in Captain Lee's account, with a sense of defeat. Pyongyang "gained" gives way, as the novel unfolds, to Pyongyang "lost." Yet *The Martyred* intimates that counterintelligence designs on North Korean territory, which take shape during the occupation, persist well beyond the city's return to "the enemy." Temporally framed by Pyongyang's brief possession by UN forces, the novel's portrait of the city is predicated on the imperative of its ideological exploitation. Of the ease of the push northward, Lee notes that as "November progressed . . . [South] Korean Infantry and various U.N. troops on the western front were busily engaged in the final stage of mopping-up operations near the Yalu River," while "on the eastern front . . . U.N. Infantry and the American Marines, encountering little opposition, steadily made their way toward the Tumen River near Siberia" (44–45). With the war's front lines pushed to the peninsula's northern limits, "everyone was cheerful and hopeful," Lee recalls, "convinced that it would be all over by Christmas" (45). He too succumbs to the euphoric mood: "for the first few weeks, I was in a state of buoyancy . . . because of the irresistible enthusiasm and affection with which the people of the city greeted all of us, their liberators" (13). What gives the lie, however, to this account of ready allegiance are the elaborate lengths to which the CIC must go in crafting a narrative of "Red" inhumanity so as to rouse the local populace against the Communist regime. Less tabula rasa than palimpsest in which insufficiently effaced traces of the past unsettle the present, Pyongyang, contra Lee's description, might have been deserted by the "Reds," yet it has not been decisively won by its occupiers. Not simply an incidental backdrop to Lee's struggle for deep meaning as he investigates the truth of Communist war atrocities, "Pyongyang" is a site of active fictionalization.

Marking the North Korean capital in its trajectory from "enemy city" to "doomed city," rollback is represented as a feverish period of limbo, of intense ideological activity within the chaos of a bloody conflict whose battle lines morphed, as historical accounts indicate, while "warfare swept south and north several times."[45] Evidence of prior combat might be visible in the "debris-ridden," "bullet-riddled" (14) cityscape, yet war is almost abstract in *The Martyred*, its usual signs absent even as it is the rationale for access to Pyongyang in the first place. It is the latent unease of the occupied city that alerts us to its instability. Pyongyang, that is to say, is less a scene of active hostilities than a site whose devastation under the "Reds" is the object of CIC investigation and the narrative it wishes to broadcast to the world. Seized in the heat of the UN counteroffensive, the city, for most of Kim's novel, is a zone of wartime occupation and a highly sensitive "area of political intelligence" (18) targeted for ideological reconstruction. Littered with "demolished . . . gray carcass[es] of cross-topped" (15) churches, Pyongyang is a far cry from the vibrant center of Christian conversion famed at the turn of the century as "the Jerusalem of the East."[46] Yet these visible signs of destruction, of houses of worship reduced to skeletal frames, if not rubble, supply malleable material for the designs of army counterintelligence. Retrievable from the desolate ruins and rumored mass executions of church leaders by the Communist regime is a potent opportunity to propagandize local Christian residents. Time and again, counterintelligence agents remark the felicitous convergence between the faith of the city's Christian believers and the propaganda of the occupying forces. That the "wall between our [CIC] fairy tale and their reality [is] very thin" (229) makes for uneasy alliances along anticommunist lines. Pointing out that the "cause of Christianity in North Korea" handily "coincide[s] with our [interests]" (43, 42), the hard-bitten Colonel Chang attempts to impress upon Lee, his conscience-plagued subordinate, that the story of the war must be conscripted to strategic ends and that questions of truth are therefore immaterial. "'Can you tell a bevy of sweet old ladies and housewives or a flock of young students,'" Chang impatiently asks, that "'all their sufferings are worthwhile because this is a noble war we are fighting, that people, many, many people will have to be sacrificed in order to make sure that the cause of individual liberty . . . will survive and be maintained for us and for our posterity?'" (172).

> "Or, would you rather tell them that this war is just like any other bloody war in the stinking history of idiotic mankind, that it is nothing but the sickening result of a blind struggle for power among the beastly states, among the rotten politicians and so on, that thousands of people have died and more will die in this stupid war, for nothing, for absolutely nothing, because they are just innocent victims, helpless pawns in the arena of cold-blooded, calculating international power politics?" (173)

In this self-reflexive novel about fiction as a special operation of the war, these two South Korean counterintelligence officers, both professed "apostates" (164) from the Christian faith, are charged with the ironic task of transforming civilian executions at the hands of the North Korean regime into resplendent narratives of Christian heroism. In his efforts to assuage Captain Lee's misgivings regarding their duties, which include planting stories in local papers with headlines blazing "Christian Intrepidity" and organizing anticommunist rallies, Chang maintains that they are helping to alleviate the distress of "miserable people" (131, 173). However palliative the effect may be, this counterconstruction of meaning, of wartime mass killings plotted into tales of martyrdom, is more than welcome fiction or benevolent lie. Presented in defamiliarizing fashion as embedded texts in the novel, the media articles, intelligence reports, transcripts of speeches and sermons, and obituaries are the narrative work of counterintelligence, and its "grand deception" (207) is a form of warfare itself.

Premised on U.S. and South Korean investment in "data about the inhuman practices of the Reds," the counterintelligence investigation at the heart of *The Martyred* must gather if not produce evidence of North Korean atrocities against Christians. Complicating the CIC's efforts to craft a tidy story of "religious persecution by the Communists" that can be hailed as a "Korean chapter in the history of Christian martyrdom" in America, if not "the entire world" (18, 19), is the baffling survival of two of the city's Christian leaders. On the challenges to spinning the story of the northward invasion, Stone's *The Hidden History of the Korean War* offers a competing insight worth mentioning here. In the wake of the obliteration wreaked by U.S. bombing campaigns, with Truman's orders of late June 1950 granting General MacArthur permission "to bomb above the 38th Parallel," the UN forces described as "liberators" in *The Martyred* faced major public relations challenges in their march north. In Stone's tongue-in-cheek observation, there was "a certain bad conscience about the destruction," with Washington conceding "the effect that the war ravages have had on the Oriental peoples, and the exploitation of it by Communist propaganda" (145). "Perhaps," Stone comments, "even some who hated Communism also felt that there had been too much unnecessary destruction by American airpower, that the bombing squads had been a little too lighthearted in their 'saturation' operations" (145). Though *The Martyred* includes descriptions of buildings blasted by "either a bomb or an artillery shell" (23), it leaves the source of the devastation unspecified and instead limits its focus to battered churches and shell-shocked Christians whose hearts and minds are at stake. In the novel, the CIC's campaign "to boost morale" (42) is impeded when the two ministers are released for unknown reasons by the Communist regime that executed twelve others on June 25, 1950. By dint of their existence, they pose a challenge to totalizing accounts of wholesale Communist brutality.

Confronted by this puzzle from Pyongyang's preoccupation past, Captain Lee understands that his task is twofold: not only must he look into the circumstances behind the two ministers' survival, but he must also participate in the CIC's cynical enterprise of "manufacturing and disseminat[ing] false information" (174). Tormented to learn from Major Jung, the captured North Korean executioner, that the "great heroes and martyrs" actually "died like dogs . . . whimpering, whining, wailing" and "denounc[ing] their god and one another," Lee, while generally averse to functioning as "an accomplice in placing haloes on false martyrs" (141, 206), is especially loath to exploit these deaths for the purpose of fomenting an anticommunist reaction amongst local churchgoers, a group whom he knows UN forces will not defend. That Jung spared the life of Hann, a church leader who had gone "crazy," because in Jung's words "I don't shoot mad men," and released Shin, the other, because "he was the only one who had enough guts to spit in my face" (141–42), makes Lee's task of producing atrocity propaganda all the more difficult. With Hann's suicide and Shin's lapse of faith, nothing about the CIC-sponsored tale of religious martyrdom appears likely to hold.

It is at this moment of narrative dissolution that Shin, the fallen minister, emerges as the antihero of the occupation army. For all the CIC's elaborate machinations behind the scenes, Shin ultimately wields the power of the spotlight as he fashions the core fiction of *The Martyred.* As Captain Lee shrinks from his duties, Shin, who discerns with great acuity the profound crisis of meaning before them, steps forward to grapple with the question of the pointlessness of mass war deaths. Going off script, he delivers a sermon to his former congregation that exults in a vision of Christian valor and resilience before death, a speech surpassing the expectations of his CIC handlers. To those parishioners wary of the reasons for "Red" mercy toward him, he falsely confesses to a craven attachment to life above faith that contrasts with the noble resolve of the "martyrs": "*I* was a sinner. *I* was a weakling. *I* was defeated. *I* submitted to the forces of evil" (196, emphasis in original). Rousing the congregation with a seductive vision of meaningful death, Shin crafts a tale of sacrifice: the "martyrs" "died in the name of our Lord, for His glory and in His glory" (196). Seated in the front pew, Lee is forced to register that the minister whose "shadow . . . stretche[s] in front of me" is but a sinister extension of himself, the novel's "professional intelligence man" (197, 31). Lee recounts, with fascination and revulsion, how Shin stood before "the hushed congregation," weaving an account of "how the martyrs resisted their captors" (197):

> The Communists wanted them to issue a public statement that the Christians in North Korea supported the Communist regime, that they upheld the "liberation" of South Korea by the North Communist regime and urged everyone to join and help the "Army of Liberation." The ministers were offered, in turn, a promise that a post in the government cabinet would be given to a representative of the Christians, that those Christians held by the Communists as political prisoners would be freed unconditionally, and the property of the churches would not be confiscated by the regime. They refused everything, and they were tortured. (197)

Refusing all worldly enticements, the twelve ministers, in Shin's hagiographic account, willingly sacrificed their lives. Bearing false witness to their memory, Shin emplots their deaths into a biblical mélange that blends elements of Christ's baptism, his persecution and martyrdom by the Romans, and Judas's betrayal. Beginning more or less descriptively—"our enemies murdered your martyrs [with] . . . volley after volley of murderous bullets shatter[ing] the dark night"—Shin then paints a portrait of the heavens parting, with "the black clouds . . . shaken asunder by the moon," and "a thundering voice" coming from above, exclaiming triumphantly, "you are my children in whom I am well pleased. Do not despair, do not despair, for you have won the battle!" (200).

A counterintelligence coup on the cusp of the occupation army's withdrawal from the North, Shin's sermon interpellates his former parishioners as soldiers of God, and this revival of their belief that they might lose their lives on earth only to gain paradise has an immediate, galvanizing effect. Whipped into a frenzy, Pyongyang's "enraged and frightened populace [take] to the streets of the tense city for a series of mass demonstrations" (217). Neither privy to CIC intelligence on the massing of Chinese troops near the northern border nor aware that UN forces will leave them to their own devices as a now assuredly unruly demographic, the city's inflamed Christians issue "impassioned calls to arms, invoking the spirit of liberty" (217, 218). That the "words of faith" (209) from Shin, a lapsed believer, have proven to be the CIC's most successful propaganda—propaganda not just as the propagation of ideas but more pointedly as the dissemination of belief—is the central internal irony of *The Martyred*.[47]

In its self-referential account of fictionalization and fabrication as cool technologies of a hot war, *The Martyred* suggests that, long after Pyongyang has been abandoned, the battle for North Korea will still be waged. With the Manichaean narrative of Christians versus Communists now set in place both as an account of the mass execution of the twelve ministers and as a forecast of the persecution of the deserted Christians in the North to come, the seeds of instability have been sown. Refusing an offer of evacuation, Shin—unlike Lee, who retreats down south—stays behind in the North. Assigned to "a special section of Army Intelligence that maintained direct communications with our agents in North Korea" (295), Lee hears from a refugee who states that "there are many people who are not from Pyongyang who say that they have seen [Shin] . . . [n]ot only alive but free" (312). If their reports are to be believed, "Shin is everywhere in North Korea" (312). With Lee's accounts of Pyongyang now all second- or thirdhand—gleaned from top-secret missives sent by Colonel Chang, who goes underground to foment counterinsurgency in the North, and from debriefings of refugees—the novel closes south of the thirty-eighth parallel. It is from this vantage that Shin, who generates the fiction at the center of *The Martyred*, can finally be seen as becoming the stuff of fiction, if not legend, himself. Everywhere at once and much larger than life, Shin, a "fellow conspirator" (204) on the loose in North Korea, cannot be pinned down in these stories and *as story* himself represents a dangerously elusive, unfixable principle. More potent than ever, "Shin," as the novel closes, has become, to borrow from Gilles Deleuze and Félix Guattari's theorization of the war machine, "the Deterritorialized par excellence," a "nomad" who possesses "absolute movement."[48] Most stories have Shin roaming free, but one places him in Pyongyang, where he was "publicly executed." Pressing the refugee from the North on the variation in rumored sightings of Shin, Lee must accept an open-ended explanation: "in such circumstances as we find ourselves here, refugees are naturally more inclined to remember *or imagine* many things they have left behind. . . . So . . . which story should one believe?" (313, 312, emphasis added).

Atrocity Fabrication

In "O My Korea!" a February 1966 article for the *Atlantic* published two years after his international best seller *The Martyred* hit the shelves, Richard Kim, a naturalized U.S. citizen originally from Hamhung in northern Korea, reported on his first visit to Korea since leaving over a decade earlier. As a seasoned Korean War veteran who had served as "a liaison officer between the American and [South] Korean armed forces," Kim offered an illuminating genealogical account of South Korea's military dictatorship.[49] Confronted by a desultory scene of students who "believe that they can always throw out any government not to their liking"—a reference to the April Revolution of 1960 that ousted U.S.-installed Syngman Rhee—and who are pitted against "a police state" premised upon anticommunism as the "*raison d'être* of the nation," Kim remarked on the strangeness of "living under democracy" (107, 117) below the thirty-eighth parallel. Fresh off the success of *The Martyred*, his Nobel Prize–nominated debut novel, and with his second, *The Innocent* (1968), a fictional twist on the 1961 coup d'etat, still in the works, Kim had returned "to the land which had taken me, a refugee from the Communist-dominated North, into its bosom," a land "for which I had fought in the bloody war [and] where I would be reunited with my parents and kin" (106). Far from a happy occasion, however, Kim's visit to the South drove home for him "the grim fact that the country was still at war with the Communists in the North" (114). Struck by the visibility of the U.S. military, the ubiquity of South Korean CIA (KCIA) agents, and the terror of the people, Kim saw fit to quote an anonymous "Korean cynic" who had dared to observe that "our intelligence bureau is the true government of Korea" (110). "Dreaded and despised by the people," with "far-reaching and deadly" influence, the KCIA, Kim noted, was a virtual "government within the government," and its genesis preceded the agency's formal inception after the 1961 rightist coup d'etat, which smashed the 1960 democratic revolution. Tracing the KCIA's lineage to army intelligence, Kim stated: "In the old days, it was the National Police"; "during the war, it was the CIC" (110).

Published over a decade after the 1953 signing of the armistice agreement, *The Martyred* marked the first time that the broad attention of the U.S. public was directed to the Korean War through the fiction of an ethnic Korean writer, yet at almost every turn the novel disavows the driving U.S. role in the war. William Stueck points out that "Americans—outsiders—remain central to the story" of the Korean War.[50] Indeed, "virtually all of the weapons and ammunition employed came from outside the peninsula," and "[a] large portion of the civilian casualties and destruction of property resulted from UN—primarily U.S.—bombing of North Korea."[51] *The Martyred*, however, offers a fictionalized account of UN rollback that obscures the U.S. agenda behind the northward campaign and that nowhere casts light on what former standing commissioner of South Korea's Truth and Reconciliation Commission (TRCK) Kim Dong-Choon describes as the "large-scale massacres conducted as part of military operations . . . led by South Korean authorities and the United States."[52] If lean on historical details, *The Martyred*, in no small part because of its self-referential treatment of fiction as a weapon of war, demands to be read critically within the active logic of the ongoing war. In 1961, three years before the novel's publication, *The Black Book on the Communist North Korea: The Record of Its Crimes*, an English-language pamphlet that was produced by the government-funded Research Institute for Internal and External Affairs in South Korea and that was aimed at an international readership, sought to write off as fabrications North Korea's charges that U.S. and South Korean forces perpetrated mass atrocities against civilians during the UN march northward in late 1950:

> Communist north [*sic*] Korea has claimed that the UN Forces massacred a great number of innocent citizens when they marched north of the 38th parallel. . . . These charges, of course, are utterly false, and are propaganda designed to sully the honor of the UN while inciting general hostility toward the UN Forces.[53]

Accusing North Korea of leveling specious charges, this South Korean anticommunist tract itself reads as disinformation. Dismissed out of hand, North Korean outrage at the brutality of the UN rollback campaign has some six decades later yet to receive a serious hearing from its historic foes, much less to be integrated into the burgeoning literature on atrocities perpetrated by U.S. and South Korean forces in the southern peninsula during the war. Whereas "atrocities committed by the North Korean Army against American prisoners have been investigated and are known to the world" and "barbaric acts by . . . communists against Korean right-wing figures and family members of police" were disclosed after the ceasefire,[54] the violence that attended the disastrous failure of UN forces to "liberate" the North and their hasty retreat down south remains—to borrow I. F. Stone's apt phrase—one of the Korean War's hidden histories.[55]

If in the abstract rollback was intended "to check and reduce the preponderant power of the USSR in Asia and elsewhere," as outlined in a classified U.S. State Department document, then "UN operations in Korea" furnished a tragically ready "stage for . . . non-communist penetration into an area under Soviet control," a hapless testing ground for U.S. Cold War foreign policy.[56] Mistaken for a mere satellite of Moscow, Pyongyang stood to go down as "the first communist capital taken in history."[57] Rollback thus presented policymakers from both major U.S. political parties with the heady fantasy of turning back Communism through application of sheer military might, of raising the Iron Curtain by blunt force, and this expansionist policy "stimulated the broadest coalition in Washington behind any Korea policy in the postwar period" (*Origins* 709). On the hypocrisy of the U.S. clamor for rollback, Cumings wryly points out the legal fungibility of the U.S.-authored thirty-eighth parallel: if North Korea's "thrust southward" across the parallel on June 25, 1950, was denounced in Washington as an unmitigated act of war, of "Hitler-style aggression" against an "inviolable 'international' boundary," the UN march north in the late months of the same year signaled "the first, last, and only time [that Americans] evinced a touching regard for Korean reunification" (709).[58] However, insofar as China's game-changing entry into the war prompted the bugout of U.S. and South Korean forces and signaled a broad policy shift to containment, rollback is typically referenced as a negative object lesson, a hubristic, "hot" experiment with military power as a crude means of achieving U.S. global dominance. Indeed, whereas containment emerged as the Cold War doctrine most identified with U.S.

anticommunist policy both at home and around the world, rollback, associated temporally and causally with the humiliation of U.S. retreat on the Korean peninsula in late 1950, has been consigned to the dustbin of history.

It is worth recalling that the impetus behind rollback was the desire to achieve "a world absent of communism" by "whatever means necessary" (*Origins* 29, 30). Published long after the official abandonment of rollback as a policy, Kim's novel, with its focus on the UN march northward, represents a rare rendering of the Cold War relative to the American literary canon. Positioned to shed much-needed light on rollback as an episode willed to obscurity within a war already deemed "forgotten" in a U.S. context, *The Martyred* offers a foil to that body of writings whose organizing logic and narrative content have been read within and against a containment paradigm. Identified with a unilateral assertion of U.S. military power, rollback does not at first glance lend itself to nuanced cultural theorization, much less to obvious aesthetic engagement. Unabashedly brutish and fascistic, rollback proceeds from a crudely territorial understanding of political geography. Yet insofar as containment falters as a description of the "cold war in non-Western territories," which was frequently "exceptionally violent . . . involving mass destruction of human lives," rollback, which speaks to the simmering if not outright hot nature of U.S. national security policies in the third world, merits revisiting.[59] As Jodi Kim argues, "the Cold War is metaphorically cold when seen from the vantage point of the United States and (western) Europe."[60] Cumings likewise points out that rollback was an "Asia-first, not Europe-first" policy (*Origins* 30). Highlighting the uneven global costs of U.S.-sponsored anticommunist campaigns, Kim Dong-Choon remarks that McCarthyism in its "Korean version caused hundreds of thousands of 'suspect civilians' to be murdered without due process."[61] Inasmuch as this cognitive mapping is naturalized in contained conceptualizations of U.S. Cold War culture that fail to account for scalar and "spatial discontinuities" between America's relatively cool home front on the one hand and its hot wars and counterinsurgencies abroad on the other, there are few established interpretive models adequate to the complexity of *The Martyred*.[62] All too often read as a war novel that transcends particulars of time and place, *The Martyred* has been touted for its universal themes of nihilism and existential despair, an interpretation fostered by the opening dedication and obvious debt to Camus. Yet such insular, dehistoricized readings leave undertheorized the novel's own provocative account of fiction, not as rupture, subversion, resistance, or containment, which are all tropological responses to political repression, but more damningly as an operation of war.

Though described in *The Martyred* as an interlude in which detective work and propaganda were the major tasks of squeamish counterintelligence agents in the occupying army, rollback was a time of counterrevolutionary terror in the North. Driven by two figures infamous for their appetites for war, Douglas MacArthur and Syngman Rhee, the Pyongyang occupation, in Cumings's pithy assessment, "was a disgrace."[63] "Operation INDIANHEAD, a multidiscipline intelligence task force," writes military historian John Patrick Finnegan, was "dispatched to sift through the rubble of Pyongyang after that North Korean capital was overrun by United Nations troops."[64] Other scholars give a fuller picture of the UN advance: "CIC detachments had personality and installation target lists," and their mission was "to reduce and exploit all targets within Pyongyang."[65] Armed with white and black lists, "American CIC personnel were present with many ROK police and intelligence units," and the brutality of "American instructions to political affairs officers on the ground in the North" jostled "with the benign, magnanimous occupation envisioned by the State Department or Acheson's messianic call to show the world the democratic way" (*Origins* 722, 721). Upon China's entry into the war, "newspapers all around the world reported eyewitness accounts of ROK [South Korean] executions of people under detention," including women, children, and the elderly whose "liquidation" was deemed necessary because "they were family members of Reds" (*Origins* 720). Due to widespread coverage of "ROK atrocities," the occupation verged on "becom[ing] an international scandal" (quoted in *Origins* 719) and an unwitting propaganda coup for North Korea. Upon their recapture of the capital, "North Korean sources claimed that fifteen thousand people had been massacred in that city alone" (*Origins* 723).

In *The Martyred*, however, the bloody history of the occupation is nowhere engaged. Stripped down to a spare drama between CIC agents and Pyongyang's Christians—with few Communists and Americans in sight—Kim's novel gives the lie to knee-jerk U.S. and South Korean accounts of wholesale Communist barbarism, but it also significantly rescripts the historical record when it comes to the savagery of rollback operations in the North. Even as the novel refuses the excess and automaticity of anticommunist caricatures in which all "blame goes to the Russians and the North Koreans," it propagates a fiction that sidesteps questions of U.S. and South Korean accountability, if not war criminality, vis-à-vis North

Korea ("Remembering" 267). That the CIC of the novel bears little resemblance to the interrogation and assassination squads of the historical record suggests more than novelistic license with or fictional rehabilitation of war's ugly realities. In a metafictional account of the destabilizing instrumentality of the fiction of war, the elision of the counterrevolutionary violence of the Pyongyang occupation and the driving role of the CIC in that political terror itself partakes of the logic of warfare; it functions, in short, as counterintelligence. Although the failure of rollback to "liberate" the North and to restore "lost territory," as Syngman Rhee put it, haunts the novel's portrait of Pyongyang, it is perversely through the deterritorializing potential of the literary, even in the description of this fiasco, that the North Korean capital is, if only fleetingly, regained.[66] Fictionalization, as *The Martyred* cannily shows, can secure and undermine political terrain long after the era of formal occupation is over. It is this metafictional insight afforded by Kim's early Korean War novel that reveals that certain strategic operations of rollback, a policy indissociable in U.S. Cold War history from a hubristic vision of North Korean regime change and of a peninsula united under UN authority, have never in fact ended.

NOTES

1. I. F. Stone, *The Hidden History of the Korean War* (New York: Monthly Review, 1952), xv. Subsequent quotations from this work will be cited parenthetically within the text.

2. Ravi Arvind Palat, *Capitalist Restructuring and the Pacific Rim* (London: Routledge-Curzon, 2004), 8, 14. See also Jodi Kim, *Ends of Empire: Asian American Critique and the Cold War* (Minneapolis: University of Minnesota Press, 2010), 24–27.

3. See John Patrick Finnegan, *Military Intelligence* (Washington, D.C.: Center of Military History—United States Army, 1998), 114.

4. Harry Truman, address on the situation in Korea, 19 July 1950. Web. http://www.trumanlibrary.org/audio/tunesCast.rss.

5. Mark E. Caprio, "Neglected Questions on the 'Forgotten War': South Korea and the United States on the Eve of the Korean War," *Asia-Pacific Journal* 9, no. 5 (31 January 2011). Web.

6. Hayden White, *Metahistory: The Historical Imagination in Nineteenth-Century Europe* (Baltimore: Johns Hopkins University Press, 1973), 7. Emphasis original.

7. Bruce Cumings, "The Korean War: What Is It That We Are Remembering to Forget?" in *Ruptured Histories: War, Memory, and the Post–Cold War in Asia*, ed. Sheila Miyoshi Jager and Rana Mitter (Cambridge, MA: Harvard University Press,

2007), 289. Subsequent quotations from this work will be abbreviated "Remembering" and cited parenthetically within the text.

8. Leo Huberman and Paul M. Sweezy, publisher's foreword to Stone, *Hidden History of the Korean War*, ix.

9. Palat, *Capitalist Restructuring and the Pacific Rim*, 14.

10. Bruce Cumings, *War and Television* (London: Verso, 1992), 148.

11. Fredric Jameson, "Cognitive Mapping," in *Marxism and the Interpretation of Culture*, ed. Cary Nelson and Lawrence Grossberg (Urbana: University of Illinois Press, 1988), 347–57.

12. Ibid., 349.

13. Frank Baldwin, introduction to *Without Parallel: The American-Korean Relationship Since 1945* (New York: Pantheon, 1974), 16.

14. Steven L. Levine, "Some Reflections on the Korean War," in *Remembering the "Forgotten War": The Korean War Through Literature and Art*, ed. Philip West and Suh Ji-moon (Armonk, NY: East Gate—M. E. Sharpe, 2001), 10.

15. William Stueck, *The Korean War: An International History* (Princeton, NJ: Princeton University Press, 1995), 198.

16. Allan Millett, "The Korean War: A 50-year Critical Historiography," *Journal of Strategic Studies* 24, no. 1 (2001): 189.

17. Kim Dong-Choon, "The War against the 'Enemy Within,'" in *The Unending Korean War: A Social History*, trans. Sung-ok Kim (Larkspur, CA: Tamal Vista Publications, 2000), 10. When referring to scholars who write in Korean and historical figures located in Korea, I have followed the conventional order of Korean names: patronym followed by given name. Rather than adhere strictly to any one system of transliteration, I have reproduced the spellings used in the scholarship I cite. Where a name of a person or an organization has been spelled differently, I have highlighted the orthographic variation.

18. Jager and Mitter, introduction to *Ruptured Histories*, 7.

19. Stueck, *Korean War*, 198.

20. Cumings, *War and Television*, 215.

21. Louis Hartz quoted in David Ryan, "Mapping Containment: The Cultural Construction of the Cold War," in *American Cold War Culture*, ed. Douglas Field (Edinburgh: Edinburgh University Press, 2005), 56. See Kuan-Hsing Chen, *Asia as Method: Toward Deimperialization* (Durham, NC: Duke University Press, 2010). On the persistence of the Cold War in Asia, Chen writes: "In East Asia, the situation has been very different. Cold-war structures in East Asia have been weakened, but by no means dismantled. Chinese Communism has not been overthrown, and Indochina has not gone the way of Eastern Europe. Korea remains divided, and Taiwan a garrison state. . . . As happened during the tensest moments of the cold war, the U.S. military continues to operate in Japan, Okinawa, and South Korea" (119).

22. Chalmers Johnson, "The Three Cold Wars," in *Cold War Triumphalism: The Misuse of History After the Fall of Communism*, ed. Ellen Schrecker (New York: New Press, 2004), 237. See Ellen Schrecker, "Introduction: Cold War Triumphalism and the Real Cold War," in Schrecker, *Cold War Triumphalism*. Schrecker writes that the narrative of the Cold War's definitive conclusion is "admittedly a Eurocentric assessment, one that gives primacy to a stable European order while ignoring violent conflicts elsewhere" (4).

23. Jon Halliday and Bruce Cumings, *Korea: The Unknown War* (New York: Pantheon, 1988), 10.

24. Rosemary Foot, "Making Known the Unknown War: Policy Analysis of the Korean Conflict in the Last Decade," *Diplomatic History* 15, no. 3 (1991): 411.

25. Bruce Cumings, *The Origins of the Korean War, Volume II: The Roaring of the Cataract, 1947–1950*. 1990 (Seoul: Yuksabipyungsa, 2002), 122. Subsequent quotations from this work will be cited parenthetically within the text.

26. Finnegan, *Military Intelligence*, 118. For an account that gestures toward integrating battlefield counterintelligence with covert operations at home, see Gary Trogdon, *A Decade of Catching Spies: The United States Army's Counter Intelligence Corps, 1943–1953* (Ann Arbor, MI: UMI, 2001), 11. For a detailed study of the operations of the FBI's counterintelligence program (COINTELPRO), see David Cunningham, *There's Something Happening Here: The New Left, the Klan, and FBI Counterintelligence* (Berkeley: University of California Press, 2004).

27. See for example Ed Evanhoe, *Dark Moon: Eighth Army Special Operations in the Korean War* (Annapolis, MD: Naval Institute Press, 1995); and William B. Breuer, *Shadow Warriors: The Covert War in Korea* (New York: Wiley, 1996).

28. Eva Horn, "Knowing the Enemy: The Epistemology of Secret Intelligence," trans. Sara Ogger, *Grey Room* 11 (2003): 64. Emphasis added. Subsequent quotations from this work will be cited parenthetically within the text.

29. See Bong-Youn Choy, *Koreans in America* (Chicago: Nelson-Hall, 1979). According to Choy, "*The Martyred* was a final nominee for the National Book Award. . . . The *New York Times* described Kim's *The Martyred* as 'a magnificent achievement . . . in the great moral and psychological tradition of Dostoyevsky and Albert Camus.' The late Pearl S. Buck said that the novel is 'a major achievement, in my opinion.' Maurice Dolbier, *New York Herald Tribune*, wrote that Kim was 'one of the ablest young novelists to appear in any nation, in decades.' Robert Kirsch, *Los Angeles Times*, said that 'Richard E. Kim's brilliant and powerful novel deserves to be included in the small group of twentieth-century novels which may be called great'" (283). See also Elaine H. Kim, "Roots and Wings: An Overview of Korean American Literature, 1934–2003," in *Korean American Literature*, ed. Young-Key Kim-Renaud et al. (Washington, D.C.: George Washington University Elliot School of International Affairs—Sigur Center Asia Papers, 2003), 1–19. Elaine Kim comments on the novel's reception: "*The Martyred* . . . remained on the

nation's best seller lists for twenty consecutive weeks and was translated into ten languages. The book remains the only work by an Asian American ever nominated for a Nobel Prize in literature" (4).

30. Richard E. Kim, *The Martyred* (New York: George Braziller, 1964), 294. Subsequent quotations from this work will be cited parenthetically within the text.

31. Trogdon, *A Decade of Catching Spies*, 173. In *The Martyred*, Richard E. Kim uses the acronym "CIC" (often modified by a possessive "our" in Colonel Chang's dialogue with Captain Lee). Although this acronym typically refers to the Counter Intelligence Corps of the U.S. Army, Kim uses it to describe the KCIC, the South Korean Counterintelligence Corps. Inaugurated during the Korean War under the direction and guidance of the American CIC, the KCIC, closely identified with Syngman Rhee's police state, was the precursor to South Korea's much-reviled Central Intelligence Agency (KCIA). Given U.S. wartime operational control over South Korea's military, confusion over which CIC Kim's novel refers to is instructive. See also Elaine Kim, "Korean American Literature," in *An Interethnic Companion to Asian American Literature*, ed. King-Kok Cheung (Cambridge: Cambridge University Press, 1997), 156–91. I follow and agree with Elaine Kim's identification of the CIC in *The Martyred* as "South Korean Army Intelligence" (161). But see also Seongho Yoon, "Richard E. Kim," in *The Greenwood Encyclopedia of Multiethnic American Literature*, vol. 3, ed. Emmanuel S. Nelson (Westport, CT: Greenwood, 2005), 1240. Reviewers such as Yoon are not entirely off the mark in describing Captain Lee as "working with a U.S. Army Counterintelligence Corps unit" (1240), insofar as KCIC agents worked under the auspices of the American CIC.

32. See David Halberstam, *The Coldest Winter: America and the Korean War* (New York: Hyperion, 2007). Halberstam describes the "full-scale retreat" of "MacArthur's army" in the winter of 1950 as the "Big Bugout": "The retreat covered some 120 miles in ten days, even though the Chinese, momentarily at least, had little offensive capacity to press any advantage. That rush south represented the total disintegration of a fighting force. . . . As the surviving men of the Second Division pulled back, they passed huge bonfires visible from miles away, as vast stores of equipment, supplies that had still been coming into the country when the great offensive started, were destroyed, lest the gear be captured by the Chinese" (483).

33. Salman Rushdie, "Imaginary Homelands," in *Imaginary Homelands: Essays and Criticism, 1981–1991* (New York: Penguin, 1991), 8.

34. Ibid., 8. Emphasis added.

35. William D. Ehrhart, "Above All, the Waste: American Soldier-Poets and the Korean War," in West and Ji-moon, *Remembering the "Forgotten War,"* 40.

36. Raymond Williams, *Marxism and Literature* (Oxford: Oxford University Press, 1978), 105. Emphasis in original.

37. Steven L. Levine, "Some Reflections on the Korean War," in West and Ji-moon, *Remembering the "Forgotten War,"* 10.

38. See Gilles Deleuze and Félix Guattari, *A Thousand Plateaus: Capitalism and*

Schizophrenia, trans. Brian Massumi (Minneapolis: University of Minnesota Press, 1987). In their theorization of the obliterations of "the war machine," Deleuze and Guattari describe the "deterritorializ[ation of] the enemy" as a "shattering [of] his territory from within" (353).

39. Arjun Appadurai, *Modernity at Large: Cultural Dimensions of Globalization* (Minneapolis: University of Minnesota Press, 1996), 31. Emphasis original.

40. Ibid., 31.

41. Fredric Jameson, *The Political Unconscious: Narrative as a Socially Symbolic Act* (London: Routledge, 1983), 134.

42. Suk-Young Kim, introduction to *Long Road Home: Testimony of a North Korean Camp Survivor* (New York: Columbia University Press, 2009), 3. See Kim Dong-Choon, *The Unending Korean War: A Social History*. Kim Dong-Choon also contends that "the Korean War was actually a civil war for the establishment of a unified state, not a war between two states, and personal retaliation was inevitable as the front line moved continuously back and forth, southward and northward" (172).

43. Pascale Casanova, *The World Republic of Letters*, trans. M. B. DeBevoise (Cambridge, MA: Harvard University Press, 2004), 81.

44. Trogdon, *A Decade of Catching Spies*, 200. See Ian Sayer and Douglas Botting, *America's Sacred Army: The Untold Story of the Counter Intelligence Corps* (New York: Franklin Watts, 1989). Sayer and Botting write: "In US Army parlance, counterintelligence (all one word) is a generic term referring to all the various measures employed by all members of the military in order to deny vital information to the enemy" (ix).

45. Kim Dong-Choon, *Unending Korean War*, 78.

46. Chung-shin Park, *Protestantism and Politics in Korea* (Seattle: University of Washington Press, 2003), 41.

47. See Jon Halliday, "The Korean War: Some Notes on Evidence and Solidarity," *Bulletin of Concerned Asian Scholars* 11, no. 3 (1979): 2–18.

48. Deleuze and Guattari, *A Thousand Plateaus*, 381.

49. Richard E. Kim, "O My Korea!" *Atlantic Monthly*, February 1966, 110. Subsequent quotations from this work will be cited parenthetically within the text.

50. William Stueck, "In Search of Essences: Labeling the Korean War," in West and Ji-moon, *Remembering the "Forgotten War,"* 189.

51. Ibid., 189.

52. Kim Dong-Choon, *Unending Korean War*, 176.

53. *The Black Book on the Communist North Korea: The Record of Its Crimes* (Seoul: Research Institute for Internal and External Affairs, 1961), 19.

54. Kim Dong-Choon, *Unending Korean War*, 75.

55. See Millett, "The Korean War: A 50-year Critical Historiography." Consider on this point Millett's argument that the "study of political and military relations between the United States and the Republic of Korea is not exactly a 'black hole'

in Korean War historiography, but it is certainly a gray crevice" with scholarship "largely silent on atrocities, corruption, nepotism, and incompetence in the ROK officer corps" (222).

56. John Allison, U.S. State Department Director of Northeast Asian Affairs, quoted in Cumings, *Origins of the Korean War, Volume II*, 710.

57. Everett Drumwright, chargé d'affaires of the U.S. Embassy in South Korea, quoted in Cumings, *Origins of the Korean War, Volume II*, 717. See Ra Jong-yil, "Governing North Korea: Some Afterthoughts on the Autumn of 1950," *Journal of Contemporary History* 40, no. 3 (2005), 521–46. Jong-yil, former national security adviser to South Korean president Roh Moo-hyun, notes: "North Korea was the first ex-communist territory 'liberated' by the 'Free World,' a place where the Iron Curtain was pushed back at the periphery of the Russian empire 'even by a few miles'" (532).

58. See Kim Dong-Choon, *Unending Korean War*. Kim Dong-Choon similarly argues: "The Korean War, first of all, was the consequence of a bloody civil conflict and guerrilla warfare. It was the result of the synchronization of war and revolution. The familiar statement that 'North Korea invaded South Korea' is thus contestable, because the thirty-eighth parallel was regarded by Korean leaders on both sides as merely a temporary or even an 'imaginary line,' as Cumings argued, rather than a national border" (78).

59. Heonik Kwon, *The Other Cold War* (New York: Columbia University Press, 2009), 11.

60. Jodi Kim, *Ends of Empire*, 16.

61. Kim Dong-Choon, *Unending Korean War*, 78.

62. Jameson, "Cognitive Mapping," 352.

63. Bruce Cumings, *Korea's Place in the Sun: A Modern History* (New York: W. W. Norton, 2005), 281.

64. Finnegan, *Military Intelligence*, 117–18.

65. Trogdon, *A Decade of Catching Spies*, 209.

66. Jong Jo Ho, Kang Sok Hui, and Pak Thae Ho, *The US Imperialists Started the Korean War* (Pyongyang: Foreign Languages Publishing House, 1993), 81.

7 THE RACE WAR WITHIN

THE BIOPOLITICS OF THE LONG COLD WAR

LEEROM MEDOVOI

> The totalitarian attempt at global conquest and total domination has been the destructive way out of all impasses. Its victory may coincide with the destruction of humanity; wherever it has ruled, it has begun to destroy the essence of man.—Hannah Arendt

> What Sphinx of cement and aluminum bashed open their skulls and ate up their brains and imagination?—Allen Ginsberg

How might we view Cold War American culture in a way that preserves the insights of the *containment* model but that moves beyond that model's limitations in dealing with nonrepressive exercises of postwar power? This chapter suggests that the most comprehensive framework for understanding the complexities of the Cold War era has been right under our nose, in the discourses and practices of war itself. In the argument presented here, I suggest that *containment* explains certain aspects of early Cold War culture well, precisely because it is one important military strategy through which the postwar political culture of permanent war was initially organized. It was not the only strategy, however. Other forms of militarized conduct were equally constitutive of the long Cold War era, a half century that took shape around a general yet highly flexible logic of permanent struggle against a radically inflected totalitarian enemy. Over multiple decades this logic was one that could be mobilized for very different political ends by strikingly different social actors. Much of the political complexity and richness of the *long* Cold War era derives from the many valences that this state of permanent war took over a long period of time.

The concept of "totalitarianism," though originally used by Mussolini to describe his own regime's practices, first took on a critical meaning when Leon Trotsky used it to analyze the "failure" of the Soviet Union.[1] It was picked up and more widely disseminated in the writings of George

Orwell.[2] It gained special influence in American political life in 1951, however, after Hannah Arendt published her influential three-volume study *The Origins of Totalitarianism*. The term became, as William Pietz has put it, "the theoretical anchor of cold war discourse."[3] In almost all its incarnations, the totalitarian thesis holds to the equation of Stalin with Hitler, and the Soviet Union with Nazi Germany. In Arendt's estimation, Nazism and Stalinism comprised the twentieth century's two major instances of a new kind of politics, one in which the state administered its population all the way down to the fine-grained level of private social life. Arendt's concept thereby reinforced and provided theoretical ammunition to the partisans of an already burgeoning Cold War security state, who called on America to defend the globe against the renewed threat of a "red fascism." As Slavoj Žižek argues, "Totalitarianism," used in this way, has served to "dismiss the leftist critique of liberal democracy" by equating all such leftisms with fascist intentions.[4]

When one recalls that the first two volumes of Arendt's book located the origins of totalitarianism in both nineteenth-century antisemitism and the new racial thought of European imperialism, however, totalitarianism begins to look like a more flexible category. For Arendt, race thinking was a basic condition of Nazism and Stalinism's emergence because both political systems work by identifying a population of racial others (unfit races and historically declining classes) against whom they must wage war. This totalitarian idea of race war provides the basis for a campaign of terror that ultimately "holds them [individual men] so tightly together that it is as though their plurality had disappeared into One Man of gigantic proportions" (465–66). Totalitarianism is always posited as the enemy of humankind itself, an inhuman system that robs its population of the social space that individuals must maintain between one another in order to inhabit personal freedom. Posed in this way as the political negation of the species, totalitarianism offers a threat against which to organize a humanist counterpolitics, one that declares as its moral imperative a permanent war on behalf of the political survival of the species.

A designation of the enemy made purposely flexible and historically unspecific, the idea of totalitarianism, if not always the word itself, thus became a mobile figure for the enemy of humanity. Arendt did not consider European racial imperialism to be itself totalitarian, despite her open admission that it had employed many terroristic means to subject colonized populations. She similarly denied that white supremacy in the United States, even in the Jim Crow South, might count as totalitarian:

> It would be a serious error to underestimate the role sheer racism has played and is still playing in the government of the Southern states, but it would be an even more serious fallacy to arrive at the retrospective conclusion that large areas of the United States have been under totalitarian rule for more than a century. (xv)[5]

Even less did Arendt entertain the question of whether to call postwar American militarism a form of totalitarianism. Furthest of all from her mind was its possible application to such terrains as the standardizations of Fordist consumer capitalism or the gender rigidities that undergird patriarchal rule. And yet totalitarianism became all of these things at different moments in the long Cold War that stretched from 1948 to 1991.

I am by no means attempting in this chapter to offer a master narrative that might exhaustively map the cultural terrains of postwar America. One can always approach the study of postwar U.S. culture by looking below or beyond the organizing frame of the Cold War. But for many decades, the logic of antitotalitarian race war served as perhaps the key mechanism for mobilizing power to political ends in the United States and, no doubt, elsewhere.

Through this lens, moreover, one discerns unexpected parallels between culturally and ideologically diverse features of American life in the second half of the twentieth century (McCarthyism and Beat literature, the Cold War security state and Black Power, Jerry Rubin and Ronald Reagan) that the containment model not only misses but would of necessity consider absurd. Finally, this frame of reference permits us to think about the Cold War as merely one episode in what is a historically far more extensive logic of permanent war that (as Arendt's analyses remind us) reaches back through the history of Western colonialism. And we need not look very far to see how it continues to shape our contemporary political life.

The Cold War as a Race War without Race

A certain paradox can be observed in the formulation *antitotalitarian race war*. As the case of Arendt shows, totalitarianism was itself the enemy of humanity because it represented the scourge of genocidal racism. Yet the war *against* totalitarianism was also practiced as a kind of race war. This paradox is best understood as a consequence of the persistent displacements of colonial logics of power in the postwar years. Nikhil Singh has suggested that we can trace a genealogy of race war as a strategy in

American politics at least as far back as Andrew Jackson, whose Indian wars represent what Michael Rogin once called the "first majority 'southern strategy' in American history."[6] Waging war is itself, as Singh puts it, a means of "race-making," one that divides the body politic from those who comprise its enemies. By the late nineteenth and early twentieth centuries, the era that Eric Hobsbawm classically terms the "age of empire," race-making had become a global vision. The human world was conceived above all as one divided between those races who would be proven fit to colonize and those fit only to be colonized. In this sense, imperialism was indeed, as Arendt puts it, conceived as a "struggle between the races for world domination," but it was also conceived as a civil war of humankind that would strengthen the victors (470). As Marcia Klotz has pointed out, this imperialist project of waging a militarized competition between the various races that composed the "human race" can be understood as a globalized biopolitics of the species.[7] Imperialism in this martial sense sought the "health" of the human species by means of what Richard Slotkin has called "regeneration through violence," projected onto a global scale."[8]

We can discern the key differences between this colonial model of power as war and the Cold War model of antitotalitarian war with which it was supplanted by comparing two works of science fiction: H. G. Wells's *War of the Worlds* (1898) and Robert Heinlein's *The Puppet Masters* (1951). Wells's famous novel narrates the story of England's extraterrestrial invasion by Martians, who quickly overwhelm the British with superior weaponry, only to succumb in the end to terrestrial bacterial infection. It is frequently noted that Wells explicitly compared the Martian assault against humanity with the imperialist genocides of European powers:

> And before we judge them [the Martians] too harshly, we must remember what ruthless and utter destruction our own species has wrought, not only upon animals, such as the vanished Bison and the Dodo, but upon its own inferior races. The Tasmanians, in spite of their human likeness, were entirely swept out of existence in a war of extermination waged by European immigrants, in the space of fifty years. Are we such apostles of mercy as to complain if the Martians warred in the same spirit?[9]

I won't dwell on Wells's book, but to the extent that it expresses what Fredric Jameson has called an "imperialist guilt," it reckons with the brutal military asymmetry typical of most colonial wars, even while drawing the reader into identification with a defense of the "human race" (against the savage other) that in fact served as the pretext for colonial wars in the first place.

To the extent that the Cold War world also conceived its politics as one of "race war," it had to do so in a manner far less explicit, one that asserted its compatibility with the repudiation of both Nazi racial ideology and the imperialist notion of non-European "inferior races." Beginning with the Truman Doctrine, the rhetoric used by the United States to declare a state of ongoing, permanent war never referred to an enemy *race*, but rather to an abstracted and nonhuman enemy force (totalitarianism) that was *exerted on* human beings. As Truman explained in his speech of March 12, 1947, world peace and human rights would be realized only if:

> we [the United States] are willing to help free peoples to maintain their free institutions and their national integrity against aggressive movements that seek to impose upon them totalitarian regimes. This is no more than a frank recognition that totalitarian regimes imposed upon free peoples, by direct or indirect aggression, undermine the foundations of international peace and hence the security of the United States.[10]

As I have noted elsewhere, the biopolitics of the Cold War moment were organized around this contradictory formulation of "totalitarianism."[11] On the one hand, totalitarianism was condemned for itself practicing the repudiated notion of race war: both fascism and Communism are understood to name politics that wage war against both their own populations (genocide) and other ones (race war). And on the other hand, the Cold War itself became understood as a politico-cultural surrogate for race war, because the "enemy" represented an ideological and terror-driven movement, not itself human, that in the "second world" created vast, dehumanized zones of life. Biological racism was repudiated, yet the idea of an enemy population inferior in its subhuman political organization was retained. With the global condemnation of racial ideology that accompanied the defeat of fascism and high imperialism, the new "war of the worlds" was to be exemplified not by differences in blood but (as in the divided nations of Germany, Korea, and Vietnam) by struggles between systems, ideologies, or ways of life.[12] Antitotalitarianism can thus be understood as a particular version of what in other work I have termed "dogma-line racism," a racism of interiority that constructs its target populations with reference to their creeds, thoughts, and loyalties rather than their blood, color, and physiognomy.[13]

Generally, this genealogical link between the racism of colonialism and its ideologically inflected offspring remained obscure. But occasionally the discursive similarities became explicit and the language of race war rose to the surface. As an early example, consider the explanation provided in George Kennan's "The Sources of Soviet Conduct" for the "particular brand of fanaticism" held by Soviet Russia's Stalinist leadership, which:

> unmodified by any of the Anglo-Saxon traditions of compromise, was too fierce and too jealous to envisage any permanent sharing of power. From the Russian-Asiatic world out of which they had emerged they carried with them a skepticism as to the possibilities of permanent and peaceful coexistence of rival forces.[14]

Here, for a moment, totalitarianism appears as an aggressive racial trait that becomes the explanation for America's impending race war with the Orient.

Communism as Racial Parasite

Just as Wells's *War of the Worlds* captures the race war logic at the heart of imperialist militarism, so this distinctive Cold War logic finds narrative expression in Robert Heinlein's pulp science fiction novel *The Puppet Masters*. First serialized in *Galaxy* magazine, *The Puppet Masters* was published in the fall of 1951, during the long stalemate of the Korean War, in the midst of the McCarthyite moment, and almost simultaneously with Arendt's publication of *The Origins of Totalitarianism*. *The Puppet Masters* reworks the alien invasion motif of *War of the Worlds* but revises it in crucial ways. One day in the year 2007, a flying saucer lands in Iowa, bringing to the United States a shipful of extraterrestrial "slugs" from Titan. These slugs attach themselves to the backs of human beings, take mental control of their hosts, and, by exploiting their social positions to obtain more hosts, rapidly seize power in much of the United States. Sam, the narrator, is an undercover operative for a U.S. government espionage agency that is the first to discover and respond to the threat. It takes quite some time for Sam's agency to persuade Congress and the president of the reality of this threat. When at last they succeed, the best that the U.S. government can manage is a stalemate in which the aliens end up controlling a "Zone Red" that extends from Iowa down through St. Louis to New Orleans, while the U.S. government maintains a free "Zone Green" on either side.

The image of the war map delineating the two zones is only one of many ways in which the agency must work hard to render this war visible, for what makes the struggle so difficult is precisely that these slug-ridden citizens are invisible enemies within the body politic, invisible parasites who, as Sam's boss the Old Man puts it to the nation's president, "are pinching off the nerve cells of our social organism before true messages get back."[15] The war goes quite badly for much of the novel as a result of this challenge. Too many congressmen, it seems, fail to be "convinced that there is a war on. Because when they [the slugs] take over a city, everything goes on as before" (77).

In its first meaningful response, the government launches "Schedule Bare Back," the "first phase of the implementation of Operation Parasite" (151), a martial law requiring all citizens to go topless so that all can plainly see who is free and who is enslaved by the parasites. This action has only limited success, however, as Sam dismayingly notes:

> By the next day it was clear that Schedule Bare Back had failed as an offensive measure. As a defense it was useful; the uncontaminated areas could be kept so, as long as the slugs could not conceal themselves. It even had mild success in offense; areas contaminated but not "secured" by the parasites were cleaned up at once . . . Washington itself, for example, and New Philadelphia . . . The entire east coast turned from red to green. But as the area down the middle of the country filled in on the map, it filled in red, and stayed so. (151)

Heinlein's *The Puppet Masters* certainly can be analyzed as an exemplar of "Red Scare" containment culture. Our protagonist is a former operative "behind the Curtain" who, from the opening page onward, stresses the interchangeability of slugs and Russian commissars, while those ridden with the slugs are equivalent to the Soviet bloc's subjugated population:

> I wondered why the titans had not attacked Russia first; Stalinism seemed tailormade for them. On second thought, I wondered if they had. On third thought I wondered what difference it would make; the people behind the Curtain had had their minds enslaved and parasites riding them for three generations. There might not be two kopeks difference between a commissar with a slug and a commissar without a slug. (205)

The military deadlock that ensues with the Titans is in fact very much in line with the Cold War stalemate that serves as the novel's historical horizon. In the future envisioned by *The Puppet Masters*, nuclear war with the Soviet Union has come and gone, and still neither side has won. Certain areas of Washington, D.C. are radioactive, and there is now a city ominously called "New Philadelphia." Yet even in the (then-distant) year of 2007, "nobody had an answer" to ending the Cold War:

> Too big to occupy and too big to ignore. World War III had not settled the Russian problem and no war ever would. The Parasites might feel right at home behind the Curtain. (148)

It is noteworthy that in this last line the equivalence of Parasites and Soviets does not really concern their common "enslavement" of human populations, but rather their intractability. With such an enemy, containment would seem to be the only effective military strategy. One cannot beat the Soviets, one can only keep them at bay. Similarly with the Titans, it seems for many pages that the defensive success of "Schedule Bare Back" may be as good as it gets.

This is not where the novel ends, however. Both the slugs and the Soviets are defeated by the end of the novel, and in the process their metaphorical equivalence is ruptured by a different kind of narrative connection: the slugs themselves prove to be history's answer to the "Russian problem." Toward its close, the novel reveals that the slugs had indeed invaded the Soviet Union first, a fact unknown to the world because the commissars had avoided seeking international help. Because the slugs ride their hosts into the ground, caring nothing for their hygienic well-being, a great "Asiatic plague" breaks out, the "only continent-wide epidemic of the Black Death since the seventeenth century" (296). Sam is initially stupefied because he knows that:

> their [the Communists'] public health measures were as good as ours and even better in some ways, for they were carried out "by the numbers" and no nonsense tolerated. . . . In such respects the commissars had even managed to clean up China to the point, at least, that bubonic plague and typhus were sporadically endemic rather than epidemic. Now both plagues were spreading like gossip across the whole Sino-Russo-Siberian axis, to the point where the soviet government system had broken down. (296)

The wrenching apart of slugs and commissars in this scene encourages us to read the novel more abstractly, not simply as an anticommunist rant (which of course it also is) but as an *antitotalitarian* war story that posits a politics organized against a universal enemy of humankind. The convergence of antitotalitarian politics with the positing of permanent war can be understood in terms of its consistency with Carl Schmitt's version of the political. In Schmitt's view, the domain of politics is not reducible to the state, but rather may be defined as any practice of power that employs a friend-enemy constellation to distinguish between a body politic and those that threaten its well-being. While politics is not exactly identical to war, it is always the hostile relationship animating any politics that establishes the potential for war. In Schmitt's view, "what always matters [for any politics] is the possibility of the extreme case taking place, the real war, and the decision whether this situation has arrived or not."[16] In a fascinating and suggestively science-fictional moment in his treatise, Schmitt suggests that:

> humanity as such cannot wage war because it has no enemy, at least not on this planet. The concept of humanity excludes the concept of the enemy, because the enemy does not cease to be a human being—and hence there is no specific differentiation in that concept.[17]

Schmitt's comment, including its aside "at least not on this planet," sheds valuable light on how Heinlein's novel mediates between a particularist politics of "race war" on the one hand, and a universalist politics of "defending humanity" on the other. We might say that the conceit of a race of "puppet masters" who enslave people allows Heinlein's novel to animate an enemy that is simultaneously human and alien. As human, the slug-ridden Zone Red occasions a national civil war, and indeed a planetary war between two rival political systems. The motif of the alien slugs, however, allows Heinlein to narrate the struggle as a war in which all genuine humanity is entirely on one side of the conflict, confronting an enemy extrinsic to the species. By the end of the novel, after the defeat of the slugs on Earth, Sam is preparing to depart for Titan in an interplanetary counterattack that is merely the human race's first foray in a defensive war without end:

> Whether we make it, or not, the human race has got to keep up its well-earned reputation for ferocity. If the slugs taught us anything, it

> was that the price of freedom is the willingness to do sudden battle, anywhere, any time, and with utter recklessness. If we did not learn that, well—"Dinosaurs, move over! We are ready to become extinct. . . . Beat the plowshares back into swords; the other was a maiden aunt's fancy." (338)

Lurking behind the equation of slug with commissar, and the friend-enemy binary that it projects, therefore, is a biopolitical logic of permanent war, the defense of the species against a generalized *inhumanity*. The explicit appeal to racial survival in Sam's final words brings to the surface the biopolitical subtext in those famous lines of John F. Kennedy's inaugural address: "Let every nation know, whether it wishes us well or ill, that we shall pay any price, bear any burden, meet any hardship, support any friend, oppose any foe, in order to assure the survival and the success of liberty."[18] To be sure, the foes that Kennedy refers to here are particular countries that might take the wrong side in a Cold War world. But Kennedy also pronounces his call to arms in that same speech as a "struggle against the common enemies of man: tyranny, poverty, disease, and war itself," thereby mapping the friend-enemy distinction in parallel fashion onto humanity (man and his freedom) and all that threatens it.

The explanation for why race would mediate here between the universal and the particular enemy is provided by Michel Foucault in his remarkable Collège de France lectures that were published under the title *Society Must Be Defended*. If modern power has arrogated to itself the goal of fostering and managing life, of seeking the "well-being" of humanity, we might say, then how, "under these conditions, is it possible for a political power to kill, to call for deaths, to demand deaths, to give the order to kill, and to expose not only its enemies but its own citizens to the risk of death?"[19]

Sam himself, as an agent of what we might call Cold War biopower, gives us the same answer as Foucault. As he puts it in the universalizing moment cited above, it is the survival of the "human race" that gives him the right to kill, and the aliens that he will kill are precisely members of a threatening "race." As Sam puts it, "this was a fight for racial survival" (26). And as the Old Man similarly insists, "the safety of all of us—and of our whole race—depends this moment on complete cooperation and utter obedience" (58).

From this perspective, characters in *The Puppet Masters* who are ridden with slugs or commissars do not count as part of humanity. Thus, when

Sam and his fellow agents kill their fellow Americans in Zone Red, they need to remind themselves that this killing "*could not be helped*" (57, emphasis original), because, after all, "we weren't shooting people, not intentionally, we were shooting parasites. . . . these things aren't human" (57). In Foucault's highly flexible understanding, racism is primarily:

> a way of introducing a break into the domain of life that is under power's control; the break between what must live and what must die. The appearance within the biological continuum of the human race of races, the distinction among races, the hierarchy of races, the fact that certain races are described as good and that others, in contrast, are described as inferior: all this is a way of fragmenting the field of the biological that power controls. (254–55)

It is also, as he stresses, an extension of the traditional relationship of war:

> "In order to live, you must destroy your enemies." But racism does make the relationship of war—"If you want to live, the other must die"—function in a way that is completely new and that is quite compatible with the exercise of biopower. . . . "The more inferior species die out, the more abnormal individuals are eliminated, the fewer degenerates there will be in the species as a whole. . . . the death of the bad race, of the inferior race . . . is something that will make life in general healthier: healthier and purer." (255)

The war of the races in Heinlein's novel—free humanity versus parasite-ridden humanity—is in fact explicitly biopoliticized as a fight against a form of contagion, a healthy population protecting itself against a diseased one. It is also this explicit model of contagion that seems most consistent with the strategy of containment, which after all is nothing other than a form of quarantine to protect the healthy.

This displacement is readily seen in the transition from Wells's *War of the Worlds* to Heinlein's *The Puppet Masters*. Wells's Martians begin victoriously because they are a more highly "evolved" race, with superior technology and stronger weapons. Heinlein's Titans, however, do not represent a different level of technology or development of civilization as much as simply a different political system that robs human beings of their freedom. The world being created by the puppet masters is still a human world, for the Titans (we are told) do not introduce anything original at the level of technology or culture. Instead, as analogues to what

Truman calls totalitarianism, they merely represent the deployment of already existing human technology and culture on behalf of human unfreedom.

In this sense, the Cold War model of power that Heinlein represents for us displaced race from the explicit scene of military confrontation. It was not blood or culture that was different, but ideologies or political systems. The contrast between Zones Red and Green in Heinlein's novel mimics what I earlier described as the Cold War's primary mode of exemplification: those divided nations that shared German, Korean, or Vietnamese blood but represented a contrast between free and unfree ways of life. As the Korean and Vietnamese cases also recall, the Cold War likewise posited a development narrative centered on the decolonizing third world poised to decide between democracy and totalitarianism. Cold War against Communism, as Truman explained, was crucial precisely because "at the present moment in world history nearly every nation must choose between alternate ways of life. The choice is too often not a free one."[20]

Cold War Dialectics

Heinlein's novel is certainly not unique in its creation of a "war of the worlds" that expresses the friend-enemy antagonism between a domain of human freedom and an inhuman realm of totalitarian servitude. But it finds company across much of the political and cultural spectrum, not only in other Red Scare texts of the right wing but equally in what scholars understand to be the opposition of the Cold War era, in the words and practices of the long Cold War's countercultures, New Leftists, antiracists, and liberationists.

Consider for instance that hypercanonical epic poem of the 1950s, Allen Ginsberg's "Howl" (1955). On the face of things, it would seem difficult to imagine texts more different than Heinlein's strident, pseudo-McCarthyite, paranoid science fiction novel and Ginsberg's anthemic postwar poem celebrating a Beat generation whose exploits included distributing "Supercommunist pamphlets in Union Square."[21] All the same, "Howl" and *The Puppet Masters* are structured by an analogous imperative defense of human freedom against the onslaught of totalitarianism. In Heinlein's novel, Americans come to serve the inhuman ends of the masters by being mentally manipulated. In Ginsberg's poem, likewise, the "minds" of his generation, while enduring a genocidal assault, resist through the spiritual poiesis of their bohemian journeys in that dark American night. In "Howl"—as would be even more emphatically the case in the 1960s—sex, drugs, and music become acts of struggle against a totalitarian inhumanity.

Ginsberg does not actually use the word *totalitarian*, yet like Heinlein, whose puppet masters bind human beings tightly together into the "groupthink" of a single organism, he offers us in "Moloch" a unitary figure of the enemy, a juggernaut with an unmistakable resemblance to the "One Man of gigantic proportions" that Arendt warns of as the end product of totalitarian terror. A bloodthirsty Canaanite god who demanded sacrifice of the firstborn, Moloch appears in the poem as "the vast stone of war" but also as:

> Robot apartments! invisible suburbs! skeleton treasuries! blind capitals! demonic industries! spectral nations! invincible mad houses! granite cocks! monstrous bombs! (22)

This litany strings together a series of deathly "others" to human life that can symbolize Moloch: machines, demons, specters, institutions, inanimate stones, or weaponry. He is a "sphinx of cement and aluminum" who has seized the "best minds" of Ginsberg's generation, "bashed open their skulls and [eaten] up their brains and imagination" (21).

The real epic thrust of "Howl" is its antitotalitarian revolt, as the mad generation, represented in the final section by the asylum inmate Carl Solomon, plots "the Hebrew socialist revolution against the fascist national Golgotha" (25). As it reaches its climactic conclusion, the poem's martial intent erupts into the open. The revolt that will release the mad generation from the confines of the Molochian Rockland mental hospital becomes a military counterattack:

> I'm with you in Rockland / where we wake up electrified out of the coma by our own souls' airplanes roaring over the roof they've come to drop angelic bombs the hospital illuminates itself imaginary walls collapse O skinny legions run outside O starry-spangled shock of mercy the eternal war is here O victory forget your underwear we're free (26)

Ginsberg's war of liberation and self-defense participates in what I have elsewhere explored as part of the explosion of politicized identity discourse in the United States, a narrative of youth revolt.[22] I am now in a better position to argue that the birth of identity discourse was itself a certain mutation in the practice of antitotalitarianism, a call to arms in the name of psycho-political freedom from a totalitarianism that had now been displaced from the second world onto the first, because of a series of overdetermined causes that included the pressures of third world decolonization, ongoing antiracist struggles in the United States, and the unmistakable anxieties attached to Fordist-era massification.

Amerikan Totalitarianism: Guerrilla Strategies

These connections emerge explicitly in Norman Mailer's famous essay "The White Negro," which like "Howl" sought to explain and justify Beat and hip countercultures. In Mailer's view, the ubiquity of totalitarian regimes, the truth of the gas chambers, the use of atomic bombs on Japan, and the continuation of militaristic regimentation into the postwar "peace" meant in essence that every man now knew:

> that when he dissented, he gave a note upon his life which could be called in any year of overt crisis. No wonder then that these have been the years of conformity and depression. A stench of fear has come out of every pore of American life.[23]

In a world such as this, one must rebel to remain human at all, to escape what Mailer calls the "totalitarian tissues of American society." As with Arendt, the terror to which the hipster responds is a kind of generalization from racism's threat to subjected populations, and it is for this reason that the hipster, responding to what is admittedly a new condition for *most* Americans, draws inspiration from the "Negro," who has "been living in the margin between democracy and totalitarianism for two centuries."[24]

Mailer's uses of race in this controversial essay have been frequently criticized, and for different reasons. My sole purpose here is to emphasize that it was crucial for Mailer to justify the hipster by appealing to "Negro" strategies of self-defense against a white supremacist system that could literally be understood to be totalitarian. Mailer was in no way alone in making such a claim. Contra Arendt, for example, the great poet of negritude Aimé Césaire had argued that colonial racism was not fundamentally different from Nazi exterminationist antisemitism. Colonialism had already borne witness to all the liquidations of humanity that Europeans later claimed to deplore in Nazi Germany, and only racism prevented an open admission of this fact. As long as the policies of terror and dehumanization remained in Africa, Europeans did not object. Once it was brought home to their own continent, they grew surprised and indignant. But in actuality:

> before they were its victims, they were its accomplices; that they tolerated that [colonial equivalent of] Nazism before it was inflicted on them, that they absolved it, shut their eyes to it, legitimized it, because, until then, it had been applied only to non-European peoples.[25]

In Césaire's account, it is not (as in Arendt's version) that colonial racism merely made totalitarianism possible. Rather, the colonial order of things was *itself* the archetypal totalitarian order, with Nazism simply one of its correlative effects, a case of the chickens coming home to roost as totalitarian methods returned to Europe in the form of a race war "defending" European (Aryan) blood against its inferior versions: Jews, Gypsies, homosexuals, Communists, and others. To confront "totalitarianism" only in its Nazi (and perhaps Stalinist) form was thus, according to Césaire's narrative, a self-serving, white supremacist disavowal of totalitarianism's actual history.

Shifting the primary focus of totalitarianism onto European and American regimes of white supremacy was a crucial and consequential discursive move in the deployment of Cold War power. The entire legacy of what Mary L. Dudziak has called "cold war civil rights" may be conceived as an indirect assertion of this sort: how could the United States claim to defend human freedom against its totalitarian enemies abroad while it waged a totalitarian race war at home every time it terrorized its own black (and other minority) populations?[26]

This political move became far more explicit among radical antiracist thinkers. In his famous speech "The Ballot or the Bullet" (1964), Malcolm X indicted in very similar terms the hypocrisy of the United States, which he represented through the Molochian image of a blood-soaked Uncle Sam who:

> still has the audacity or the nerve to stand up and represent himself as the leader of the free world. Not only is he a crook, he's a hypocrite. There he is standing up in front of other people, Uncle Sam, with the blood of your and mine mothers and fathers on his hands, with the blood dripping down his jaws like a bloody-jawed wolf, and still got the nerve to point his finger at other countries. You can't even get civil rights legislation. And this man has got the nerve to stand up and talk about South Africa, or talk about Nazi Germany, or talk about [inaudible]. Nah, no more days like those.[27]

Once again, in Malcolm X's account, the real war against a genocidal totalitarianism needs to begin right here at home by gathering the victims of Uncle Sam together to "fight for the right to live as free humans,"[28] a universal struggle that in the era of anti-imperialist decolonization also takes the form of a global race war:

> the racial sparks that are ignited here in America today could easily turn into a flaming fire abroad, which means it could engulf all the people of this earth into a giant race war. What happens to a black man in America today happens to the black man in Africa . . . in Asia and to the man down in Latin America.[29]

In his New Left best seller *Soul on Ice* (1968), Eldridge Cleaver drew these various threads of antitotalitarian war into a complete vision. The vivid struggle of that era between left and right, black power and white supremacy, needed to be understood as nothing less than a war over what kind of future America would face: one that forged a genuinely "free world" for humanity, or the grim alternative. The world had reached a:

> decisive fork in the road, and this is at the heart of our national crisis. . . . The road to the right is refusal to submit to the universal demand for national liberation, economic justice, peace, and popular sovereignty. To walk this last path, the decision-makers must be prepared to unleash worldwide genocide, including the extermination of America's Negroes. The people within these countries who try to stand against the will of the overwhelming majority of the human race must be willing to forgo the last traces of their own liberty and see their governments turned into totalitarian regimes tolerating no dissent.[30]

Much of the power of the 1960s, read in this way, can be understood as a kind of strategic reversal of the Cold War security state's exercise of the politics of antitotalitarianism, one that drew its strength from the grand appeals to humanity's confrontation with its twentieth-century Molochian enemies.

In *The Armies of the Night*, Norman Mailer's award-winning account of the 1967 march on the Pentagon, the student revolt against the Vietnam War is itself part of a larger struggle against an America in which "the republic was now managing to convert the citizenry to a plastic mass, ready to be attached to any manipulative gung ho."[31] Mailer's favorite name for this kind of nightmare America, "technologyland," suggests a fascistic machine-logic that is materially and visually embodied in:

> floods of totalitarian architecture, totalitarian superhighways, totalitarian smog, totalitarian food (yes, frozen), totalitarian communications. . . . The machine would work, grinding out mass man and his surrealistic wars until the machine was broken. (176)

Mailer's title *The Armies of the Night* specifically refers to a military understanding of the confrontation between American protesters and American soldiers on the steps of the Pentagon, itself the primary symbol of the state's war-making power. He thus figures the protests of the 1960s as a renewed American civil war, musing at one point as the protesters have begun smoking pot in the darkness of the standoff's final night:

> Can this be one of the moments when the Secretary of Defense looks out from his window in the Pentagon at the crowd on the Mall and studies their fires below? They cannot be unreminiscent of the other campfires in Washington and Virginia little more than a century ago. (263)

Once again, the great war at hand is one waged between two American populations. On one side we find antiwar protesters, whom the anticommunist state phobically racializes as a "pullulating unwashed orgiastic Communist-inspired wave of flesh" that threatens to "roll over" the American troops (257). On the other side are the troops themselves, mere working-class American boys whom the protesters associate with the "profound turpitude of the American military might in Asia" and who must be expected to commit "any conceivable brutality here" (256). Seeking to give us this bird's-eye view of the two armies from above, Mailer discerns their mirror-image, dehumanizing "racializations" of one another. Each side, as he puts it, is "coming face to face with its own conception of the devil!" (256).

Yet this particularized account of an American civil war is always balanced by Mailer's theory of American totalitarianism, the machine-logic of technologyland that ultimately serves as the "puppet master" behind the American troops. They may be human, but what rides them is assuredly not. Any hope for the future of American freedom rests (as surely as it does for Allen Ginsberg, Malcolm X, or Eldridge Cleaver) with the defeat of a genocidal, inhuman juggernaut.

Mailer's antitotalitarian war (like that of Ginsberg, Cleaver, and Malcolm X) does not adopt the strategy of containment, and it is for this reason that the scholarly rubric of "containment culture" cannot help us to analyze it. Unlike Kennan's Soviet Union, this is not an enemy one can wait out until it collapses under the weight of its own contradictions, though it may be one that can be defeated by other means. Rather, the logic is borrowed from decolonization struggles against imperialist powers, the idea of guerrilla war. As Malcolm X famously put it: "Any time Uncle Sam, with all his machinery for warfare, is held to a draw by some rice-eaters, he's lost the battle. . . . Modern warfare today won't work. This is the day of the guerrilla."[32] Often, guerrilla tactics in the context of the domestic civil war meant waging what Mailer understood as "symbolic war," struggling for semiotic advantage in a propaganda battle raging across a mass-mediated landscape. In more radical New Left circles, however, the struggle could be understood quite literally as a strategic use of paramilitary tactics in an increasingly fascistic world of "Amerikan" domination.

Late Antitotalitarianism: Domestic Counterinsurgency

In 1976, Hollywood released its third Dirty Harry vehicle, *The Enforcer*. Throughout the immensely popular series, Clint Eastwood plays Dirty Harry as a semipathological vigilante cop whose outrageous actions are expected both to astound us and ultimately to be accepted because the police force on which he serves is otherwise too incompetent to protect its citizens adequately. From the start, Dirty Harry represents the waging of a real "war on crime," signaling what Stuart Hall and his coauthors once called "policing the crisis" through a military campaign of "law-and-order."[33] This new permutation in the practice of permanent war was perhaps the decisive strategy of power that enabled the Reagan revolution and the rise of the New Right. Reagan, it should be remembered, built his political career by running against the "permissiveness" of 1960s culture, with the result that he was elected governor of California. He excoriated Clark Kerr for being too soft on the Berkeley Free Speech Movement, and on taking office as governor he carried out a brutal crackdown on the Black Panther Party that can now be seen as an opening gambit in the building of what Ruth Wilson Gilmore has called California's "golden gulag," the greatest single network in the nation's now-enormous prison-industrial complex.[34]

Perhaps the key insight into the fate of antitotalitarianism in the late phase of the Cold War is the way in which it invigorated a right-wing political narrative of domestic counterinsurgency by targeting the movements of the 1960s as themselves the national enemy and thus as an occasion for a call to arms. In *The Enforcer*, these strategies come into striking view. Like the first two Dirty Harry movies, *The Enforcer* showcases a weak—because overly sensitive and liberal—police force and city hall, whose rules and red tape make it all but impossible to ensure the defense of society. In this third film, however, society's internal enemy becomes explicitly politicized. The murderous villains are actually a New Left paramilitary group calling itself the People's Revolutionary Strike Force, which is made up of a racial cross section of the city: a couple of whites, a Latino, and a black man. Harry's partner, who often sides with the liberal authorities against Harry's tactics, is fatally knifed by the group's lead killer as it breaks into a military installation to steal powerful weapons in order to blackmail the San Francisco mayor's office.

In a striking early scene, a woman officer who has been badly rattled by the knifing turns to Harry and asks: "It's a war, isn't it? I guess I never really understood that." Later, when Harry confronts a "liberationist" preacher who has been offering safe haven to the guerrillas, the preacher shouts back, "Sacrifices have to be made, Mister. These people are at WAR," to which Harry replies, "So am I." With whom or what exactly is Harry at war? Early in the film, one might think that he is at war with a group that believes its fight is for the people. Halfway through, however, it becomes clear that this populism is in bad faith. It is money that they are interested in, and ethical responsibility that they have sacrificed to get it. Bobby Maxwell, the leader of the strike force, proves to be a pimp who has joined the group for the sake of the blackmail money he might get. His violence has no real political end but instead expresses a sadistic streak that he acquired in Vietnam (itself an interesting admission that opens the film up to alternative, antiwar meanings).

Over and over again, the sign of political corruption is confirmed. When Harry spots the black member of the strike force and chases him down, they crash through a skylight at one point, quite literally into the bed where a pornographer is making a blue movie. Harry follows up by visiting the black militant group that this man was formerly a part of, a group known as Yuhuru and run by someone named Big Ed Mustafa. But once again, Mustafa reveals that he harbors no deep political ambitions but is ultimately intent only on his own aggrandizement. It slowly becomes clear that the war at hand is one between Harry, someone who uses violence to defend the "people," and an unholy cabal that includes a soft, corrupt city government, a bureaucratically inept police force, and paramilitary groups that claim to fight for the people while only peddling immorality, violence, and self-interest. Real totalitarianism in the form of the Soviet Union is offstage, but the implication is clear enough: the liberals who control government and the radicals of the 1960s are collaborators in the external war against the United States simply in the way that they are rotting the nation's security from within.

Reagan's famous "Evil Empire" speech of March 8, 1983, in which he rededicated himself to the global struggle against Soviet totalitarianism, was in fact a speech to none other than the National Association of Evangelicals, whose attention he directed toward the second front of his war:

> While America's military strength is important, let me add here that I've always maintained that the struggle now going on for the world will never be decided by bombs or rockets, by armies or military might. The real crisis we face today is a spiritual one; at root, it is a test of moral will and faith.[35]

What distinguishes the new right-wing antitotalitarianism that gathered force in the 1970s and achieved hegemony by the 1980s was its full and systematic narrative incorporation of liberals and 1960s radicals alike as forces of immorality that necessitated a whole *new series* of wars of self-defense: wars against crime, against drugs, and against sexual permissiveness as key battlefronts in any meaningful war against the inhumanity of totalitarianism. The final years of the Cold War thus saw a *multiplication* of permanent wars with which we are still not done. They effectively opened the door to the "culture wars" declared by Patrick Buchanan (which the Right uses to this day for purposes of electoral self-mobilization) and to the more recent return with George W. Bush to a geopolitics of renewed war.[36]

If this reading makes sense, then a deeper understanding of the Cold War would attend to this full range of strategic narratives—containment, guerrilla war, counterinsurgency, and no doubt others—through which its historical actors articulated their various antitotalitarian, biopolitical projects. Are we still in an age of antitotalitarianism? There is no doubt that George W. Bush sought to deploy its power in his September 20, 2001, speech when he pronounced the 9/11 terrorists as:

> heirs of all the murderous ideologies of the 20th century. By sacrificing human life to serve their radical visions—by abandoning every value except the will to power—they follow in the path of fascism, Nazism, and totalitarianism.[37]

In an incisive interpretation that he wrote in the early Bush years, Nikhil Singh analyzed this "recycling" of totalitarianism by Bush, focusing in particular on how Bush replayed the Cold War original's disavowal of American racism.[38] The years that followed, however, have suggested an even bleaker picture. It may be that the principal enemy remains conceived as totalitarian, but the disavowal of race is becoming less and less necessary to that task, as we see in the explicit mobilization of Tea Party militancy against an image of Barack Obama as a foreign, crypto-Muslim enemy. The Cold War era's pursuit of a "race war without race" may finally have come to an end. But if so, we have not gotten there by dispensing with war but by returning openly again to race.

NOTES

1. Trotsky uses the term in chapters 5 and 11 of Leon Trotsky, *The Revolution Betrayed: What is the Soviet Union and Where is it Going?* trans. Max Eastman. Web. http://www.marxists.org/archive/trotsky/1936/revbet/index.htm. Trotsky suggests that the Soviet Union had adopted Germany's "totalitarian" methods of rule.

2. See Orwell's famous 1940 essay: George Orwell, "Literature and Totalitarianism," in *Essays* (New York: Alfred A. Knopf, 2002), 587–89.

3. Hannah Arendt, *The Origins of Totalitarianism* (New York: Harcourt Brace Jovanovich, 1973), originally published in 1951. Subsequent quotations from this work will be cited parenthetically within the text. William Pietz, "The Post-Colonialism of Cold War Discourse," *Social Text* 19 and 20 (August 1988): 55–75. Although I agree with Pietz's claim, my understanding of how totalitarianism serves as the Cold War "theoretical anchor" differs significantly. For Pietz, the concept only ever served to bolster anticommunism by appealing to an orientalizing racism (55). I too suggest that race lay at the heart of the totalitarian idea, but that the concept could also work in other directions, for example to make the case for liberationist struggles against a concept of imperialist race war. My understanding of the "post-colonialism" of totalitarianism is therefore that it functioned more broadly and served a more diverse set of political ends.

4. Slavoj Žižek, *Did Somebody Say Totalitarianism? Five Interventions in the (Mis)use of a Notion* (New York: Verso, 2002), 3.

5. Nikhil Singh offers a truly outstanding discussion of the way in which the question of racism haunted the totalitarian thesis during the Cold War and remains a problem for us as we seek to navigate the post-9/11 "war on terror." See Nikhil Pal Singh, "Cold War Redux: On the 'New Totalitarianism,'" *Radical History Review* 85 (Winter 2003): 171–81.

6. Quoted in Nikhil Pal Singh, "Beyond the 'Empire of Jim Crow': Race and War in Contemporary U.S. Globalism," *Japanese Journal of American Studies*, no. 20 (2009): 89–111, 101. I am indebted to Singh not only for these insights in his writ-

ten work but also for the ongoing informal exchange we have conducted in recent years.

7. See Marcia Klotz, "Global Visions: From the Colonial to the National Socialist World," *European Studies Journal* 16, no. 2 (1999): 37–68, which also offers a far more convincing explanation of the connections between colonial racism and Nazi antisemitism than Arendt's unreflectively racist account.

8. See Richard Slotkin, *Regeneration through Violence: The Mythology of the American Frontier, 1600–1860* (Norman: University of Oklahoma Press, 1975). Slotkin's book makes this perceptive argument about "regeneration through violence" in the particular imperialist context of U.S. overland expansion to the West. The argument can be usefully applied to much of nineteenth-century imperialist warfare, however, in which such vitalistic thinking was rampant.

9. See John Rieder, *Colonialism and the Emergence of Science Fiction* (Middletown, CT: Wesleyan University Press, 2008) for a much broader account of how and why the new genre of science fiction played such a central role in the representation of late nineteenth-century European colonial imperialism.

10. Quoted from Harry Truman, "President Harry S. Truman's Address before a Joint Session of Congress, March 12, 1947," Avalon Project at Yale Law School. Web. http://avalon.law.yale.edu/20th_century/trudoc.asp.

11. The following paragraphs revisit a discussion of race war and the Cold War that I first developed in Leerom Medovoi, "Global Society Must Be Defended," *Social Text*, no. 91 (Summer 2007): 53–79. That essay is focused on explaining the globalization of the biopolitical frame in George W. Bush's "war on terror," but my discussion of the Cold War in this chapter expands and develops the one I began there.

12. All the same, the Cold War occasionally resurfaced as race war.

13. I develop this idea in an article titled "Dogma-Line Racism: Islamophobia and the Second Axis of Race," *Social Text* 30 (Summer 2012): 43–74. The focus there is on constructing a working genealogy of contemporary Islamophobic racism, but I would argue that antitotalitarianism has a place in such a genealogy, particularly in its anticommunist form.

14. This passage comes from George Kennan, "The Sources of Soviet Conduct," *Foreign Affairs* (July 1947). William Pietz has explored these orientalist elements in anticommunist theories of totalitarianism in greater detail in "The 'Post-Colonialism' of Cold War Discourse."

15. Robert Heinlein, *The Puppet Masters* (New York: Del Rey, 1951), 31. Subsequent quotations from this work will be cited parenthetically within the text.

16. Carl Schmitt, *The Concept of the Political*, trans. George Schwab (Chicago: University of Chicago Press, 1995), 35. One does not need to agree with Schmitt that all politics *must* take the form of the friend-enemy decision in order to see how it certainly applied to the political form of the Cold War, a presumption of necessary and ongoing hostility (as a permanent war-in-potentia) that only occa-

sionally broke out into open conflict but even at other times channeled and organized the circuits of power and their self-legitimation, on both planetary and domestic levels. This turn to Schmitt may at first seem surprising, given that in my book *Rebels* I sought to bypass the containment model by stressing that the Cold War conflict was always triangulated in relationship to the third world and a liberationist conception of identity. The turn to Schmitt's friend-foe distinction may seem like a regressive return to an "us-versus-them" approach to the Cold War. What I ultimately suggest is that the Schmittian model of politics actually helps us discern how the "us-versus-them" moment of the Cold War and the liberationist moment (linked variously to the "other 1950s," the "1960s," to rebels, activists, civil rights, social movements, and countercultures) actually represent a unitary political moment at a higher level of abstraction.

17. Ibid., 54.

18. John F. Kennedy, "Inaugural Address." 20 January 1961. Web. http://www.americanrhetoric.com/speeches/jfkinaugural.htm.

19. Michel Foucault, *Society Must Be Defended: Lectures at the Collège de France, 1975–1976*, trans. David Macey (New York: Picador, 2003), 254. Subsequent quotations from this work will be cited parenthetically within the text.

20. "President Harry S. Truman's Address before a Joint Session of Congress, March 12, 1947."

21. "Howl," in Allen Ginsberg, *Howl and Other Poems* (San Francisco: City Lights Books, 1981), 64. Subsequent quotations from this work will be cited parenthetically within the text.

22. See Leerom Medovoi, *Rebels: Youth and the Cold War Origins of Identity* (Durham, NC: Duke University Press, 2005).

23. Norman Mailer, "The White Negro," in *Advertisements for Myself* (New York: G. P. Putnam's Sons, 1959), 337–58, 338.

24. Ibid., 340.

25. Aimé Césaire, *Discourse on Colonialism*, trans. Joan Pinkham (New York: Monthly Review Press, 1972), 3.

26. Mary L. Dudziak, *Cold War Civil Rights: Race and the Image of American Democracy* (Princeton, NJ: Princeton University Press, 2002).

27. Malcolm X actually gave several versions of the speech titled "The Ballot or the Bullet." This particular quotation is taken from the April 12, 1964, version delivered in Detroit, Michigan. I also cite the April 3, 1964, version presented in Cleveland, Ohio. To my knowledge, only the latter has been published in print, but the former is accessible on-line. Malcolm X, "The Ballot or the Bullet" (April 3, 1964, version), in *Malcolm X Speaks*, ed. George Breitman (New York: Grove Press, 1966), 23–44. Malcolm X, "The Ballot or the Bullet" (April 12, 1964, version). Web. http://lybio.net/malcolm-x-the-ballot-or-the-bullet/speeches/.

28. Malcolm X, "The Black Revolution," in Breitman, *Malcolm X Speaks*, 45–57, 51.

29. Ibid., 48.

30. Eldridge Cleaver, *Soul on Ice* (New York: Ramparts, 1972), 119, originally published in 1968.

31. Norman Mailer, *The Armies of the Night: History as a Novel, the Novel as History*. 1968 (New York: Plume, 1994), 15. Subsequent quotations from this work will be cited parenthetically within the text.

32. Malcolm X, "The Ballot or the Bullet" [April 3, 1964, version], 36–37.

33. See Stuart Hall, Chas Critcher, Tony Jefferson, John N. Clarke, and Brian Roberts, *Policing the Crisis: Mugging, the State, and Law and Order* (London: Palgrave, 1978).

34. Ruth Wilson Gilmore, *Golden Gulag: Prisons, Surplus, Crisis, and Opposition in Globalizing California* (Berkeley: University of California Press, 2006).

35. Ronald Reagan, "'Evil Empire' Speech." Web. http://www.fordham.edu/halsall/mod/1982reagan1.as.

36. See Patrick Buchanan, "August 17, 1992 Speech at the Republican National Convention." Web. http://buchanan.org/blog/1992-republican-national-convention-speech-148.

37. George W. Bush, "September 20, 2001 Address to Joint Meeting of Congress." Web. http://www.americanrhetoric.com/speeches/gwbush911jointsessionspeech.htm.

38. Singh, "Cold War Redux."

8 THE EMPIRE STRIKES OUT

STAR WARS (IV, V, AND VI) AND THE ADVENT OF REAGANISM

ALAN NADEL

Reaganism is a phenomenon from long ago in a galaxy far, far away that, despite its extraterrestrial (that is, cinematic) origins, was able to snatch the body politic of the United States by reconnecting the umbilical cord of its national imaginary to the bipolar global-political antipathies of the 1950s. An important aspect of that alien seduction is that Reaganism found a story able to serve, as had the conquest of the West through the early 1960s, as an informing narrative for American identity. When Reagan came into office in 1981, the era of Vietnam and Watergate in American politics had in effect reoriented the poles of East and West so radically that the term *West* had lost much of its mythology, and the gold standard, like the dollar it had supported, had become historical trivia akin to the fact that for over a quarter of a century the United States government had managed to mistake the island of Formosa (Taiwan), with a population smaller than that of New York State, for the largest country in the world.

The virtual demise in the 1960s of the American Western, which at one time was the most widespread genre in American popular culture, is symptomatic of the conditions under which the notion of the West could no longer connect the territorial conquests of the United States to its leadership in the global anticommunist crusade. In that context, I show that the first *Star Wars* trilogy (1977–1983) reinvigorated the glorification of Western conquest through a disavowal of historical specificity, in the same way that Reaganism reinvigorated a Cold War sensibility that bridged the Vietnam era, constructing a version of containment that connected the Berlin Airlift in 1948 to the fall of the Berlin Wall in 1989. President Reagan's affinity for cinematic narratives in general, for science fiction more particularly, and for *Star Wars* most specifically, thus underscores how Reagan exploited a public imaginary crucial to the concept of a "long Cold War." If the first film of the trilogy (*Star Wars* IV) revives and revises the Western, the second introduces the philosophical basis of that narrative, for which the final episode provides practical policy applications. The *Star Wars* trilogy (IV, V, and VI), to put it another way, not only glosses but also is instrumental in the performance of President Reagan's Cold War endgame.

What Does the West Stand For?

Because a spherical surface has no absolute east or absolute west, the directions that delimit a military front in a genuinely global conflict eventually and logically redouble as a rear action. For this reason, broad geographical labels designate political orientations rather than actual places in what we have called the Cold War. Countries aligned with the West thus were not located solely in the Western Hemisphere, any more than the Eastern Bloc consisted only of countries behind the Iron Curtain. Initially China and subsequently Taiwan, along with South Korea and Japan, while geographically in the Far East, resided irrefutably in the geopolitical West.

In the three-centuries-long settlement and expansion of the United States, however, the labels *East* and *West* distributed different connotations, for initially in American history the East had exemplary rather than adversarial status. It represented what the West had to become: settled, civilized, systematized within the flow of commerce and the generation of capital. In this context, the concepts associated with the term *West* in American popular discourse located topical antipathies within the broader framework of American triumphalism, such that in the westward expansion of the United States, the West—understood simultaneously as history, destiny, and mythology—signified the fact of transcontinental nationalism as well as the means by which that fact was established. That activity, however, entailed a linguistic inversion; while *doxa* made Eastern manners, practices, and laws requisite to the assimilation of Western regions, in the process of placing Western territory under the East's control the entire nation nominally assumed the mantle and identity of the West. More than just a facile irony, this substitution of West for East suggests how much the interests of the United States' Eastern establishment profited from having the Western mythos serve as the national ethos. Richard Slotkin has extensively detailed the ways in which the United States, as a "gunfighter nation," effected this conversion and the extent to which cultural and historical practice continues to sustain it.[1]

This form of "victory culture," as Tom Engelhardt calls it, found its apotheosis in the World War II success of the West (with the crucial help of Russia on Germany's *eastern* front).[2] For the United States, that victory was as much social, cultural, and economic as military. Winning a devastating war that affected more than half of the planet without incurring any damage to its homeland, the United States was uniquely positioned among Allied nations to profit immediately from its triumphs. The spoils were multifarious and plentiful: American corporations, like American currency, became the strongest in the world, allowing the standard of living in the United States rapidly to surpass all rivals. Nor was this merely a secular victory, because the same events at Hiroshima and Nagasaki that ended World War II initiated the atomic age such that, as Paul Boyer has shown, Americans frequently associated the ascent to atomic power with the divine will: the capacity to cause nuclear devastation demonstrated the destiny of the West.[3]

Nevertheless, another image of America's westward expansion—that of covered wagons in a circle—remains in vital counterpoint to the triumphalist narratives that Slotkin has delineated. In the Cold War, despite economic and military superiority, an exchange rate that made dollars themselves the ultimate colonialist instrument, and the plethora of creature comforts this economic colonialism facilitated, the United States proliferated narratives representing the self-proclaimed "leader of the Free World" as surrounded and outnumbered by hostile adversaries. A fear—legitimate, paranoid, or a little bit of both—haunted the postwar period with almost hysterical intensity, suggesting the fragility of Western power that from the late 1940s until the early 1960s saw itself as subject to insidious subversion and, at any moment after 1949, to immediate annihilation.[4]

By the end of the 1960s, however, in the face of the military and ethical failure of the Vietnam War, the legends of the American West that had so graphically merged divine destiny and Cold War supremacy were unable to project a story of virtuous triumph. Everything about the Vietnam War disproved the premise that the conquest of the American West symbolized the spread of democracy. As the war escalated exponentially throughout the 1960s, the West was more and more visibly engaged in perpetuating tyranny rather than in preserving freedom. North Vietnam's victory, moreover, disproved the notion of a world Communist monolith that mandated strategies of containment. Since these had been cornerstones of American foreign policy since World War II, and since the Vietnam War was "hot" rather than "cold," in many ways the Vietnam era can aptly be seen as the culmination of the Cold War.

This admittedly arbitrary historical and cultural division works well in delimiting a form of high Cold War sensibility in the United States, in which an array of clichés about freedom, subversion, nuclear holocaust, and (Judeo-Christian) moral superiority operated broadly enough to justify consensus about multiple overt and covert activities in an ideologically and politically bifurcated world. The high Cold War period was thus the era when these clichés were able to inflect cultural practice, public discourse, educational curricula, and popular media strongly. By the same token, nostalgia—not just for Cold War sensibilities but, perhaps more importantly, for the sanctimonious pride they inspired—unquestionably connects the post-Vietnam period to the high Cold War, creating a "long Cold War" starting with what some view as politically motivated genocide at Nagasaki in 1945 and culminating with the collapse of the Berlin Wall in 1989.[5]

The central thesis of my book *Containment Culture* is that the (high) Cold War was full of dualities, contradictions, and diversities that the rigid social conformity and the political and sexual repression of the late 1940s and 1950s never succeeded in suppressing fully.[6] Even when the apparatuses of repression—HUAC investigations, FBI surveillance, blacklisting, film and television censorship, and television network monopolies[7]—combined to iterate relentlessly the narratives of America as a white, homogeneous, heterosexual, and middle-class nation, dualities were nevertheless ubiquitous. Their expression occurred chiefly in textual contradictions (such as Holden Caulfield's attempt to achieve veracity without telling the truth). At the same time, moreover, alternative cultural values, such as those represented by *Playboy* magazine, acquired popular reception. Thus, by the end of the 1950s, cultural containment started to break down and suppressed contradictions were replaced by visible dualities in works such as *The Man Who Shot Liberty Valance* and *Catch-22*, and, more importantly, in political actions such as the Bay of Pigs invasion and the Free Speech Movement at Berkeley.

The 1960s, therefore, did not end the Cold War as much as make visible its contradictions. In this sense the Vietnam War era, rather than following the Cold War era, vividly exposed it. After Vietnam (and to a lesser degree Watergate), therefore, it was hard to view the history of the West as consistent with the mythology of the Western, as the two no longer seemed to portend a common, desirable destiny.

The Western Goes Galactic

To put it another way, reviving (or extending) Cold War narratives in the post-Vietnam period posed the rhetorical problem of tying a morally and geopolitically bifurcated allegory to a multifarious geographical and conceptual terrain. Thus, when the first *Star Wars* (IV) film in 1977 transferred the tropes and conventions of the Western from Earth to another galaxy, it recontextualized America's Cold War ethos because the object-specific terrain delimited by *East* and *West* lost its meaning when the orbiting gravity of a small planet was put in a multigalactic perspective. As Will Wright aptly points out, "while the Western is a historical, and therefore legitimating myth . . . [o]n the face of it . . . the *Star Wars* films direct us toward . . . a myth in which heroism, love, and success are made to look accessible only through the setting aside of all social, historical, and even natural realities."[8]

Nor does it take an Einstein to see that *Star Wars*' change in perspective is temporal as well as spatial, for however futuristic its weaponry and its command of distance, *Star Wars* represents this technological destiny as the product of an already-unfolded history. We are, as the opening titles tell us, not in the future but in the past—"A long time ago in a galaxy far, far away"—so that, just as the story of the West made contemporary audiences (and American citizens) the advocates of the destiny of the West, it made them so by virtue of being the historical products of the story that they were positioned to champion anew.

In this context, President Reagan's infamous penchant for revisionist history is completely consistent with the way in which *Star Wars* (IV) conflates an imaginary past with a desired future.[9] The iconography of an earlier age, when "warriors" carried ammo in belts across their chests, holstered handguns gunslinger-style, and fought with sabers, constantly tempers *Star Wars*' visual world of intergalactic flight, advanced robotics, and cosmic weaponry. The costumes also suggest that the technological focus in this distant galaxy falls completely on robotics, blasters, and nifty ways to go places really fast, with none devoted to textile manufacturing or sewing machines. Luke and his cohorts perform facile technological feats dressed in clothing resembling homespun togas, and Obi-Wan Kenobi wears the hooded cloak of a medieval monk, which is made from hopsack and colored with dung, as does the Emperor, who apparently shops from the same rack for superannuated monks at the galactic Goodwill store.

Apparently, both Obi-Wan Kenobi and the Emperor shop at the galactic Goodwill store. From *Star Wars* IV.

Star Wars' pastiche of pastness privileges particularly the period associated with the Old West. In this "Western in intergalactic drag," as Wright calls it,[10] Han Solo sports his ray gun gunslinger-style and wears a leather vest direct from the Wyatt-Earp-of-Uranus collection.[11] Luke's adoptive parents live in an adobelike structure located on what looks like the vacated site of a John Ford Western, and his relationship to them echoes that of Martin Pauly, the adoptive son of Ethan's (John Wayne's) brother and sister-in-law in *The Searchers*. Even complex computer repairs are done by hand, in something like the garage or barn, in much the way one might fix a wagon wheel. The computer science necessary to maintain the robots is treated as a kind of quotidian farm work, an everyday task learned at home, and the robots are discussed as though they were ranch hands. "Your only concern," Luke's uncle tells him, "is to prepare those new droids for tomorrow. In the morning, I want them up there on the south ridge working on those condensers." One almost expects to find in the outtakes a scene in which R2-D2 and C-3PO, to the tune of raspy trumpets and punctured car mufflers, accompany the campfire serenade produced by Blazing Saddles trail hands.

Luke's little pueblo on the mesa also resembles the nineteenth-century American Southwest in that it is surrounded by hostile adversaries of the two sorts most common in Westerns: the savage and the violent gang. If he strays too far from home, especially after dark, Luke is open to attack by the Sand People, who resemble Native Americans auditioning for what not to wear. Luke's home is also vulnerable to outlaw massacre. In this futuristic place, in other words, science and technology do not tame the West but rather allow for the constant restaging of its vulnerability, in-

Han Solo sports his ray gun gunslinger-style. From *Star Wars* IV.

The massacre of Luke's home and a comparable scene in *The Searchers*. From *Star Wars* IV.

cluding the massacre of Luke's home and family, which resembles a comparable event in *The Searchers*. Violent annihilation and frontier justice circumscribe the simple life Luke leads.

The trailer for *Star Wars* (IV), moreover, which proclaims "the most extraordinary motion picture of all time: *Star Wars*," participates in the same act of temporal dislocation as does the film when it claims, even before the film's release, its historical status as the exceptional representative of both the past and the future. The exceptionalism entailed in the word "extraordinary" reflects the same duality that has characterized American exceptionalism as representative of the ordinary (the norm meaning the average) and the extraordinary (the norm meaning the ideal). The trailer extends that claim of American exceptionalism into the future: "No legendary adventure of the past could be as exciting as this romance of the future." This is not, however, a romance *of* the future but a romance *with* the future, which constructs the future as a place in the aftermath of Vietnam where once again war will be romantic, that is, the way war was in the past or, rather, the way it was represented by movie stars. The trilogy thematizes this aspect of *Star Wars* by having the narrative of the three episodes (IV, V, and VI) pivot crucially around competition for very specific stars, because the winning over of those in whom the Force is strong guarantees control of the galaxy. The *Star Wars* saga, in other words, is as much about the Hollywood studio system as it is a replica of the classic Westerns that that system produced.

Which Side Are We On?

In this regard, Darth Vader and the Emperor, on the one hand, and Obi-Wan and Yoda, on the other, resemble rival studio heads competing for the star on whose appeal the future of the studio depends. The casting gives this competition additional resonance, for neither Vader nor Yoda speaks in his own voice. Yoda is a puppet voiced by longtime Jim Henson staffer Frank Oz, and Vader is a performer miming the role of a machine that houses the remnants of a person. His voice comes from black actor James Earl Jones, associated at that point in his career with the boxer Jack Johnson, whom he portrayed on stage and on screen. At least subliminally, the two rivals for Luke's affiliation thus turn the struggle into a fight between Jack Johnson and Miss Piggy (which makes the outcome inevitable, for, as all Muppet fans know, hell hath no adversary like a porcine scorned). If the Dark Side is represented by a black outfit through which a black man speaks, then Luke is de facto the Great White Hope; in fact, both Obi-Wan and Yoda consider Luke the last *hope* to defeat the *Dark* Side.

He is not, however, the only hope, in that Princess Leia is his sister and thus by virtue of genetic disposition another in whom the Force is strong. The fact that Leia is played by Carrie Fisher echoes yet another Hollywood rivalry, because she too came from a gene pool of warring stars. Like Leia's father Vader, Carrie Fisher's father Eddie Fisher was a celebrity who went over to the dark side when he abandoned his wife Debbie Reynolds to marry Elizabeth Taylor. Carrie Fisher, who currently has a one-woman show chronicling the follies of her background, could easily have named that show "star wars," thereby conflating, in the same way that her life did, the film trilogy's mythic battle for control of the galaxy with the on- and offscreen celebrity wars that Hollywood has produced for a century. (In her show, Fisher recounts being recognized recently by a fan, who told her that he had thought about her every day when he was in high school. "*Every* day?" she asked. "Well, actually four times a day," he replied.)

This concern over star allegiance, in both the extradiegetic and the master plot of *Star Wars*, is one of many affinities between the saga and Ronald Reagan. If Lou Cannon's history of the Reagan presidency is called *President Reagan: The Role of a Lifetime*, it was a role Reagan acquired after decades of combat in Hollywood's star wars, including a largely unsuccessful attempt to battle his way out of B pictures. In the 1940s, "Reagan was battling Warner's for hefty dramatic roles that the studio believed were over his head."[12] One of the reasons for the dissolution of his marriage to Jane Wyman, in fact, was that her career was on an upward trajectory while his was flatlining. Another aspect of Reagan's star wars related to his Screen Actors Guild activity, especially as it was engaged with Congressional hearings, Communist witch hunts, and the industry blacklist. "As President of the Screen Actors Guild from 1947 to 1952, . . . Reagan enforced the blacklist. He supported a provision in the guild constitution barring Communists from membership. He acted as an informant for the FBI, naming actors and actresses who 'follow the Communist party line.'"[13] From one perspective, Reagan's shift from liberal to supporter of HUAC and Barry Goldwater could suggest that he went over to the dark side; alternatively, however, his rejection of liberalism could be viewed as a testament to his virtue. In any case, the two heroes of *Star Wars* (IV, V, and VI) reflect two aspects of Reagan's personal narrative: Han Solo is the dashing Western hero, the kind of role for which Reagan yearned and which went instead to stars such as Errol Flynn, Clark Gable, or John Wayne. Luke, on the other hand, is the earnest man from modest origins whose stardom is more potential than actual, more a function of his will than of his ability. Because it turns out in *Star Wars* that Luke is not fighting for a side as much as the two sides are fighting over Luke, he becomes, as Reagan did late in his life, a de facto star, despite the observation by Yoda when Luke first meets him: "Grr . . . Great warrior? Grr . . . Wars not make one great."

The question of which side Luke will end up on, however, diverts us from a more troubling question: which side is the Rebel Alliance on? "It is a period of civil war," the opening titles of *Star Wars* (IV) tell us, making clear in the second sentence that our sympathies *must* lie with the "Rebels," as they have "won their first victory against the *evil* Galactic Empire" (emphasis added). Made in the wake of American withdrawal from Vietnam, the a priori choice to make the Rebels good and the Empire evil could suggest a sympathetic identification with the Viet Cong, who had rebelled against and eventually defeated the imperialist forces first of the French and then of the United States, despite the technological superiority of these global powers. This allegorical reading is further reinforced by the fact that the Empire has the weaponry, the Death Star, "with enough power to destroy an entire planet," that is, with the equivalent of the United States' unmatched nuclear arsenal.

Very rapidly, however, the film undermines this reading, not only because it associates the Rebels with Western settlers and heroes but also because it populates the evil Empire with soldiers and henchmen outfitted for a Stalinist regime. The initiating premise of *Star Wars* (IV), in other words, is exactly the inverse of the Vietnam War, in that the West is represented by the technologically inferior Rebels rather than by an invading war machine that used napalm and Agent Orange to defoliate the landscape and eradicate "unfriendly" villages, that mined Hai Phong Harbor, and that dropped over 7 million tons of bombs on Vietnam. *Star Wars* (IV) thus starts by reviving the narrative that the Vietnam War discredited, that the South Vietnamese Army comprised the freedom fighters, and the North Vietnamese were the agents of a monolithic, evil, Communist empire set on world domination.

This too was the position that Ronald Reagan took when in 1980 he proclaimed that the war in Vietnam "was, in truth, a noble cause. A small country newly free from colonial rule sought our help in establishing self-rule and the means of self-defense against a totalitarian neighbor bent on conquest."[14] While this brief quotation, like the speech from which it is excerpted, is replete with historical errors,[15] it accurately describes the tenets of *Star Wars* (IV, V, and VI), the next episode of which, *The Empire Strikes Back* (V), premiered almost exactly three months before Reagan made this speech. Just as Reagan's cowboy image helped identify him with the kind of Western hero he wanted to play, his gravitation toward the *Star Wars* Rebels helped attach that image to a post-Vietnam West, for the "way of the West" has strong kinship ties to what the *Star Wars* trilogy calls the "way of the Jedi."

The Empire Strikes Back

If *Star Wars* (IV) resuscitated the Western as the definitive scaffold for national ideals, *The Empire Strikes Back* (V) connected that narrative to its underpinnings in American Emersonian transcendentalism. When Yoda advises Luke: "Try not. Do, or do not. There is no try" (V), it is hard to miss the echo of Emerson's assertion in "Compensation" that the "law of nature is, do the thing, and you shall have the power: but they who do not the thing have not the power."[16]

Yoda understood the power of the Force to rest in a belief system that rendered one's state of mind more powerful than facts, one's perceptions more valid than history. As Obi-Wan explains to Luke: "What I told you [about your father being dead] was true from a certain point of view." "You're going to find," he further explains, "that many of the truths we cling to depend greatly on our own point of view" (V). Similarly, as Shanti Fader notes, "Yoda's primary lesson is that in order to use the Force, one must look beyond appearances."[17] After all, according to Emerson, "one man's justice is another's injustice; one man's beauty another's ugliness; one man's wisdom another's folly; as one beholds the same objects from a higher point."[18] "Mind is the only reality," says Emerson at his most Platonic, "of which men and all other natures are better or worse reflections."[19] With the image of the cave, as Julia Barrad points out, "Plato wants to show us that most people are ignorant of their true selves and reality."[20] This is the reason, Barrad points out, that Yoda "makes Luke enter the recesses of a dark cave. . . . [H]e doesn't know himself as well as he should."[21] "For Yoda, Obi-Wan, and Plato," according to Christopher M. Brown, "true power is spiritual power—having control over one's own self."[22] An explication of this principle that Emerson provides in "Self-Reliance" may be read as providing a transcendentalist gloss on the Force that powers the Jedi:

> The magnetism which all original action exerts is explained when we inquire the reason of self-trust. Who is the Trustee? What is the aboriginal Self, on which a universal reliance may be grounded. . . . The inquiry leads us to that source, at once the essence of genius, of virtue, and of life, which we call Spontaneity or Instinct. We denote this primary wisdom as Intuition, whilst all later teachings are tuitions. In that deep force . . . all things find their common origin.[23]

"Every thing in nature controls all the powers of nature,"[24] Emerson tells us in "Compensation," providing a more succinct and coherent version of Yoda's instruction to Luke that "you must feel the Force around you. Here, between you . . . me . . . the tree . . . the rock . . . everywhere!"

Make no mistake, *Star Wars* is dumbed-down Emerson, and my target here, like that of Ralph Ellison in his allusions to Emerson in *Invisible Man*,[25] is not Emerson per se but the way in which his ideas, filtered through the minds of simplistic thinkers, have provided an echo chamber for those who, like Reagan and his adoring base, would grapple with historical and political realities aphoristically and anecdotally, who would see well-crafted phrases as resolving contradictions rather than wrestling with them. Such people, even if they had never read Emerson, were among the 27 percent of eligible voters choosing Reagan in 1980 and describing as "important" "the intensity of his convictions."[26] Pointing out the historical antecedent to Reagan's predilection, William Kleinknecht quotes a passage from "Self-Reliance" that applies with equal cogency to Yoda: "To believe your own thought, to believe that what is true for you in your private heart is true for all men—that is genius."[27]

When one reads Emerson today, it may be hard to understand his reputation in the nineteenth century as a public speaker, in much the same way that Reagan's speeches do little (pace Peggy Noonan) to justify his reputation as the "great communicator." The same holds true for Yoda as the wellspring of Jedi wisdom. Anthony Lane, reviewing *Revenge of the Sith* for the *New Yorker*, made this general characterization of Yoda's communication skills: "What's with the screwy syntax? Deepest mind in the galaxy, apparently, and you still express yourself like a day-tripper with a dog-eared phrase book. 'I hope right you are.' Break me a fucking give."[28]

Like Yoda, Reagan's communication skills were as much the subject of ridicule as reverence. To complement their shared belief in "self-reliance" and their physical resemblance, Reagan and Yoda share one of Emerson's rhetorical traits. Much has been made of what F. O. Matthiessen described as Emerson's "organic" style;[29] Harold Bloom has called the linguistic process of Emerson's essays a form of "gnosis";[30] and Richard Poirier has identified it with Emerson's genius.[31] Another way to describe his style is to say that the unit of organization for Emerson is the assertion, which may be seen as a form of linguistic self-reliance, as the crafting of standalone utterances that make the world anew, sometimes in startling ways. Like Emerson, in other words, Reagan's organization of utterances does not depend on their place in a logical sequence. Rather, they are all excerpts, meant more for the mode of the sound bite than for that of the argument. These sound bites are linked not by logos but by ethos, by our sense of the speaker as more coherent than the speech.

The Force, as Reagan thus demonstrated, was public relations, the same Force that the heroes of *Star Wars* shared with its makers. Both George Lucas and Reagan understood the value of packaging a utopian vision as lapsarian rather than as progressive, and both did so by resusci-

Reagan's resemblance to Yoda. Reagan portrait by Michael J. Deas. Yoda from *The Empire Strikes Back*.

tating the West through the redemption of the Western. *Star Wars* provided a template for these strategies, as did the concept of Reaganism. "The Reagan Revolution," Kleinknecht succinctly explains, "has rested on a fallacy—that somewhere in the American past shimmers a halcyon era when the masses lived happily and private enterprise flourished without interference from the dead hand of government. Ronald Reagan—nothing if not a dreamer, a man who made crucial decisions on the advice of an astrologer, who believed in extraterrestrials, who again and again confused Hollywood images with reality—tried to take America back on a journey to a Shangri-la that never existed."[32]

The Return of the Gipper

The year 1983 was a watershed for Reagan.[33] At the beginning of the year, it was clear that, even with the revenue generated by his tax increases, his economic policies had doubled rather than reduced the national debt; in the words of his budget director David Stockman, he had "cooked the books." In light of his low approval ratings, there were suggestions early in the year that he might use his age as an excuse to avoid seeking a second term. But by the end of the year, everything had changed. The turning point started in March, when Reagan delivered his "Evil Empire" speech to a gathering of evangelicals, which was the first of four events that helped convert the mythology of *Star Wars* (IV) and the philosophy of *The Empire Strikes Back* (V) into their pragmatic consequences and that made the trilogy an explicit cornerstone of Reaganism.[34] In the "Evil Empire" speech, he extolled the importance of spiritual over material values. Characterizing the Cold War in language that aptly describes Luke's challenge—"The real crisis we face today is a spiritual one; at root, it is a test of moral will and faith"—Reagan connected that challenge to the high Cold War by citing for support the writing of the McCarthy-era anticommunist witness Whittaker Chambers.

On March 23, Reagan made another allusion to the *Star Wars* lexicon when he introduced his strategic defense initiative by using the title from episode IV and calling it "a new hope" for the children of the twenty-first century. This new hope, quickly known as "Star Wars," was a strategic defense initiative to build a technology "that could intercept and destroy strategic ballistic missiles before they reached our own soil and that of our neighbors."[35]

These key speeches not only allude to the titles of the first two *Star Wars* episodes (IV and V) but also manifest, especially in combination, the dual consciousness that informs the trilogy. As with the settling of the West, Reagan figures the nation as advancing economic civilization and forging the frontiers of freedom through the sheer mass of its material goods and technological know-how; at the same time, he sees it beleaguered and outnumbered like the Rebel forces, the wagons in a proverbial circle. Exaggerating at both extremes, Reagan represents the nation as simultaneously overwhelming and overwhelmed. If the nation is a futuristic place that replicates "long ago," Reagan sees that return to the future as spiritual as well as material, and the nation as a place where school prayer is a necessity of national security.

All of these themes inform the third instantiation of *Star Wars* in 1983: the opening of *Return of the Jedi* (*Star Wars* VI) took place on May 25. In this final episode, the ragtag Rebel coalition reunites to destroy yet a second Death Star, but the information that leads them to this mission is a ruse of the Emperor to lure Luke. For the final battle, it turns out, is over Luke's soul. And Luke, ever the optimistic Reaganite, continues to underestimate the power of the Dark Side until his sheer persistence turns the tables, making the saving of Vader's soul rather than the preservation of his own the ultimate victory.

The spiritual dimension of Reagan's Cold War endgame uncannily replicates this narrative, with his rapprochement with Mikhail Gorbachev replicating Luke's turning Vader away from the Dark Side. Instrumental in this process was Suzanne Massie, a deeply religious Russophile who developed a very strong personal—but not romantic—relationship with Reagan. Over a series of private meetings spanning several years, usually upstairs in the White House family quarters, Massie convinced Reagan of the inherent goodness of the Russian people. Reagan was entranced by her history of Russia *Land of the Firebird: The Beauty of Old Russia* (1980), a book that a *New York Times* review had characterized as a "heavy breathing comic strip" and "a lollipop speaking baby-talk."[36]

According to James Mann:

> At Geneva and in its aftermath, Reagan seemed to be wondering whether Gorbachev might secretly be a religious believer—a question that was closely linked to his discussions with Massie about the spiritual nature of the Russian people. "Strangely enough in those meetings he twice invoked God's name," Reagan wrote in a letter. . . . When Gorbachev briefly used the phrase "God bless" at a subsequent summit meeting, Reagan took notice and pointed it out to Colin Powell.[37]

About the 1986 accident at Chernobyl, Mann explains:

> Massie told Reagan and Secretary of State George Shultz that ordinary Russians viewed the disaster as confirmation of a biblical prophecy. The Book of Revelations refers to a star called Wormwood, which falls to the earth, poisoning the waters and killing many people. Wormwood is the name for a common herb, and the Ukrainian name for it is *chernobyl*.[38]

The constant reinforcement of Reagan's conception of the Russian people as spiritual, that is, as capable of rejecting the Dark Side, some believe, may have been far more instrumental in ending the Cold War than Reagan's "Star Wars" strategic defense initiative or his "tear down this wall" speech in Berlin.

If Reagan's softening toward Gorbachev imitates Luke's overtures to Vader, his hardening policy in Central America makes his October invasion of Grenada the fourth *Star Wars* event of 1983. National Security Council (NSC) operative Oliver North's extralegal arms sales to Iran and his funneling of the proceeds to the Nicaraguan Contras reflect the ad hoc militarism typified in the *Star Wars* saga by Han Solo, the lone ranger who with his faithful companion Chewbacca rides from out of the west "with the speed of light and a hearty hi-yo Silver."[39]

The defeat of the first Death Star, we discover at the outset of *Return of the Jedi*, was only a temporary setback for the forces of evil, which are now working on an even more powerful space station. "When completed," the opening titles tell us, "this ultimate weapon will spell certain doom for the small band of rebels struggling to restore freedom to the galaxy." In other words, the Rebels are not fighting for freedom *from* the Empire; rather, they want to replace the Empire and become the governing force of the entire galaxy. The task is disproportionately large for the *small* band of Rebels, and, even more significantly, their ambition compared to their size is astronomical. It is as if the Viet Cong wanted not only to expel foreign forces but also to topple the French and American governments. Similarly, Castro might overthrow a dictator and then be invaded by counterrevolutionaries backed by America, but the converse is preposterous: although Castro could endure an attack at the Bay of Pigs, he could hardly launch one on Boca Raton or Fort Lauderdale, despite the claims of American rhetoric throughout the long Cold War. According to a "domino theory," that rhetoric held that if for example South Vietnam fell to the North Vietnamese, a sequence of adjacent nations would also fall in an endless cascade subsuming not just Saigon, Cambodia, and Thailand but also Malaysia, Australia, Japan, Samoa, et cetera, until Guam remained the last free outpost west of Hollywood. The fifty-year boycott of Cuba is similarly due to the belief that the country, located only ninety miles from Florida, could "export" revolution (to a place such as Miami Beach, where no doubt thousands of seniors watching the Home Shopping Network in their assisted-living communities would jump at the chance to import the hirsute guerrillas Castro was exporting).

Nor were these references purely platitudinous. The dual heroic identities as Rebel force and rightful heir to the universal Force that were implicit in the *Star Wars* saga found concrete expression in President Reagan's Central American policy. Throughout the 1980s, the Reagan administration supported what it deemed the "legitimate" government in El Salvador (responsible for rampant death squads) against insurgency, at the same time that it supported the Contra rebels attempting to overthrow the government of El Salvador's neighbor Nicaragua. To justify his violation of the Boland Amendment, which prohibited aid to the Contras, Oliver North, echoing the sentiments of the *Star Wars* saga, called those Contras "freedom fighters." Thus, the violated interdiction of the Contras exposed an inherent *contra*diction: the Contras could fight for independence as long as they depended upon global power. Without the United States' capacity for Death Star destruction, it would have been unlikely, for instance, that the Reagan administration would have dared in 1983 to violate international law by mining Nicaragua's harbors. To the extent that the United States supported freedom fighting, therefore, the freedom for which the Contras were fighting was not their own but that of the United States. As Reagan stated in a speech in 1986:

> Using Nicaragua as a base, the Soviets and Cubans can become the dominant power in the crucial corridor between North and South America. Established there, they will be in a position to threaten the Panama Canal, interdict our vital Caribbean sea lanes, and ultimately, move against Mexico. Should that happen, desperate Latin peoples by the millions would begin fleeing north into the cities of the southern United States, or to wherever some hope of freedom remained.[40]

Holly Sklar points out:

> President Reagan has called Nicaragua a "totalitarian dungeon"; the Sandinistas are "infinitely worse than Somoza," he says. He has branded Nicaragua an "outlaw state," part of "a confederation of terrorist states," also including Iran, Libya, North Korea and Cuba. He told the American Bar Association these "outlaw states" were "run by the strangest collection of misfits, Looney Tunes and squalid criminals since the advent of the Third Reich." . . . George Shultz has taken to referring to the Nicaraguan government as "a cancer, right here on our land mass."[41]

If Shultz's use of the term "our land" to describe Central America treats the United States as an empire, the Iran-Contra scandal makes clear that in the Nicaraguan portion of *our* land mass, we side with the Rebel Alliance. But that loyalty to the Rebels should not be taken as anti-imperialist, as *Return of the Jedi* makes clear in its species hierarchy, vividly illustrated in the saga's final segments relating to Ewoks, who are one step down from the Wookie (the ethnically and genetically inferior sidekick of the sort that often populates Western literature and film). Importantly, both the Rebel Alliance and the "Evil Empire" are run by the same species, the only group from which the masters of the universe can come. The other species are ancillary and subordinate, whether unruly and troublesome or loyal and cooperative. If Chewbacca is a Tonto, the narrative and visual systems in *Return of the Jedi* code the Ewoks as African "natives" who, much like the tribesmen in the Tarzan series and its kindred African adventures, confuse Western technology with a magic that demands worship. Thus, the tribal reverence that the Ewoks show for C-3PO confirms

Three dead patriarchs return to celebrate a monarchy of adventurism. Hayden Christensen (left), who played Anakin Skywalker (later Darth Vader) in the more recent films, was retroactively inserted into the earlier *Return of the Jedi* for DVD release. From *Star Wars* VI.

the natural order of colonialism, with the lowest form of humanoid—actually a gold-plated piece of technological bling—demonstrating clear superiority over the more animalistic natives. That superiority, moreover, makes intellectual superiority synonymous with moral superiority, in that their worship of C-3PO not only avails the Ewoks of a technologically superior way of life but also stops them from practicing cannibalism. When their service to the Rebel Alliance incorporates them within its sphere of influence, they participate with their primitive weapons, celebrate with songs, and dance to a roughly calypso beat. It is hard to pinpoint, however, exactly what the Ewoks are celebrating, in that they did not seem to be in danger from the "Evil Empire," nor did the "Evil Empire" seem interested in duping them into worshipping false idols. By inference, they rejoice in the triumph of the Rebel Alliance, regardless of the implications for their own civilization.

But the confusing politics of *Star Wars* that might surface at this moment is instead marked by an ostensible dissolution of class distinctions, implied in the triumph of the Rebels. Not only do Ewok and Wookie participate, but the nobility consisting of Luke and Leia, as well as the outsider Han, celebrates in a more ceremonial event marking the restoration of royal rule: they don't call her *Princess* Leia for nothing. In effect, the Eastern establishment and the European aristocracy acknowledge their appreciation for the lone ranger, just as he acknowledges his commitment to their benevolent monarchy.

As I argued in *Flatlining on the Field of Dreams*, Reaganism reasserted patriarchal power by convincing Americans that their patriarchs would be stronger posthumously than they were in their vitality, which is certainly true at the end of *Star Wars* (IV, V, and VI), where three dead patriarchs—Obi-Wan, Yoda, and the redeemed Vader—return to celebrate this marriage of Western adventurism and Eastern monarchy in scenes that confirm the union's implicit hierarchy as part of a natural order.[42] Only the Force allows such cosmic agency to what ought to have been by 1983 a moribund patriarchy. The (dead) founding fathers, one per episode, thus become eternal forces of nature, as well as the father, son, and holy ghost of the long Cold War.

NOTES

1. See Richard Slotkin, *Gunfighter Nation: The Myth of the Frontier in Twentieth-Century America* (New York: Atheneum, 1992).

2. Tom Engelhardt, *The End of Victory Culture: Cold War America and the Disillusioning of a Generation* (New York: Basic Books, 1995).

3. Paul Boyer, *By the Bomb's Early Light: American Thought and Culture at the Dawn of the Atomic Age* (New York: Pantheon, 1985).

4. See Richard Hofstadter, *The Paranoid Style in American Politics: And Other Essays* (Cambridge, MA: Harvard University Press, 1996); and Michael Rogin, *Ronald Reagan, the Movie: And Other Episodes in Political Demonology* (Berkeley: University of California Press, 1988). This is but one incarnation of a long-standing national theme that contributed to what Richard Hofstadter long ago called the "paranoid style in American politics" and what Michael Rogin more recently described as the politics of demonization. The nativism that the twenty-first-century Tea Party shares with the antebellum Know-Nothing Party participates in the same kinds of fears that have been directed toward "Papists," Freemasons, the Irish, or more recently, Mexicans and Arabs.

5. The most extensive argument that Hiroshima was bombed as a function of the United States' Soviet policy is made by Gar Alperovitz, *The Decision to Use the Atomic Bomb* (New York: Vintage, 1996); see also Ronald Takaki, *Hiroshima: Why America Dropped the Atomic Bomb* (New York: Back Bay Books, 1996).

6. Alan Nadel, *Containment Culture: American Narratives, Postmodernism, and the Atomic Age* (Durham, NC: Duke University Press, 1995).

7. See Alan Nadel, *Television in Black-and-White America: Race and National Identity* (Lawrence: University of Kansas Press, 2005).

8. Will Wright, "The Empire Bites the Dust," *Social Text*, no. 6 (Autumn 1982): 120–25, 121.

9. See Lou Cannon, *President Reagan: The Role of a Lifetime* (New York: Simon and Schuster, 1991); Susan Jeffords, *Hard Bodies: Hollywood Masculinity in the Reagan Era* (New Brunswick, NJ: Rutgers University Press, 1994); Alan Nadel, *Flatlin-*

ing on the Field of Dreams: Cultural Narratives in the Films of President Reagan's America (New Brunswick, NJ: Rutgers University Press, 1997); Rogin, *Ronald Reagan, the Movie*; and Garry Wills, *Reagan's America: Innocents at Home* (New York: Doubleday, 1987).

10. Wright, "Empire Bites the Dust," 120.

11. See Wright, "Empire Bites the Dust." Wright lists a number of other traits that *Star Wars* shares with the Western, including the designation of white hats for good guys and black hats for bad guys, and the way in which Han's spaceship the *Millennium Falcon* stands in for talismanic animals such as Trigger or Silver.

12. Cannon, *President Reagan*, 191.

13. Rogin, *Ronald Reagan, the Movie*, 31.

14. Ronald Reagan, "Peace: Restoring the Margin of Safety" (speech, Veterans of Foreign Wars Convention, Chicago, 18 August 1980). Web. http://www.reagan.utexas.edu/archives/reference/8.18.80.html.

15. For example, Reagan claimed that Vietnam was threatening Thailand and that Vietnam's strategy in the Vietnam War was to win the propaganda war in the United States, because it could not win on the battlefield.

16. Ralph Waldo Emerson, *The Essential Writings of Ralph Waldo Emerson*, ed. Brooks Atkinson (New York: Random House, 2000), 165.

17. Shanti Fader, "'A Certain Point of View': Lying Jedi, Honest Sith, and the Viewers Who Love Them," in *Star Wars and Philosophy: More Powerful Than You Can Possibly Imagine*, ed. Kevin S. Decker and Jason T. Eberl (Chicago: Open Court Publications, 2005), 192–204, 197.

18. Emerson, *Essential Writings of Ralph Waldo Emerson*, 259.

19. Ibid., 83.

20. Julia Barrad, "The Aspiring Jedi's Handbook of Virtue," in Decker and Eberl, *Star Wars and Philosophy*, 57–68, 63.

21. Ibid.

22. Christopher M. Brown, "'A Wretched Hive of Scum and Villainy': *Star Wars* and the Problem of Evil," in Decker and Eberl, *Star Wars and Philosophy*, 69–79, 73.

23. Emerson, *Essential Writings of Ralph Waldo Emerson*, 141.

24. Ibid., 158.

25. See Alan Nadel, *Invisible Criticism: Ralph Ellison and the American Canon* (Iowa City: University of Iowa Press, 1988), 111–23.

26. William Kleinknecht, *The Man Who Sold the World: Ronald Reagan and the Betrayal of Main Street* (New York: Nation Books, 2009), xxvi.

27. Ibid., xxvi.

28. Anthony Lane, "Space Case," *New Yorker*, 23 May 2005. Web.

29. F. O. Matthiessen, *American Renaissance: Art and Expression in the Age of Emerson and Whitman*. 1941 (New York: Oxford University Press, 1968).

30. Harold Bloom, *Agon: Towards a Theory of Revisionism* (New York: Oxford University Press, 1983).

31. Richard Poirier, *The Renewal of Literature: Emersonian Reflections* (New Haven, CT: Yale University Press, 1988).

32. Kleinknecht, *Man Who Sold the World*, 71.

33. For a discussion of key films of 1983 as reflections of themes and issues related to Reaganism, see Alan Nadel, "1983: Movies and Reaganism," in *American Cinema of the 1980s: Themes and Variations*, ed. Stephen Prince (New Brunswick, NJ: Rutgers University Press, 2007), 82–106.

34. Ronald Reagan, "Speech to Evangelicals," 8 March 1983. Web. http://www.nationalcenter.org/ReaganEvilEmpire1983.html.

35. Ronald Reagan, "Address to the Nation on Defense and National Security" (23 March 1983). Web. http://www.reagan.utexas.edu/archives/speeches/1983/32383d.htm.

36. James Mann, *The Rebellion of Ronald Reagan: A History of the End of the Cold War* (New York: Viking, 2009), 66.

37. Ibid., 93.

38. Ibid., 95. Emphasis original.

39. Alvin H. Marill, *Television Westerns: Six Decades of Sagebrush, Sheriffs, Scalawags, and Sidewinders* (Lanham, MD: Scarecrow Press, 2011), 5.

40. Quoted in Michael Weiler and W. Barnett Pearce, *Reagan and Public Discourse in America* (Tuscaloosa: University of Alabama Press, 1992), 198.

41. Holly Sklar, *Reagan, Trilateralism and the Neoliberals: Containment and Intervention in the 1980s* (Cambridge, MA: South End Press, 1986), 37.

42. See Andrew Gordon, "'The Empire Strikes Back': Monsters from the Id," *Science Fiction Studies* 7, no. 3 (November 1980): 313–18. Gordon notes "the deliberate suggestion of 'Death Father' in the name 'Darth Vader'" (314).

BIBLIOGRAPHY

Adler, Bill, ed. *Kids' Letters to the F.B.I.* Illustrated by Arnold Roth. Englewood Cliffs, NJ: Prentice-Hall, 1966.

Allport, Gordon W. "Liabilities and Assets in Civilian Morale." *Annals of the American Academy of Political and Social Science* 216 (July 1941): 88–94.

Alperovitz, Gar. *The Decision to Use the Atomic Bomb.* New York: Vintage, 1996.

American Poetry: The Twentieth Century, Volume Two: E. E. Cummings to May Swenson. New York: Literary Classics of the United States, 2000.

Amis, Martin. *The Moronic Inferno and Other Visits to America.* New York: Viking, 1987.

Anderson, Jack. "Edwin Denby, Dance Critic, Dies at 80." *New York Times*, 14 July 1983. Web.

Appadurai, Arjun. *Modernity at Large: Cultural Dimensions of Globalization.* Minneapolis: University of Minnesota Press, 1996.

Apter, Emily. "On Oneworldedness: Or Paranoia as a World System." *American Literary History* 18, no. 2 (2006): 365–89.

Arendt, Hannah. *The Origins of Totalitarianism.* New York: Harcourt Brace Jovanovich, 1973.

Auden, W. H. "Ballet's Present Eden: Example of *The Nutcracker.*" In *The Complete Works of W. H. Auden, Volume III (1949–1955): Prose*, ed. Edward Mendelson, 393–95. Princeton, NJ: Princeton University Press, 2008.

Baldwin, Frank. Introduction to *Without Parallel: The American-Korean Relationship Since 1945*, 3–37. New York: Pantheon, 1974.

Barrad, Julia. "The Aspiring Jedi's Handbook of Virtue." In Decker and Eberl, *Star Wars and Philosophy*, 57–68.

Bateson, Gregory. *Steps to an Ecology of Mind.* Chicago: University of Chicago Press, 1972.

Becker, Patti Clayton. *Books and Libraries in American Society during World War II: Weapons in the War of Ideas.* New York: Routledge, 2005.

Belgrad, Daniel. *The Culture of Spontaneity: Improvisation and the Arts in Postwar America.* Chicago: University of Chicago Press, 1998.

Belletto, Steven. *No Accident, Comrade: Chance and Design in Cold War American Narratives.* New York: Oxford University Press, 2012.

Benjamin, Bret. *Invested Interests: Capital, Culture, and the World Bank.* Minneapolis: University of Minnesota Press, 2007.

Berlant, Lauren. "Intimacy: A Special Issue." *Critical Inquiry* 24 (1998): 281–88.

The Black Book on the Communist North Korea: The Record of Its Crimes. Seoul: Research Institute for Internal and External Affairs, 1961.

Blair, John, et al. *Economic Concentration and World War II*. Report of the Smaller War Plants Corporation to the U.S. Senate Special Committee to Study Problems of American Small Business. Washington, D.C.: Government Printing Office, 1946.

Bloom, Harold. *Agon: Towards a Theory of Revisionism*. New York: Oxford University Press, 1983.

———, ed. *John Updike*. New York: Chelsea House, 1987.

Borlaug, Norman. "The Green Revolution, Peace, and Humanity." Nobel Lecture, 11 December 1970. In *Nobel Lectures in Peace (1951–1970)*, ed. Frederick W. Haberman, 454–78. Hackensack, NJ: World Scientific Publishing Co., 1999.

Boyer, Paul. *By the Bomb's Early Light: American Thought and Culture at the Dawn of the Atomic Age*. New York: Pantheon, 1985.

Brand, Stewart. "Both Sides of the Necessary Paradox." *Harper's*, November 1973, 20–37.

———. "Review of *Steps to an Ecology of Mind*." *Rolling Stone*, 9 November 1972.

Breuer, William B. *Shadow Warriors: The Covert War in Korea*. New York: Wiley, 1996.

Briggs, John, and F. David Peat. *Turbulent Mirror: An Illustrated Guide to Chaos Theory and the Science of Wholeness*. New York: Harper and Row, 1989.

Brown, Christopher M. "'A Wretched Hive of Scum and Villainy': *Star Wars* and the Problem of Evil." In Decker and Eberl, *Star Wars and Philosophy*, 69–79.

Brown, Julia Clarice. *I Testify: My Years as an F.B.I. Undercover Agent*. Boston: Western Islands, 1966.

Brunner, Edward. *Cold War Poetry*. Urbana: University of Illinois Press, 2001.

Buber, Martin. *I and Thou*. Translated by Walter Kaufmann. New York: Scribner, 1970.

Buchanan, Patrick. "August 17, 1992 Speech at the Republican National Convention." Web. http://buchanan.org/blog/1992-republican-national-convention-speech-148.

Bush, George W. "September 20, 2001 Address to Joint Meeting of Congress." Web. http://www.americanrhetoric.com/speeches/gwbush911jointsession speech.htm.

Cage, John. *M: Writings '62–'72*. Middletown, CT: Wesleyan University Press, 1973.

———. *Silence: Lectures and Writings*. London: Marion Boyars, 1995.

———. *A Year from Monday*. Middletown, CT: Wesleyan University Press, 1967.

Cannon, Lou. *President Reagan: The Role of a Lifetime*. New York: Simon and Schuster, 1991.

Caprio, Mark E. "Neglected Questions on the 'Forgotten War': South Korea and the United States on the Eve of the Korean War." *Asia-Pacific Journal* 9, no. 5 (31 January 2011). Web.

Caruth, Cathy. "Interview with Gayatri Spivak." *PMLA* 125, no. 4 (October 2010): 1020–25.

Casanova, Pascale. *The World Republic of Letters*. Translated by M. B. DeBevoise. Cambridge, MA: Harvard University Press, 2004.

Caute, David. *The Great Fear: The Anti-Communist Purge Under Truman and Eisenhower*. New York: Simon and Schuster, 1978.

———. *Politics and the Novel During the Cold War*. Piscataway, NJ: Transactions Publishers, 2010.

Césaire, Aimé. *Discourse on Colonialism*. Translated by Joan Pinkham. New York: Monthly Review Press, 1972.

Chakrabarty, Dipesh. *Provincializing Europe: Postcolonial Thought and Historical Difference*. Princeton, NJ: Princeton University Press, 2000.

Chen, Kuan-Hsing. *Asia as Method: Toward Deimperialization*. Durham, NC: Duke University Press, 2010.

Choy, Bong-Youn. *Koreans in America*. Chicago: Nelson-Hall, 1979.

Clark, Suzanne. *Cold Warriors: Manliness on Trial in the Rhetoric of the West*. Carbondale: Southern Illinois University Press, 2000.

Cleaver, Eldridge. *Soul on Ice*. New York: Ramparts, 1972.

Coale, Samuel Chase. *In Hawthorne's Shadow: American Romance from Melville to Mailer*. Lexington: University of Kentucky Press, 1985.

Corber, Robert. *In the Name of National Security: Hitchcock, Homophobia, and the Political Construction of Gender in Postwar America*. Durham, NC: Duke University Press, 1993.

Cordle, Daniel. *States of Suspense: The Nuclear Age, Postmodernism, and United States Fiction and Prose*. Manchester, UK: Manchester University Press, 2008.

Corkin, Stanley. *Cowboys as Cold Warriors: The Western and U.S. History*. Philadelphia: Temple University Press, 2004.

Cornis-Pope, Marcel. *Narrative Innovation and Cultural Rewriting in the Cold War Era and After*. New York: Palgrave, 2001.

Cruse, Harold. *The Crisis of the Negro Intellectual*. New York: William Morrow, 1967.

Culler, Jonathan. "Why Lyric?" *PMLA* 123, no. 1 (January 2008): 201–6.

Culleton, Claire A. "Extorting Henry Holt and Co.: J. Edgar Hoover and the Publishing Industry." In *Modernism on File: Writers, Artists, and the FBI, 1920–1950*, edited by Claire A. Culleton and Karen Leick, 237–52. New York: Palgrave, 2008.

Cumings, Bruce. "The Korean War: What Is It That We Are Remembering to Forget?" In Jager and Mitter, *Ruptured Histories*, 266–90.

———. *Korea's Place in the Sun: A Modern History*. New York: W. W. Norton, 2005.

———. *The Origins of the Korean War, Volume II: The Roaring of the Cataract, 1947–1950*. 1990. Seoul: Yuksabipyungsa, 2002.

———. *War and Television*. London: Verso, 1992.

Cunningham, David. *There's Something Happening Here: The New Left, the Klan, and FBI Counterintelligence*. Berkeley: University of California Press, 2004.

Davidson, Michael. *Guys Like Us: Citing Masculinity in Cold War Poetics*. Chicago: University of Chicago Press, 2003.

Davidson, Sara. "A Visit with Joan Didion." In Friedman, *Joan Didion*, 13–21.

de Man, Paul. "Anthropomorphism and Trope in the Lyric." Chap. 9 in *The Rhetoric of Romanticism*. New York: Columbia University Press, 1984.

Decker, Kevin S., and Jason T. Eberl, eds. *Star Wars and Philosophy: More Powerful Than You Can Possibly Imagine*. Chicago: Open Court Publications, 2005.

Deleuze, Gilles, and Félix Guattari. *A Thousand Plateaus: Capitalism and Schizophrenia*. Translated by Brian Massumi. Minneapolis: University of Minnesota Press, 1987.

Denby, Edwin. *The Complete Poems*. Edited with an introduction by Ron Padgett, and with essays by Frank O'Hara and Lincoln Kirstein. New York: Random House, 1986.

———. *Dance Writings*. Edited by Robert Cornfield and William MacKay. Gainesville: University Press of Florida, n.d. [1986].

———. *Dance Writings and Poetry*. Edited by Robert Cornfield. New Haven, CT: Yale University Press, 1998.

———. *Dancers, Buildings and People in the Streets*. With an introduction by Frank O'Hara. New York: Horizon Press, 1965.

———. "A Good Libretto." *Modern Music* 13, no. 3 (March 1936): 14–21.

———. *Looking at the Dance*. New York: Pellegrini and Cudahy, 1949.

———. *Mediterranean Cities*. New York: George Wittenborn, Inc., 1956.

———. "On the Soul's Reaction to Gymnastics." Translated by George Jackson and J. Michael Whitman, M.D. *Ballet Review* 13, no. 1 (Spring 1985): 44–50.

Didion, Joan. *A Book of Common Prayer*. 1977. New York: Vintage, 1995.

———. *Democracy*. 1984. New York: Vintage, 1995.

———. *The Last Thing He Wanted*. New York: Vintage, 1996.

———. *Slouching Towards Bethlehem*. 1968. New York: Farrar, Straus and Giroux, 1990.

———. *The White Album*. 1979. New York: Farrar, Straus and Giroux, 1990.

Diggory, Terence, ed. *Encyclopedia of the New York School Poets*. New York: Facts on File, 2009.

Dittmer, John. *Local People: The Struggle for Civil Rights in Mississippi*. Urbana: University of Illinois Press, 1994.

Douglas, Ann. "Periodizing the American Century: Modernism, Postmodernism, and Postcolonialism in the Cold War Context." *Modernism/Modernity* 5, no. 3 (September 1998): 71–98.

Duberman, Martin. *The Worlds of Lincoln Kirstein*. New York: Alfred A. Knopf, 2007.

Dudziak, Mary L. *Cold War Civil Rights: Race and the Image of American Democracy*. Princeton, NJ: Princeton University Press, 2002.

Edwards, Brian. *Morocco Bound: Disorienting America's Maghreb, from Casablanca to the Marrakech Express*. Durham, NC: Duke University Press, 2005.

Ehrhart, William D. "Above All, the Waste: American Soldier-Poets and the Korean War." In West and Ji-moon, *Remembering the "Forgotten War,"* 40–54.

Eisele, John. "The Wild East: Deconstructing the Language of Genre in the Hollywood Eastern." *Cinema Journal* 41, no. 4 (Summer 2002): 68–94.

Eklund, Doug. "The Pursuit of Happiness: Rudy Burckhardt's New York, 1935–1940." In *New York, N. Why? Photographs by Rudolf Burckhardt, Poems by Edwin Denby*. 1938. New York: Nazraeli Press/Metropolitan Museum of Art, 2008, unpaginated.

Ellis, R. J. "Frank Herbert's *Dune* and the Discourse of Apocalyptic Ecologism in the United States." In *Science Fiction Roots and Branches: Contemporary Critical Approaches*, edited by Rhys Garnett and R. J. Ellis, 104–24. New York: St. Martin's, 1990.

Emerson, Ralph Waldo. *The Essential Writings of Ralph Waldo Emerson*. Edited by Brooks Atkinson. New York: Random House, 2000.

Engelhardt, Tom. *The End of Victory Culture: Cold War America and the Disillusioning of a Generation*. New York: Basic Books, 1995.

Ernst, David. *The Evolution of Electronic Music*. New York: Macmillan, 1977.

Evanhoe, Ed. *Dark Moon: Eighth Army Special Operations in the Korean War*. Annapolis, MD: Naval Institute Press, 1995.

Fader, Shanti. "'A Certain Point of View': Lying Jedi, Honest Sith, and the Viewers Who Love Them." In Decker and Eberl, *Star Wars and Philosophy*, 192–204.

"The FBI Reviews a Book." *Nation*, 27 January 1951, 86.

FBI.gov. 2008. Federal Bureau of Investigation. 29 January 2008. Web. http://www.fbi.gov/.

Field, Douglas, ed. *American Cold War Culture*. Edinburgh: Edinburgh University Press, 2005.

Finnegan, John Patrick. *Military Intelligence*. Washington, D.C.: Center of Military History—United States Army, 1998.

Flader, Susan L. *Thinking Like a Mountain: Aldo Leopold and the Evolution of an Ecological Attitude toward Deer, Wolves, and Forests*. Madison: University of Wisconsin Press, 1974.

———, and J. Baird Callicott. Introduction to *The River of the Mother of God and Other Essays by Aldo Leopold*, 3–31. Madison: University of Wisconsin Press, 1991.

Foertsch, Jacqueline. *Enemies Within: The Cold War and the AIDS Crisis in Literature, Film, and Culture*. Urbana: University of Illinois Press, 2001.

Foot, Rosemary. "Making Known the Unknown War: Policy Analysis of the Korean Conflict in the Last Decade." *Diplomatic History* 15, no. 3 (1991): 411–32.

Ford, Mark, ed. *New York Poets II: An Anthology*. Manchester, UK: Carcanet Press, 2006.

Foreman, Joel, ed. *The Other Fifties: Interrogating Midcentury American Icons*. Urbana: University of Illinois Press, 1997.

Foucault, Michel. *Society Must Be Defended: Lectures at the Collège de France, 1975–1976*. Translated by David Macey. New York: Picador, 2003.

Friedman, Ellen G., ed. *Joan Didion: Essays and Conversations*. Princeton, NJ: Ontario Review Press, 1984.

Galison, Peter. "The Americanization of Unity." In *Science in Culture*, edited by Peter Galison, Stephen R. Graubard, and Everett Mendelsohn, 45–72. New Brunswick, NJ: Transaction Publishers, 2001.

Gardiner, Judith Kegan. "Evil, Apocalypse and Feminist Fiction." *Frontiers: A Journal of Women Studies* 7, no. 2 (1983): 74–80.

Gayle, Addison, Jr. Introduction to *The Black Aesthetic*, edited by Addison Gayle, Jr., xv–xxiv. 1971. Garden City, NY: Anchor-Doubleday, 1972.

Gentry, Curt. *J. Edgar Hoover: The Man and the Secrets*. New York: W. W. Norton, 1991.

Gilman, Nils. *Mandarins of the Future: Modernization Theory in Cold War America*. Baltimore: Johns Hopkins University Press, 2003.

Gilmore, Ruth Wilson. *Golden Gulag: Prisons, Surplus, Crisis, and Opposition in Globalizing California*. Berkeley: University of California Press, 2006.

Ginsberg, Allen. *Composed on the Tongue: Literary Conversations, 1967–1977*. San Francisco: Grey Fox Press, 1980.

———. *Howl and Other Poems*. San Francisco: City Lights Books, 1981.

Gordon, Andrew. "'The Empire Strikes Back': Monsters from the Id." *Science Fiction Studies* 7, no. 3 (November 1980): 313–18.

Gornick, Vivian. "The Prose of Nothingness." *Women's Review of Books* 14, no. 3 (December 1996): 6–7.

Grausam, Daniel. *On Endings: American Postmodern Fiction and the Cold War*. Charlottesville: University of Virginia Press, 2011.

Guilbaut, Serge. *How New York Stole the Idea of Modern Art: Abstract Expressionism, Freedom, and the Cold War*. Translated by Arthur Goldhammer. Chicago: University of Chicago Press, 1983.

Halberstam, David. *The Coldest Winter: America and the Korean War*. New York: Hyperion, 2007.

Hall, Stuart, Chas Critcher, Tony Jefferson, John N. Clarke, and Brian Roberts. *Policing the Crisis: Mugging, the State, and Law and Order*. London: Palgrave, 1978.

Halliday, Jon. "The Korean War: Some Notes on Evidence and Solidarity." *Bulletin of Concerned Asian Scholars* 11, no. 3 (1979): 2–18.

Halliday, Jon, and Bruce Cumings. *Korea: The Unknown War*. New York: Pantheon, 1988.

Hammond, Andrew, ed. *Cold War Literature: Writing the Global Conflict*. New York: Routledge, 2006.

———, ed. *Global Cold War Literature, Volume 2: Western, Eastern and Postcolonial Perspectives*. New York: Routledge, 2012.

Hardwick, Elizabeth. "In the Wasteland: Joan Didion." In Elizabeth Hardwick, *Sight-Readings: American Fictions*, 147–57. New York: Random House, 1998.

Harred, Jane. "The Heart of Darkness in Joan Didion's *Salvador*." *College Literature* 25, no. 2 (1998): 1–16.

Harris, Trudier. "Lance Jeffers." In *The Oxford Companion to African American Literature*, edited by William L. Andrews, Frances Smith Foster, and Trudier Harris, 397–98. New York: Oxford University Press, 1997.

Hartz, Louis. *The Liberal Tradition in America*. 1955. New York: Harvest, 1991.

Heinlein, Robert. *The Puppet Masters*. New York: Del Rey, 1951.

Herbert, Frank. *Dune*. 1965. New York: Ace, 1990.

———. "Dune Genesis." *Omni*, July 1980, 72–74.

———. *Dune Messiah*. New York: G. P. Putnam's Sons, 1969.

———. "When I Was Writing *Dune*." In Frank Herbert, *Heretics of Dune*, v–vi. 1984. New York: Ace, 1987.

Higashida, Cheryl. "To Be(come) Young, Gay, and Black: Lorraine Hansberry's Existentialist Routes to Anticolonialism." *American Quarterly* 60, no. 4 (December 2008): 899–924.

Ho, Jong Jo, Kang Sok Hui, and Pak Thae Ho. *The US Imperialists Started the Korean War*. Pyongyang: Foreign Languages Publishing House, 1993.

Hoberek, Andrew. *The Twilight of the Middle Class: Post–World War II American Fiction and White-Collar Work*. Princeton, NJ: Princeton University Press, 2005.

Hobsbawm, Eric. *The Age of Empire: 1875–1914*. New York: Vintage, 1989.

———. *The Age of Extremes: A History of the World, 1914–1991*. New York: Pantheon, 1994.

Hoffman, Elizabeth Cobbs. *All You Need Is Love: The Peace Corps and the Spirit of the 1960s*. Cambridge, MA: Harvard University Press, 1998.

Hofstadter, Richard. *The Paranoid Style in American Politics: And Other Essays*. Cambridge, MA: Harvard University Press, 1996.

Hollowell, John. "Against Interpretation: Narrative Strategy in *A Book of Common Prayer*." In Friedman, *Joan Didion*, 164–76.

Hoover, J. Edgar. "How U.S. Reds Use 'Pseudo Liberals' [*sic*] as a Front." *U.S. News and World Report*, 13 April 1956, 138–39.

Horn, Eva. "Knowing the Enemy: The Epistemology of Secret Intelligence." Translated by Sara Ogger. *Grey Room* 11 (2003): 58–85.

Howard, Richard. "Luminous Paradigms." *New Republic*, 6 April 1987, 37–39.

Hubbs, Nadine. *The Queer Composition of America's Sound: Gay Modernisms, American Music, and National Identity*. Berkeley: University of California Press, 2004.

Huberman, Leo, and Paul M. Sweezy. Publisher's foreword to Stone, *Hidden History of the Korean War.*

Hult, Carol. "Metonymy and Metaphor in Joan Didion: A Personal Grammar of Style." In *The Peirce Seminar Papers*, vol. 3, edited by Michael Shapiro, 59–73. New York: Peter Lang, 1998.

"International Unity: Address by Secretary Dulles." *Department of State Bulletin* 30, no. 782 (21 June 1954): 935–39.

Itzkoff, Dave. "Dune Babies." *New York Times*, 24 September 2006: 20.

Jackson, Virginia W. *Dickinson's Misery: A Theory of Lyric Reading.* Princeton, NJ: Princeton University Press, 2005.

Jacobson, Matthew Frye, and Gaspar González. *What Have They Built You to Do?* The Manchurian Candidate *and Cold War America.* Minneapolis: University of Minnesota Press, 2006.

Jager, Sheila Miyoshi, and Rana Mitter. Introduction to *Ruptured Histories: War, Memory, and the Post–Cold War in Asia*, edited by Sheila Miyoshi Jager and Rana Mitter, 1–14. Cambridge, MA: Harvard University Press, 2007.

Jameson, Fredric. "Cognitive Mapping." In *Marxism and the Interpretation of Culture*, edited by Cary Nelson and Lawrence Grossberg, 347–57. Urbana: University of Illinois Press, 1988.

———. *The Political Unconscious: Narrative as a Socially Symbolic Act.* 1981. London: Routledge, 1983.

Jefferson, Thomas. *Notes on the State of Virginia.* Edited with an introduction and notes by Frank Shuffleton. New York: Penguin, 1999.

Jeffords, Susan. *Hard Bodies: Hollywood Masculinity in the Reagan Era.* New Brunswick, NJ: Rutgers University Press, 1994.

Jeffreys-Jones, Rhodri. *The FBI: A History.* New Haven, CT: Yale University Press, 2007.

Johnson, David K. *The Lavender Scare: The Cold War Persecution of Gays and Lesbians in the Federal Government.* Chicago: University of Chicago Press, 2006.

Johnson, Diane. *Terrorists and Novelists.* New York: Alfred A. Knopf, 1982.

Joseph, Gilbert, and Daniela Spenser, eds. *In from the Cold: Latin America's New Encounter with the Cold War.* Durham, NC: Duke University Press, 2007.

Joseph, Peniel E. *Waiting 'Til the Midnight Hour: A Narrative History of Black Power in America.* New York: Henry Holt, 2006.

Kakutani, Michiko. "Joan Didion: Staking Out California." *New York Times*, 10 June 1979. Web.

Kauffman, David. "Denby on Dance." *Horizon* 30, no. 6 (July–August 1987): 38–40.

Kazin, Alfred. *The Bright Book of Life.* Notre Dame, IN: University of Notre Dame Press, 1980.

Keenaghan, Eric. *Queering Cold War Poetry: Ethics of Vulnerability in Cuba and the United States*. Columbus: Ohio State University Press, 2009.

Kennan, George. "The Sources of Soviet Conduct." *Foreign Affairs* (July 1947). In "The History Guide Website, Lectures on Twentieth Century Europe." Web. http://www.historyguide.org/europe/kennan.html.

Kennedy, John F. *"Let the Word Go Forth": The Speeches, Statements, and Writings of John F. Kennedy*. Edited by Theodore C. Sorensen. New York: Delacorte, 1988.

———. *The Strategy of Peace*. Edited by Allan Nevins. New York: Harper and Row, 1960.

Kim, Dong-Choon. "The War against the 'Enemy Within.'" In Dong-Choon Kim, *The Unending Korean War: A Social History*, translated by Sung-ok Kim. Larkspur, CA: Tamal Vista Publications, 2000.

Kim, Elaine. "Korean American Literature." In *An Interethnic Companion to Asian American Literature*, edited by King-Kok Cheung, 156–91. Cambridge: Cambridge University Press, 1997.

Kim, Elaine H. "Roots and Wings: An Overview of Korean American Literature, 1934–2003." In *Korean American Literature*, edited by Young-Key Kim-Renaud et al., 1–19. Washington, D.C.: George Washington University Elliot School of International Affairs—Sigur Center Asia Papers, 2003.

Kim, Jodi. *Ends of Empire: Asian American Critique and the Cold War*. Minneapolis: University of Minnesota Press, 2010.

Kim, Richard E. *The Martyred*. New York: George Braziller, 1964.

———. "O My Korea!" *Atlantic Monthly*, February 1966, 106–17.

Kim, Suk-Young. Introduction to *Long Road Home: Testimony of a North Korean Camp Survivor*. New York: Columbia University Press, 2009, 1–18.

Klein, Christina. *Cold War Orientalism: Asia in the Middlebrow Imagination, 1945–1961*. Berkeley: University of California Press, 2003.

Kleinknecht, William. *The Man Who Sold the World: Ronald Reagan and the Betrayal of Main Street*. New York: Nation Books, 2009.

Klinghoffer, David. "Putting Down Didion Thriller is the Last Thing Reader Will Do." *Washington Times*, 15 September 1996. Web.

Klotz, Marcia. "Global Visions: From the Colonial to the National Socialist World." *European Studies Journal* 16, no. 2 (1999): 37–68.

Knoespel, Kenneth J. "The Emplotment of Chaos: Instability and Narrative Order." In *Chaos and Order: Complex Dynamics in Literature and Science*, edited by N. Katherine Hayles, 100–24. Chicago: University of Chicago Press, 1991.

Kostelanetz, Richard, ed. *John Cage*. New York: Praeger, 1970.

Kuehl, Linda. "Joan Didion: The Art of Fiction No. 71." *Paris Review* (Fall–Winter 1978). Web.

Kwon, Heonik. *The Other Cold War*. New York: Columbia University Press, 2009.

Lane, Anthony. "Space Case." *New Yorker*, 23 May 2005. Web.

Larson, Cedric. "The Council for Democracy." *Public Opinion Quarterly* 6, no. 2 (Summer 1942): 284–90.

Latham, Michael E. *Modernization as Ideology: American Social Science and "Nation Building" in the Kennedy Era*. Chapel Hill: University of North Carolina Press, 2000.

Lawrence of Arabia. VHS. Directed by David Lean. 1962. Sony Pictures, 2001.

Lehman, David, and John Brehm, eds. *The Oxford Book of American Poetry*. New York: Oxford University Press, 2006.

Leopold, Aldo. *A Sand County Almanac*. New York: Oxford University Press, 1966.

Levine, Steven L. "Some Reflections on the Korean War." In West and Ji-moon, *Remembering the "Forgotten War,"* 3–11.

Lipset, David. *Gregory Bateson: The Legacy of a Scientist*. Englewood Cliffs, NJ: Prentice-Hall, 1980.

Lipsitz, George. *Rainbow at Midnight: Labor and Culture in the 1940s*. Chicago: University of Illinois Press, 1994.

Litvak, Joseph. *Strange Gourmets: Sophistication, Theory, and the Novel*. Durham, NC: Duke University Press, 1997.

Locke, John. *Two Treatises on Civil Government, Preceded by Sir Robert Filmer's "Patriarcha."* London: G. Routledge, 1884.

Lowenthal, Max. *The Federal Bureau of Investigation*. New York: William Sloane, 1950.

Lukin, Josh, ed. *Invisible Suburbs: Recovering Protest Fiction in the 1950s United States*. Jackson: University Press of Mississippi, 2008.

Macdonald, Dwight. "The Root Is Man (Part I)." *Politics* 3 (April 1946): 97–115.

Mailer, Norman. The *Armies of the Night*: *History as a Novel, the Novel as History*. 1968. New York: Plume, 1994.

———. "Superman Comes to the Supermart." *Esquire*, November 1960, 119–27.

———. "The White Negro." In Norman Mailer, *Advertisements for Myself*, 337–58. New York: G. P. Putnam's Sons, 1959.

Malcolm X. "The Ballot or the Bullet." April 3, 1964, version. In *Malcolm X Speaks*, edited by George Breitman, 23–44. New York: Grove Press, 1966.

———. "The Ballot or the Bullet." April 12, 1964, version. Web. http://lybio.net/malcolm-x-the-ballot-or-the-bullet/speeches/.

———. "The Black Revolution." In Breitman, *Malcolm X Speaks*, 45–57.

Mann, James. *The Rebellion of Ronald Reagan: A History of the End of the Cold War*. New York: Viking, 2009.

Marable, Manning. *Race, Reform, and Rebellion: The Second Reconstruction and Beyond in Black America, 1945–2006*. 3rd ed. Jackson: University Press of Mississippi, 2007.

Margulis, Lynn, and James Lovelock. "The Atmosphere as Circulatory System of the Biosphere—the Gaia Hypothesis." In *News that Stayed News: Ten Years of "CoEvolution Quarterly," 1974–1984*, edited by Art Kleiner and Stewart Brand, 15–25. San Francisco: North Point Press, 1986.

Marill, Alvin H. *Television Westerns: Six Decades of Sagebrush, Sheriffs, Scalawags, and Sidewinders*. Lanham, MD: Scarecrow Press, 2011.

Markon, Jerry, and Philip Rucker. "The Suspects in a Russian Spy Ring Lived All-American Lives." *Washington Post* (30 June 2010). Web.

Maus, Derek C. *Unvarnishing Reality: Subversive Russian and American Cold War Satire*. Columbia: University of South Carolina Press, 2011.

Maxwell, Mary. "Edwin Denby's New York School." *Yale Review* 95, no. 4 (October 2007): 65–96.

May, Elaine Tyler. *Homeward Bound: American Families in the Cold War Era*. New York: Basic Books, 1988.

May, Lary, ed. *Recasting America: Culture and Politics in the Age of Cold War*. Chicago: University of Chicago Press, 1989.

McCann, Sean. "The Imperiled Republic: Norman Mailer and the Poetics of Anti-Liberalism." *English Literary History* 67, no. 1 (Spring 2000): 293–336.

McClure, John A. *Late Imperial Romance*. New York: Verso, 1994.

McConachie, Bruce. *American Theater in the Culture of the Cold War: Producing and Contesting Containment*. Iowa City: University of Iowa Press, 2003.

McGurl, Mark. *The Program Era: Postwar Fiction and the Rise of Creative Writing*. Cambridge, MA: Harvard University Press, 2009.

Mead, Margaret. "The Comparative Study of Culture and the Purposive Cultivation of Democratic Values." In *Science, Philosophy, and Religion, Second Symposium*, edited by Lymon Bryson and Louis Finkelstein, 56–69. New York: Conference on Science, Philosophy and Religion in their Relation to the Democratic Way of Life, Inc., 1942.

Medovoi, Leerom. "Cold War American Culture as the Age of Three Worlds." *minnesota review*, nos. 55–57 (Fall 2000 and Spring–Fall 2001): 167–86.

———. "Global Society Must Be Defended: Biopolitics Without Boundaries." *Social Text*, no. 91 (Summer 2007): 53–79.

———. *Rebels: Youth and the Cold War Origins of Identity*. Durham, NC: Duke University Press, 2005.

Melley, Timothy. *Empire of Conspiracy: The Culture of Paranoia in Postwar America*. Ithaca, NY: Cornell University Press, 2000.

Merivale, Patricia. "Through Greene-Land in Drag: Joan Didion's *A Book of Common Prayer*." *Pacific Coast Philology* 15 (1980): 45–52.

Mickenberg, Julia. *Learning from the Left: Children's Literature, the Cold War, and Radical Politics in the United States*. New York: Oxford University Press, 2006.

Miller, D. Quentin. *John Updike and the Cold War: Drawing the Iron Curtain*. Columbia: University of Missouri Press, 2001.

Miller, Nancy K. "The Entangled Self: Genre Bondage in the Age of the Memoir." *PMLA* 122, no. 2 (March 2007): 537–48.

Millett, Allan. "The Korean War: A 50-year Critical Historiography." *Journal of Strategic Studies* 24, no. 1 (2001): 188–224.

Mills, C. Wright. *The Power Elite*. New York: Oxford University Press, 1956.

———. "The Powerless People: The Role of the Intellectual in Society." *Politics* 1, no. 4 (April 1944): 69–71.

———. "The Structure of Power in American Society." *British Journal of Sociology* 9, no. 1 (March 1958): 29–41.

Morris, Gay. "Modernism's Role in the Theory of John Martin and Edwin Denby." *Dance Research* 22, no. 2 (Winter 2004): 168–84.

Motherwell, Robert. "Beyond the Aesthetic." In *The Collages of Robert Motherwell*, edited by E. A. Carmean, Jr., 91. Houston: Museum of Fine Arts, 1972.

Mowitt, John. *Re-takes: Postcoloniality and Foreign Film Languages*. Minneapolis: University of Minnesota Press, 2005.

Nadel, Alan. "1983: Movies and Reaganism." In *American Cinema of the 1980s: Themes and Variations*, edited by Stephen Prince, 82–106. New Brunswick, NJ: Rutgers University Press, 2007.

———. *Containment Culture: American Narratives, Postmodernism, and the Atomic Age*. Durham, NC: Duke University Press, 1995.

———. *Flatlining on the Field of Dreams: Cultural Narratives in the Films of President Reagan's America*. New Brunswick, NJ: Rutgers University Press, 1997.

———. *Invisible Criticism: Ralph Ellison and the American Canon*. Iowa City: University of Iowa Press, 1988.

———. *Television in Black-and-White America: Race and National Identity*. Lawrence: University of Kansas Press, 2005.

"Negro FBI Agents in Action." *Ebony*, October 1947, 9–13.

Nelson, Deborah. *Pursuing Privacy in Cold War America*. New York: Columbia University Press, 2002.

Neuhaus, Max. Liner notes for Max Neuhaus, *Fontana Mix—Feed (six realizations of John Cage)*. Alga Margnen, 2003.

Oates, Joyce Carol. "A Taut Novel of Disorder." *New York Times Book Review*, 3 April 1977. Web.

O'Hara, Frank. "Rare Modern." *Poetry* 89, no. 5 (February 1957): 313–16.

Olmstead, Kathryn S. *Real Enemies: Conspiracy Theories and American Democracy, World War I to 9/11*. New York: Oxford University Press, 2009.

O'Reilly, Kenneth. *"Racial Matters": The FBI's Secret File on Black America, 1960–1972*. New York: Free Press, 1989.

O'Reilly, Timothy. *Frank Herbert*. New York: Frederick Ungar, 1981.

Orwell, George. "Literature and Totalitarianism." In George Orwell, *Essays*, 587–89. New York: Alfred A. Knopf, 2002.

Palat, Ravi Arvind. *Capitalist Restructuring and the Pacific Rim*. London: Routledge-Curzon, 2004.

Park, Chung-shin. *Protestantism and Politics in Korea*. Seattle: University of Washington Press, 2003.

Paterson, Thomas G., J. Garry Clifford, and Kenneth J. Hagan. *American Foreign Policy: A History since 1900*. 2nd ed. Lexington, MA: D. C. Heath and Company, 1983.

Pearce, Kimber Charles. *Rostow, Kennedy, and the Rhetoric of Foreign Aid*. East Lansing: Michigan State University Press, 2001.

Peel, Robin. *Writing Back: Sylvia Plath and the Cold War*. Madison, NJ: Fairleigh Dickinson University Press, 2002.

Pettet, Simon. *Conversations with Rudy Burckhardt about Everything*. New York: Vehicle Editions, 1987.

Piette, Adam. *The Literary Cold War: 1945 to Vietnam*. Edinburgh: Edinburgh University Press, 2009.

Pietz, William. "The 'Post-Colonialism' of Cold War Discourse." *Social Text* 19 and 20 (August 1988): 55–75.

Plath, James, ed. *Conversations with John Updike*. Jackson: University Press of Mississippi, 1994.

"The Plowboy Interview: Frank Herbert. Science Fiction's Yellow Journalist Is a Homesteading 'Technopeasant.'" *Mother Earth News* 69 (May–June 1981): 17–23.

Poirier, Richard. *The Renewal of Literature: Emersonian Reflections*. New Haven, CT: Yale University Press, 1988.

Pollack, Howard. *Aaron Copland: The Life and Work of an Uncommon Man*. New York: Henry Holt and Company, 1999.

Posnock, Ross. "A Great Memoir! At Last!" *New Republic*, 19 February 2010. Web.

Powers, Richard Gid. *Broken: The Troubled Past and Uncertain Future of the FBI*. New York: Free Press, 2004.

Prescott, Peter S. "Didion's Grace." In *The Critical Response to Joan Didion*, edited by Sharon Felton, 97–98. Westport, CT: Greenwood, 1994.

Ra, Jong-yil. "Governing North Korea: Some Afterthoughts on the Autumn of 1950." *Journal of Contemporary History* 40, no. 3 (2005): 521–46.

Reagan, Ronald. "Address to the Nation on Defense and National Security." 23 March 1983. Web. http://www.reagan.utexas.edu/archives/speeches/1983/32383d.htm.

———. "Address to the Nation on the Situation in Nicaragua." 16 March 1986. Web. http://www.reagan.utexas.edu/archives/speeches/1986/31686a.htm.

———. "Peace: Restoring the Margin of Safety." Speech at Veterans of Foreign Wars Convention, Chicago, 18 August 1980. Web. http://www.reagan.utexas.edu/archives/reference/8.18.80.html.

———. "Speech to Evangelicals." 8 March 1983. Web. http://www.nationalcenter.org/ReaganEvilEmpire1983.html.

Redding, Arthur. *Turncoats, Traitors, and Fellow Travelers: Culture and Politics of the Early Cold War.* Jackson: University Press of Mississippi, 2008.

Rieder, John. *Colonialism and the Emergence of Science Fiction.* Middletown, CT: Wesleyan University Press, 2008.

Ripp, Joseph. "Middle America Meets Middle Earth: American Discussion and Readership of J. R. R. Tolkien's *The Lord of the Rings*, 1965–1969." *Book History* 8 (2005): 245–86.

Rogin, Michael. *Ronald Reagan, the Movie: And Other Episodes in Political Demonology.* Berkeley: University of California Press, 1988.

Roman, Camille. *Elizabeth Bishop's World War II–Cold War View.* New York: Palgrave, 2001.

Rostow, W. W. *The Stages of Economic Growth: A Non-Communist Manifesto.* 1960. New York: Cambridge University Press, 1965.

Roth, Moira, and Jonathan D. Katz. *Difference/Indifference: Musings on Postmodernism, Marcel Duchamp, and John Cage.* Amsterdam: G+B Arts International, 1998.

Rushdie, Salman. "Imaginary Homelands." In Salman Rushdie, *Imaginary Homelands: Essays and Criticism, 1981–1991*, 9–21. New York: Penguin, 1991.

Rustin, Susanna. "Legends of the Fall." *Guardian*, 21 May 2005. Web.

Ryan, David. "Mapping Containment: The Cultural Construction of the Cold War." In *American Cold War Culture*, edited by Douglas Field, 50–68. Edinburgh: Edinburgh University Press, 2005.

Saldaña-Portillo, María Josefina. *The Revolutionary Imagination in the Americas and the Age of Development.* Durham, NC: Duke University Press, 2003.

Salt. DVD. Directed by Phillip Noyce. Sony Pictures, 2010.

Sayer, Ian, and Douglas Botting. *America's Sacred Army: The Untold Story of the Counter Intelligence Corps.* New York: Franklin Watts, 1989.

Schaub, Thomas. *American Fiction in the Cold War.* Madison: University of Wisconsin Press, 1991.

Schell, Jonathan. *The Time of Illusion.* New York: Vintage, 1976.

Schlesinger, Stephen, and Stephen Kinzer. *Bitter Fruit: The Story of the American Coup in Guatemala.* Cambridge, MA: Harvard University Press, 1999.

Schmitt, Carl. *The Concept of the Political.* Translated by George Schwab. Chicago: University of Chicago Press, 1995.

Schmitt, Natalie Crohn. *Actors and Onlookers: Theater and Twentieth-Century Scientific Views of Nature.* Evanston, IL: Northwestern University Press, 1990.

Schrecker, Ellen. *Many Are the Crimes: McCarthyism in America.* Princeton, NJ: Princeton University Press, 1998.

———, ed. *Cold War Triumphalism: The Misuse of History After the Fall of Communism.* New York: New Press, 2004.

Schreiber, Rebecca M. *Cold War Exiles in Mexico: U.S. Dissidents and the Culture of Critical Resistance*. Minneapolis: University of Minnesota Press, 2008.

Schulman, Bruce. *The Seventies: The Great Shift in American Culture, Society, and Politics*. New York: Free Press, 2001.

Seed, David. *Brainwashing: The Fictions of Mind Control*. Kent, OH: Kent State University Press, 2004.

Shane, Scott, and Charlie Savage. "In Ordinary Lives, U.S. Sees the Work of Russian Agents." *New York Times*, 28 June 2010. Web.

Shaw, Lytle. *Frank O'Hara: The Poetics of Coterie*. Iowa City: University of Iowa Press, 2006.

Sherif, Ann. *Japan's Cold War: Media, Literature, and the Law*. New York: Columbia University Press, 2009.

Sherry, Michael S. *Gay Artists in Modern American Culture: An Imagined Conspiracy*. Chapel Hill: University of North Carolina Press, 2007.

Singh, Nikhil Pal. "Beyond the 'Empire of Jim Crow': Race and War in Contemporary US Globalism." *Japanese Journal of American Studies* 20 (2009): 89–111.

———. "Cold War Redux: On the 'New Totalitarianism.'" *Radical History Review* 85 (Winter 2003): 171–81.

Sklar, Holly. *Reagan, Trilateralism and the Neoliberals: Containment and Intervention in the 1980s*. Cambridge, MA: South End Press, 1986.

Slotkin, Richard. *Gunfighter Nation: The Myth of the Frontier in Twentieth-Century America*. New York: Atheneum, 1992.

———. *Regeneration through Violence: The Mythology of the American Frontier, 1600–1860*. Norman: University of Oklahoma Press, 1975.

Spivak, Gayatri Chakravorty. *A Critique of Postcolonial Reason: Toward a History of the Vanishing Present*. Cambridge, MA: Harvard University Press, 1999.

———. *Death of a Discipline*. New York: Columbia University Press, 2003.

———. *Outside in the Teaching Machine*. New York: Routledge, 1993.

———. "Righting Wrongs." *SAQ* 103, nos. 2 and 3 (2004): 523–81.

Stanley, Alessandra. "Cold War–Style Spying Is Back (How Quaint)." *New York Times*, 13 June 2010, C1.

Stimpson, Catharine. "The Case of Miss Joan Didion." *Ms.*, January 1973, 36–41.

Stone, I. F. *The Hidden History of the Korean War*. New York: Monthly Review, 1952.

Stoneley, Peter. *A Queer History of the Ballet*. New York: Routledge, 2007.

Stout, Janis P. *Strategies of Reticence: Silence and Meaning in the Works of Jane Austen, Willa Cather, Katherine Anne Porter and Joan Didion*. Charlottesville: University Press of Virginia, 1990.

Strandberg, Victor. "Passion and Delusion in *A Book of Common Prayer*." In Friedman, *Joan Didion*, 147–63.

Stratton, Susan. "The Messiah and the Greens: The Shape of Environmental

Action in *Dune* and *Pacific Edge*." *Extrapolation* 42, no. 4 (Winter 2001): 303–16.

Stueck, William. "In Search of Essences: Labeling the Korean War." In West and Ji-moon, *Remembering the "Forgotten War,"* 187–202.

———. *The Korean War: An International History*. Princeton, NJ: Princeton University Press, 1995.

Takaki, Ronald. *Hiroshima: Why America Dropped the Atomic Bomb*. New York: Back Bay Books, 1996.

Taylor, Gordon O. *Studies in Modern American Autobiography*. New York: Macmillan, 1983.

Tooker, Dorothy. "The Editors Meet William Carlos Williams." Interview with the editors of *A.D.*, 1952. In *Interviews With William Carlos Williams: "Speaking Straight Ahead,"* edited by Linda Welshimer Wagner, 27–40. New York: New Directions Publishing Corporation, 1976.

Touponce, William F. *Frank Herbert*. Boston: Twayne, 1988.

Trogdon, Gary. *A Decade of Catching Spies: The United States Army's Counter Intelligence Corps, 1943–1953*. Ann Arbor: UMI, 2001.

Trotsky, Leon. *The Revolution Betrayed: What Is the Soviet Union and Where Is It Going?* Translated by Max Eastman. Web. http://www.marxists.org/archive/trotsky/1936/revbet/index.htm.

Truman, Harry. Address on the Situation in Korea. 19 July 1950. Web. http://www.trumanlibrary.org/audio/tunesCast.rss.

———. "President Harry S. Truman's Address before a Joint Session of Congress, March 12, 1947." Avalon Project at Yale Law School. Web. http://avalon.law.yale.edu/20th_century/trudoc.asp.

Turner, Frederick Jackson. *The Frontier in American History*. New York: Holt, Rinehart and Winston, 1962.

United States Federal Bureau of Investigation. James Baldwin file obtained under provisions of the Freedom of Information Act. Assorted documents dated [?] October 1958 to 20 February 1974. Internal case file no. 62-108763.

———. Amiri Baraka file self-deposited in the Amiri Baraka Papers, Moorland-Spingarn Research Center, Howard University, Washington, D.C. Assorted documents dated 28 January 1957 to 3 March 1971. Internal case file no. 100-425307.

———. Frank London Brown file obtained under provisions of the Freedom of Information Act. Assorted documents dated 19 December 1955 to 27 December 1957. Internal case file no. 100-30890.

———. Alice Childress file obtained under provisions of the Freedom of Information Act. Assorted documents dated 11 April 1951 to [?] 1957. Internal case file no. 100-379156.

———. Harold Cruse file obtained under provisions of the Freedom of

Information Act. Assorted documents dated 7 August 1950 to 9 January 1969. Internal case file no. 100-370842.

———. Shirley Graham Du Bois file obtained under provisions of the Freedom of Information Act. Assorted documents dated 8 August 1950 to 28 July 1975. Internal case file no. 100-370965.

———. Lonne Elder III [Lonnie Williams] file obtained under provisions of the Freedom of Information Act. Document dated 3 September 1954. Internal case file no. 100-116777.

———. Ralph Ellison file obtained under provisions of the Freedom of Information Act. Assorted documents dated 19 April 1950 to 10 December 1964. Internal case file no. 100-428862.

———. E. Franklin Frazier file obtained under provisions of the Freedom of Information Act. Assorted documents dated 25 June 1953 to 13 July 1961. Internal case file no. 138-825.

———. Hoyt Fuller file obtained under provisions of the Freedom of Information Act. Assorted documents dated 27 April 1954 to 25 March 1974. Internal case file no. 157-16554.

———. Lorraine Hansberry file obtained under provisions of the Freedom of Information Act. Assorted documents dated 21 July 1952 to 22 January 1965. Internal case file no. 100-107297.

———. Ollie Harrington file obtained under provisions of the Freedom of Information Act. Assorted documents dated 4 May 1951 to 22 June 2002. Internal case file no. 100-379980.

———. Calvin Hernton file obtained under provisions of the Freedom of Information Act. Assorted documents dated 14 March 1955 to 29 August 1969. Internal case file no. 100-417598.

———. Lance Jeffers file obtained under provisions of the Freedom of Information Act. Assorted documents dated 8 February 1949 to 15 July 1966. Internal case file no. 100-359726.

———. Charles S. Johnson file obtained under provisions of the Freedom of Information Act. Assorted documents dated 21 February 1952 to 1 October 1956. Internal case file no. 138-3218.

———. Bob Kaufman file obtained under provisions of the Freedom of Information Act. Assorted documents dated 31 January 1950 to 18 August 1970. Internal case file no. 100-366937.

———. Julian Mayfield file obtained under provisions of the Freedom of Information Act. Assorted documents dated 16 August 1954 to 6 September 1974. Internal case file no. 100-412872.

———. Willard Motley file obtained under provisions of the Freedom of Information Act. Assorted documents dated 16 July 1951 to 12 October 1972. Internal case file no. 100-382070.

———. William Pickens file obtained under provisions of the Freedom of Information Act. Assorted documents dated 22 October 1947 to 12 May 1964. Internal case file no. 121-4978.

———. Andy Razaf [Andrea Razafkeriefo] file obtained under provisions of the Freedom of Information Act. Assorted documents dated 3 May 1949 to 19 May 1949. Internal case file no. 100-361384.

———. J. Saunders Redding file obtained under provisions of the Freedom of Information Act. Assorted documents dated 13 February 1953 to 15 August 1968. Internal case file no. 123-14868.

———. William Gardner Smith file obtained under provisions of the Freedom of Information Act. Assorted documents dated 5 May 1951 to 7 November 1974. Internal case file no. 100-379969.

Updike, John. *The Centaur.* New York: Alfred A. Knopf, 1963.

———. "Packed Dirt, Churchgoing, a Dying Cat, a Traded Car." In John Updike, *Olinger Stories.* New York: Vintage, 1964.

———. *Self-Consciousness: Memoirs.* New York: Alfred A. Knopf, 1989.

———. "Why Write?" In John Updike, *Picked-Up Pieces.* New York: Alfred A. Knopf, 1975.

Waldman, Anne, and Lewis Warsh, eds. *Angel Hair Sleeps With a Boy in My Head: The Angel Hair Anthology.* New York: Granary Books, 2001.

Weiler, Michael, and W. Barnett Pearce. *Reagan and Public Discourse in America.* Tuscaloosa: University of Alabama Press, 1992.

West, Philip, and Suh Ji-moon, eds. *Remembering the "Forgotten War": The Korean War Through Literature and Art.* Armonk, NY: East Gate—M. E. Sharpe, 2001.

Westad, Odd Arne. *The Global Cold War: Third World Interventions and the Making of Our Times.* Cambridge: Cambridge University Press, 2005.

White, Daniel R., and Gert Hellerich. *Labyrinths of the Mind: The Self in the Postmodern Age.* Albany: State University of New York Press, 1998.

White, Edmund. "The Man Who Understood Balanchine." *New York Times Book Review*, 8 November 1998. Web.

White, Hayden. *Metahistory: The Historical Imagination in Nineteenth-Century Europe.* Baltimore: Johns Hopkins University Press, 1973.

Whole Earth Catalog, Fall 1969.

Whyte, William H., Jr. *The Organization Man.* New York: Simon and Schuster, 1957.

Wiener, Jon. "J. Edgar Hoover, Author." *Nation*, 22 May 2008. Web.

Wilcox, Leonard. "Narrative Technique and the Theme of Historical Continuity in the Novels of Joan Didion." In Friedman, *Joan Didion*, 68–80.

Williams, Kevin. "Imperialism and Globalization: Lessons from Frank Herbert's *Dune.*" *Reconstruction: Studies in Contemporary Culture* 3, no. 3 (Summer 2002). Web.

Williams, Raymond. *Marxism and Literature.* Oxford: Oxford University Press, 1978.

Willis, Ellen. "From Democracy to Demagogy." *Women's Review of Books* 19, no. 2 (November 2001): 7–8.

Wills, Garry. *Reagan's America: Innocents at Home*. New York: Doubleday, 1987.

Wright, Will. "The Empire Bites the Dust." *Social Text*, no. 6 (Autumn 1982): 120–25.

Yanagi, Soetsu. *The Unknown Craftsman: A Japanese Insight into Beauty*. New York: Kodansha International, 1978.

Yoon, Seongho. "Richard E. Kim." In *The Greenwood Encyclopedia of Multiethnic American Literature*, vol. 3, edited by Emmanuel S. Nelson, 1240. Westport, CT: Greenwood, 2005.

Young, John K. *Black Writers, White Publishers: Marketplace Politics in Twentieth-Century African American Literature*. Jackson: University Press of Mississippi, 2006.

Žižek, Slavoj. *Did Somebody Say Totalitarianism? Five Interventions in the (Mis)use of a Notion*. New York: Verso Press, 2002.

CONTRIBUTORS

Daniel Belgrad is the author of *The Culture of Spontaneity: Improvisation and the Arts in Postwar America*. He teaches in the Department of Humanities and Cultural Studies at the University of South Florida.

Andrew Hoberek teaches twentieth- and twenty-first-century American literature at the University of Missouri–Columbia and is the author of *The Twilight of the Middle Class: Post–World War II American Fiction and White-Collar Work*. His chapter is drawn from a book in progress on post-1960 U.S. fiction and foreign policy.

Christine Hong is assistant professor in the Literature Department at the University of California, Santa Cruz, where she specializes in transnational Asian American, Korean diaspora, and critical Pacific Rim studies. She is at work on a book that examines the historic relationship of post-1945 Afro-Asian human rights literature to the Pax Americana, the U.S. military "peace" that restructured the Asia-Pacific region following Japan's defeat in the Pacific war.

Catherine Gunther Kodat is dean of the Division of Liberal Arts at the University of the Arts. She has published widely on U.S. literature, music, dance, and film in journals such as *American Literary History*, *American Quarterly*, *Boston Review*, and *Representations*. During the 1980s, she was the dance critic for the *Baltimore Sun*.

William J. Maxwell is associate professor of English and African and African American studies at Washington University in St. Louis, where he teaches courses in twentieth-century American and African American literatures. He has published two books: *New Negro, Old Left: African-American Writing and Communism between the Wars* and an annotated edition of Claude McKay's *Complete Poems*.

Leerom Medovoi is professor of English at Portland State University and founding director of the Portland Center for Public Humanities. His book *Rebels: Youth and the Cold War Origins of Identity* was published in 2005. He has published articles on Cold War culture, popular music, age studies, postcolonial American studies, cultures of globalization, critical race theory, and the war on terror in journals such as *Cultural Critique*, *minnesota review*, *Interventions*, *Social Text*, *American Literary History*, and *New Formations*.

Alan Nadel, William T. Bryan Chair of American Literature and Culture at the University of Kentucky, is the author of several books, including *Containment Cul-*

ture: American Narratives, Postmodernism, and the Atomic Age, *Flatlining on the Field of Dreams: Cultural Narratives in the Films of President Reagan's America*, and *Television in Black-and-White America: Race and National Identity*. He is the editor of two books on August Wilson, *May All Your Fences Have Gates* and *August Wilson: Completing the Twentieth-Century Cycle*, and he is the coeditor with Susan Griffin of *Henry James and Alfred Hitchcock, the Men Who Knew Too Much*.

Karen Steigman is assistant professor of English at Otterbein University. She teaches twentieth-century American literature, postcolonial literature, and film. An essay on Graham Greene's *The Quiet American* is forthcoming in *College Literature*.

INDEX